D1242157

GROWING UP WORKING CLASS

Contents

Library of Congress Cataloging-in-Publication Data

Wegs, J. Robert.
Growing up working class.

Bibliography: p.
Includes index.
1. Labor and laboring classes—Austria—Vienna—
History. 2. Youth—Austria—Vienna—History.
3. Family—Austria—Vienna—History. 4. Sex role—
Austria—Vienna—History. I. Title.
HD8420.V52W45   305.2'35'0943613   87–43188
ISBN 0-271-00637-4

GROWING UP
WORKING CLASS

Continuity and Change Among
Viennese Youth, 1890–1938

J. Robert Wegs

THE PENNSYLVANIA STATE UNIVERSITY PRESS
UNIVERSITY PARK AND LONDON

Preface

This study examines a number of generalizations about working-class culture and youth behavior in a Central European setting. In testing the important theories of John Gillis, Louise Tilly, Joan Scott, Peter Stearns, Stephen Humphries, and others, it establishes the importance of their findings while adding a strata dimension to the laboring population's experience that enriches our understanding of a complicated group. In addition, it will complement the many studies of the Austrian Social Democratic subculture and recent cultural and social-political studies of Vienna, such as those of Carl Schorske and John Boyer. As Schorske's study examines the world of high culture and Boyer's work the experiences of a political party (Christian Socialism), my work investigates the experiences and attitudes of those ordinary people who comprised the bulk of the population. Since a full-scale social history of Vienna has not yet been written, this study will be one of the few works to begin to fill this gap.

Although recognizing the period 1890–1938 as an important transitional period, this study establishes the importance of tradition in guiding youths' and parents' choices. As turn-of-the-century Europe was being transformed by powerful economic and demographic forces, numerous traditional (peasant and artisanal) practices and attitudes, such as the centrality of the family wage economy, the inclination to work rather than continue school beyond the elementary grades, and the inferior position of daughters, slowed the changes among working-class youth. It argues, contrary to those who stress only the negative aspects of the urban experience, that the social networks in working-class districts protected youth from the most destructive aspects of the urban experience. Finally, it maintains that there was a great diversity among working-class youth, which must be taken into account when discussing the working-class experience.

This study uses oral-history evidence to bring the experience of youth alive. Only a few book-length studies of English youth (Stephen Humphries and Elizabeth Roberts) have done this. The oral evidence is used to recover the human and individual dimensions of working-class life that are missing in traditional sources. Although I use only 120 oral interviews (70 that I carried out in 1978–79, 31 carried out by the Institute for Economic and Social History in the University of Vienna between 1980 and 1984, and 19 collected by Eva Viethen in 1982–83), most are lengthy and are supported by a great deal of other evidence. While interviewing, I compared the impressions I was gaining through those conversations with the archival and published sources. It was therefore the intermingling of these various sources of information that brought me to the conclusions that I present here.

I wish to thank the American Council of Learned Societies for a summer Grant-in-Aid in 1978 and the University of Notre Dame's Institute for Scholarship in the Liberal Arts for summer grants in 1982 and 1983 to collect information in Vienna. I owe my Viennese colleague Dr. Reinhard Sieder much gratitude for making available some of the interviews carried out by the Institute for Economic and Social History and for our many conversations that helped clarify some of my views on Viennese youth. Thanks go to the Institute for Folklore for permitting me to use Eva Viethen's interviews.

I am indebted to the following archives and libraries for providing me with information: the Austrian National Library, The Center for the Study of the Working-Class Movement, the Document Archive of the Austrian Resistance, the Chamber of Labor Library, the Administrative Archive, and the district archives in Favoriten and Liesing.

Particular thanks go to Dr. Kurt Liepold, the former director of the Center for the Study of the Working-Class Movement, and its present director Dr. Wolfgang Maderthaner. School officials who provided indispensible aid: Otto Hois of the School Advisory Office of Vienna, Dr. Werner Stöckl, Director of the Bundesrealgymnasium in Ottakring (Schuhmeierplatz), and Maria Springschitz in the office of St. Johann Evangelist parish provided much help. Both Dr. Renate Banik-Schweitzer and Dr. Gerhard Meissl gave me constant encouragement and friendship throughout this project. I am particularly grateful to Hannelore Veit for transcribing most of the interviews and to Professor Albert Wimmer for his aid with the trickier aspects of Viennese dialect.

I owe a great debt to all those elderly Viennese who took the time to talk about their youth experiences. Finally, I wish to thank my wife, who managed to take time to read many versions of my manuscript despite pursuing her own career, first in academia and then in business.

Introduction

This is a study of lower-class youth from 1890 to 1940. I chose 1890 because it was about this time that Vienna began to experience the rapid growth of large-scale factories and 1940 because the period prior to World War II was characterized more by its continuity with the nineteenth century than with the post–World War II period. These dates, by providing approximately a generation on both sides of World War I, permit me to compare the experiences of youth more clearly as to long-term trends. Although this is primarily a study of the children of manual laborers and small-scale artisans, it will sometimes include the children of other socially disadvantaged groups who lived, played, and went to school with them in the working-class districts. As this work will argue, the social divisions among manual laborers and between manual laborers and those immediately above them—lower-level service workers and small-scale shopkeepers—was fluid and often not based upon economic criteria alone. Among youth, social divisions were even less distinct since street activities normally brought children of manual workers together with those of small-shop owners and ill-paid government and city employees who could not afford the rents in other districts.

Major attention will be directed toward that period of youth that is commonly known as adolescence. While this concept can be fixed in the life course as that period of youth following childhood and preceding adulthood, when youth were not yet involved in adult concerns such as marriage, parenthood, and full-time employment, history has shown that it is not merely a biological concept but is milieu- and gender-specific and changes over time. It can also have positive or negative connotations depending upon societal attitudes and historical circumstances. During times of historical stress, for example, adolescence has been perceived negatively due to adults' fears of an excessive teenage precocity and juvenile delinquency. Although bourgeois parents began to treat their teenage children as adolescents as early as the mid-nineteenth century in the advanced European countries, no consensus has been reached on when adolescence came to the working class. The problem is further complicated due to the different social strata in the working class and gender considerations. While some artisan and skilled-worker families began to free their teenagers from adult duties before World War I, most of the working class treated their children as young wage-earners even as late as the interwar period.

Reductionist paradigms have dominated the studies of Central European workers. Geographic, social, gender, and time differences have given way to all-encompassing models that imposed a unity on the laborers that did not in reality exist. In studies of Central Europe, socialist reformers have overlooked the often extreme heterogeneity of the culture of manual laborers in the larger cities in order to establish the evils of capitalist society. To paint this picture of misery, writers relied extensively on worker autobiographies that normally stressed the authors' bleak youth and subsequent rise from poverty to positions of importance, usually within socialist parties. Structural-functionalists, in attempting to prove that only the isolated nuclear family with the mother in the home and the husband in the factory is suited to the industrial period, have overlooked the fact that most work forces, especially those of large cities, were diversified.[2] An equally one-sided cultural-deprivation theory has held that poverty led automatically to cultural and social degeneration among the working class. This theory views working-class society as violent, authoritarian, and intolerant.[3] But all these perspectives are similar to the extent that they tend to concentrate on the negative aspects of life in the city, to lump all workers together, and fail to investigate how the laboring poor dealt with scarcity.

These reductionist views of the working class have given way in the last decade to a search for the diversity and individual initiative within the laboring population. Inspired in some cases by Gramsci's stress on the heterogeneity of cultures or by the American and British attempts to rewrite history from "the bottom up," historians have begun to study the mentality of individual workers as well as studying them as a group. John Clarke, Richard Johnson, and Chas Critcher summed up much of this new orientation by instructing students of culture to begin with everyday life—with work, community, and family—and then build toward the explication of cultural phenomena.[4] This new emphasis has produced some outstanding studies on working-class English youth. Most successful have been those studies that get at the real experiences of working-class youth through the addition of oral-history evidence.[5] These studies have elaborated some of the issues raised by John Gillis's pathbreaking study of youth, especially his conclusion that concentration on the real historical experiences of youth would show the diversity of experiences and even different cultures within a class and a particular locality.[6] These studies have gone far beyond Philippe Aries's study of what adults thought about children.[7]

Until recently, studies of the Austrian working class have centered on the socialist movement or on the more strictly economic aspects of working-class existence. Works that broke from this mold in the last decade still tended to study labor culture from an institutional—primarily Social Democratic Party—perspective.[8] These studies tended to produce broad generalizations but neglected the enormous variety in the working-class experience. As Gillis argues, "Social history cannot be separated from institutional history, but the latter must not be allowed to obscure the existence of those autonomous traditions of youth associated with class, ethnicity, and locality."[9] Austrian researchers began to penetrate the complex world of working-class youth only in the 1970s.[10]

But except for a few recent articles, no modern full-scale study of Austrian youth exists. Those that were written in the interwar period were heavily influenced by a cultural-deprivation theory that permeated the Social Democratic Party (SDAP). Writers such as Otto Rühle and Otto Kanitz, in their attempts to paint a picture of total deprivation, concentrated on the bleaker aspects of life among working-class youth.[11] A few studies, such as those by Margarete Rada, Charlotte Bühler, and Hildegard Hetzer, did note differences among working-class children but offered little explanation as to why differences in behavior existed.[12] During the authoritarian and

Nazi periods, works of a social and cultural nature ceased to be written except among a few socialist exiles. In the post–World War II period, Austrian scholars were more concerned with describing the reasons for Austria's fall to the authoritarian and Nazi regimes. Attention to social questions came as a result of outside stimulation. British and American studies of society, family, and youth began to influence similar investigations in Austria in the 1970s. The Institute for Economic and Social History at the University of Vienna under the direction of Michael Mitterauer was responsible for most of these studies. Mitterauer and his associates produced numerous books on the European family and society but, with the exception of Mitterauer's general study of youth, paid only limited attention to working-class youth.[13] Other studies of youth within the social democratic movement have appeared, but they contain little information on the everyday life of working-class children.[14] My effort, then, will be the first full-scale attempt to describe the life of Viennese working-class youth from "the bottom up."[15]

In order to learn as much as possible about those who inhabited the lower-class areas of Vienna during the period 1890–1940, I utilized 120 oral interviews: the 70 interviews that I carried out in 1978 and 1979, 31 others carried out in 1980–82 by the Institute for Economic and Social History and put at my disposal by Reinhard Sieder, and 19 others put together by Eva Viethen for her dissertation, "Wiener Arbeiterinnen Leben zwischen Familie, Lohnarbeit und politischen Engagement," provide one of the major sources of information for this study.[16] They are an important addition to the mountain of information that is available in government documents, periodicals, newspapers, worker autobiographies, contemporary descriptions, and school and parish records. They make it possible to obtain information about such topics as children's work that was never fully reported to government authorities and on experiences such as daily routines and life strategies, for which there is little information at all from that period.

For example, it is possible through an examination of government and city documents to ascertain income and living costs, but not how a family dealt with scarcity on a day-to-day basis. Published and archival records tend also to give information for an entire city or district with no strata differentiation. Since Vienna's predominantly working-class districts contained many small business and government/city employees, economic and demographic conditions appear better than they actually were. Also, as chapter

1 will argue, the Viennese working class was divided into three economic and occupational strata that were held together only by behavioral and cultural norms that produced some common attitudes and practices. Those I interviewed came primarily from the upper two strata. Since the mean age of my interviewees was the low eighties, very few of those from the lowest strata survived to this age. Still, 17 of the 70 interviewees were at one time a part of the lower stratum.

Oral interviewing commonly produces as much information about the present, in terms of attitudes, as it does about the past. The elderly tend to develop a collective memory of the past, in addition to their specific recollections of family experiences. Political phenomena are conditioned overwhelmingly by perceptions that have been shaped by scores of discussions over the years. For example, Viennese workers' political attitudes about the 1920s have been structured by a major trial (the Schattendorf trial) and the acquittal of several Austrian nationalists who had killed two workers in 1927. Almost all my respondents used the Schattendorf trial to explain their opposition to the government of Monsignor Seipel and their reason for leaving the Catholic Church during the interwar years. Their memories of everyday life are also conditioned to a certain extent by this collective memory. When describing their childhood, the elderly tend to compare it to the present. This often leads them to paint a rosier picture of the past than actually existed, since they perceive that present-day youth suffer from problems such as drugs, broken families, and violence much more than their generation. Therefore, in constructing a reasonably accurate picture of the past, it is necessary to subject oral-history evidence to constant critical examination and compare it to all other kinds of evidence.[17]

Oral history made it possible to uncover the extreme diversity among Vienna's working population. In Vienna there was no one economically and culturally homogeneous working class as might exist in a mining community or a small industrial town. Among the manual workers there were marked economic, social, and behavioral differences well into the twentieth century. Factory workers were normally recent immigrants and often ethnic minorities, but most of the artisanal work force had lived in Vienna for several generations and was distributed throughout the city rather than being concentrated in the predominantly working-class districts such as Favoriten, Ottakring, or Floridsdorf. Having more contact

with other classes and a better standard of living, the master artisans were often a group between the lower-middle-class service
workers and the upper strata of the factory workers in terms of
their behavior and lifestyle. Still, some of these artisans, especially
in the period before 1914, earned very little and were subordinant
to more well-to-do masters for whom they produced products.[18]

As chapter 5 will make clear, the condition of apprentices in the
many small artisanal shops in Vienna was no better and in most
cases was worse than factory workers. Therefore, it is not a hard
and fast rule that artisans are always economically superior to
factory workers, although they tended to be superior in a social
sense because unskilled factory workers were accorded lower es-
teem. In addition to these occupational differences, the location
and condition of one's housing separated the working class.[19] Workers housed in inferior company-provided quarters near factories or
areas housing predominantly manual workers were often rejected
by the workers in the more mixed occupational neighborhoods.
Although subletting was a common practice in Vienna prior to
World War I, those who had to take in subtenants normally ranked
lower in the minds of the skilled workers in the upper stratum of
laborers. What were, then, the most important factors in the life of
the working-class child between 1890 and 1940?

Viennese working-class youth were influenced primarily by family, strata, gender, economic conditions, neighborhood, peer group,
schools, a Social Democratic subculture, and the time period. Although the family lost influence during the 1890–1938 period, it
remained the major socializing agent among working-class youth.
The welfare of the family predominated, especially in the period
before World War I, over any individual considerations. If children
were needed for work at home, attendance at school was sacrificed.
Children accepted the necessity to work and contribute their often
meager earnings to the family. While this was the dominant practice, family well-being, size, gender, time, and attitudes determined how much a child worked and the amount of earnings contributed to the family.

Among the large, impoverished families at the bottom of working-
class society, little consideration was given to the welfare of the
child. But among the other working-class strata, especially among
the skilled workers in the upper strata, increasing attention was
given to the children. Also, the smaller families of the interwar period permitted closer attention to youths' needs and aspirations. In

comparison with the prewar generation, interwar working-class youth exercised more independence in job choice and had greater opportunities to obtain occupational training. Throughout this work, attention will be given to the important strata divisions in working-class society and how they influenced youths' leisure, work, and attitudes toward school.

 It was among the casual laborers, primarily ethnic minorities during the prewar period and Austrian peasants in the interwar years, that children were most subjected to family priorities. Long-term considerations, such as achieving a better job through schooling or training, had to take second place to family well-being. It was not, as some have argued, that the working class could not defer gratification; it was a matter of immediate survival. Therefore, the occupational possibilities of those among the lowest working-class stratum were extremely limited. The possibility of an occupational move up the ladder was rarely within the realm of possibility for the children of unskilled ethnic minorities.

Of course, not all ethnic minorities were unskilled. Some of the Czech immigrants were ambitious skilled artisans who left their native Bohemia or Moravia in order to increase their chance for success in the city. Immediately before World War I, 28 percent of the Czech-speaking inhabitants worked in the clothing industry.[20] Still associated with tailoring in popular consciousness, many of these immigrants settled in the better districts of Vienna or at least the better-off sections of the working-class districts. While immigrants comprised an important segment of the working class in the period before World War I, the collapse of the Habsburg Monarchy and poor Viennese economic conditions in the interwar period sharply reduced the percentage of migrant families in the working-class areas. In addition, immigrants during the interwar period came primarily from the German-speaking provinces of Austria and were therefore more rapidly assimilated than the Bohemian and Moravian immigrants of the prewar period.

Since the family came first among all but the better-off artisanal and skilled-worker families, the schools, as chapter 4 argues, occupied an inferior position in working-class consciousness. Schools, with their class-specific ethos, clashed with a dominant working-class family and community ethos. Youth among the higher reaches of the working class tended to take on more of the ethos that pervaded the schools. Parents, especially those in the lowest working-class strata, often rejected schools and subjects that seemed to have no practical significance for their children. This attitude no doubt influenced their children. Since working-class youth could often not see the purpose behind studying such subjects as history or literature and often performed poorly in such subjects because of linguistic and cultural inadequacies, deep chasms of misunderstanding separated them from their predominantly middle-class-oriented teachers. In the interwar years, attempts were made to instruct working-class children in Viennese dialect in order to overcome the linguistic and grammatical problems they encountered in the schools. For the children of unskilled ethnic minorities, the problems were even greater. In some cases, the clash in the schools resulted in severe disciplining of students and violent reactions on the part of working-class students and parents. But in most cases, the student became disengaged from the school and sought solace in the streets among his peers.

The streets, as chapter 3 shows, provided a milieu free of authoritarian figures where youth, overwhelmingly male, formed their own subculture. These youth groupings (not gangs in the post-1945 sense of the term) were therefore not distinct from society, as the generational theorists of the postwar period claim, but a result of society's closing off all other areas for autonomy. In the interwar period, the smaller working-class families, the lack of jobs for youth, and the emphasis placed on education by the Social Democratic administration of Vienna brought about a greater acceptance of schools in the working-class areas. But the harsh economic conditions of the war and interwar period restricted the number who could take advantage of this change in attitude.

Although a general trend toward more equal treatment for young women occurred during the period 1890–1938, gender continued to be a decisive factor in job opportunity, education, and leisure. Only in the late nineteenth century in the German-speaking lands did the concept *Jugendliche*—a common designation for all youth—come to replace the gender-specific and romantically oriented concepts of *Jungling* (young man) and *Jungfrau* (young woman).[21] Change came about as a result of new occupational possibilities (factories and white-collar work), the smaller families of the interwar years that permitted greater opportunity, and the actions taken by numerous government and private organizations to treat youth as a distinctive phase in the life-course. But economic need and traditional attitudes among working-class parents, especially the lower reaches of laboring families, slowed all efforts to bring equal treatment for girls.

Some working-class youth, as chapter 1 details, were influenced by the many cultural and social activities of the Austrian Social Democratic party. Particularly in the interwar period, when the Social Democrats took over the administration of the city of Vienna, a multitude of organizations and activities for youth helped shape the attitudes of those who took part. As a result of their association with this socialist subculture, some took on a class-based interpretation of history that continued to inform them throughout their life. Others took part in the activities because it gave them something to do but never fully accepted the party position. Most had very little to do with the party and its organizations. The party itself sent youth a mixed message. Some leaders took a basically middle-class position that youth needed to solve its economic and social problems through the adoption of a middle-class strategy. Countless numbers of self-help agencies and programs were set up for youth with an emphasis on self-control, frugality, deferred gratification, cleanliness, etc. These leaders tended to see youths' problems as resulting more from some internal failures brought on by their poverty that could be corrected. The party spent most of its efforts on cultural and educational activities in what was essentially a reformist effort to improve youths' behavior rather than attempting to change the conditions in society that had produced such behavior. Many socialist youth began to reject the party in the late 1920s because of its concentration on cultural tasks rather than engaging its political enemies in battle.[22] This was a generational revolt with a strong class aspect and not one resulting from youths' natural hedonism and rebelliousness, as was argued for the youth rebellions of the 1960s.

One overriding conclusion of this work is that the working class is a very complex group, and therefore any general conclusions about youth will need to be qualified in terms of strata, gender, family attitudes, neighborhood, etc. Such complexity will necessarily complicate the search for change or continuity in youth experience and attitudes. The decline in family size in the interwar period, for example, made it possible for some working-class families to consider secondary education or occupational training for most of their children. Smaller families also permitted a better diet and increased attention for each child. Nevertheless, interwar eco-

nomic conditions and traditional working-class attitudes often hindered a full utilization of the existing opportunities. For example,
chapter 5 will argue that the increased educational and occupational opportunities for women resulting from smaller families
were not fully realized due to some lower-stratum parents' traditional attitudes concerning women's work and place in family and
society and the poor economic conditions of the interwar period. It
is hoped, however, that this more complex picture will more
closely approximate the real youth experiences.

1

Workers' World, 1890–1938

Mother was very much against our associating with kids from the lumpenproletariat, since we could not learn anything worthwhile from them.[1]

—Son of a seamstress abandoned by her father at age 12

There was a lower stratum among the working class, right. A lower and an upper. It has always been a matter of character, right. Because when someone has a bad character, he will have gone into debt, isn't that so.[2]

—Daughter of a bricklayer

Until recently, few social analysts had anything positive to say about the influence of industrialization on workers' communities. Middle-class reformers wrote of a despair and fatalism among the working class that could only lead to apathy and crime. In fact, poverty and crime were inextricably tied together in popular consciousness. Youth were viewed as especially powerless victims of a culture of poverty. Late nineteenth- and early twentieth-century Vienna provides an excellent workshop for discussion of industrialism's impact on workers' families and youth. Due to Austria's slow-paced industrialization, many of the poor conditions described by social reformers would have been most in evidence at the end of the nineteenth century. Certainly large factories and the economic and social dislocation they caused among both factory and arti-

Table 1.1   Industrial Production in
Austria, 1880–1913

(1880 = 100)	
1880	100
1885	129
1890	165
1895	205
1900	228
1905	247
1910	303
1913	333

Source: Richard Rudolf, "The Pattern of
Austrian Industrial Growth," table 1. *Austrian History Yearbook*, 11, 1975.

sanal families occurred on a mass basis only at this time. But
working-class culture and consciousness were shaped not only by
economic, demographic, and political factors but, as will be described at the end of this chapter, also by social perceptions that
did not always correspond to existing conditions.

A recent study of Viennese family structure and industrialization
correctly argues that one cannot discuss the labor force or, in this
case, working-class youth unless one establishes the stage of industrialization and the corresponding type of society in which the discussion will take place.[3] While Austrian industrialization proceeded
at a slower pace than that of Germany in the latter half of the nineteenth century, few would deny that Austria had reached a mature
industrial stage by the late nineteenth century. Despite the growing
domestic turmoil between the dominant German-speaking population and the largely Slavic minorities in the last two decades before
the war, Table 1.1 shows that the Austrian economy grew at a steady
if not rapid rate. Figure 1 reveals that much of this growth occurred
in the territory of present-day Austria and that the economic development in that territory was not significantly inferior to economic
development in Germany. David Good calculated that the real GNP
growth per capita in the Austrian Republic territory and Germany
between 1870 and 1913 was 1.46 and 1.51 percent, respectively.[4]
Moreover, Table 1.2 indicates that industrial workers were concentrated in a few urban centers such as Vienna. During the period
1890–1914, the quickened industrial pace brought about significant
changes in workers' families. The dislocation caused by the influx of

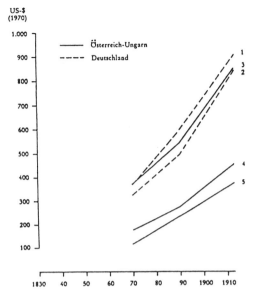

US-$
(1970)

1. Territory of present-day German Federal Republic
2. German Empire
3. Territory of present-day Austria
4. Austrian half of the Monarchy
5. Austro-Hungarian Monarchy

FIG. 1. Real gross domestic product per inhabitant in Germany and Austria 1870–1913 (in 1970 U.S. dollars). From Renate Banik-Schweitzer, "Zur Bestimmung der Rolle Wiens als Industriestadt für die wirtschaftliche Entwicklung der Habsburgermonarchie," in Renate Banik-Schweitzer and Gerhard Meissl, *Industriestadt Wien* (Vienna: Franz Deuticke, 1983), 49.

labor, the rationalization of industry, and the rapid growth of predominantly labor districts was offset among better-off workers—primarily skilled factory workers—by a reduction in working hours, increased real wages, and a large reduction in children employed outside the home.

Vienna, although one of the rapidly growing centers of industry in the Habsburg Monarchy, retained many small (primarily artisanal) shops and medium-sized factories. In 1902, Vienna had a total of 48,722 firms (*Betriebe*) with fewer than twenty employees.[5] Of 133,870 firms in 1902, 87 percent employed five or fewer workers.[6] These small firms (*Kleinbetriebe*) were involved primarily in supplying the larger clothing factories or in repair work. But large and medium-sized factories were increasing rapidly. Meissl shows that in the machine industry, firms with 100–1,000 workers increased from 69 in 1902 to 115 in 1913 and those with more than 1,000 workers from 5 to 17.[7] The larger factories were located primarily in the *Vororte* outer districts (10–21): from a total of 29 with

Table 1.2 Occupational Composition of the Austrian[a] and Viennese Population (percent)

	1890		1900		1910	
	Austria	Vienna	Austria	Vienna	Austria	Vienna
Agriculture & Forestry	62.4	1.2	58.2	.7	53.1	.8
Industry	21.2	55.3	22.2	51.5	24.0	46.6
Transport & Trade	6.2	21.4	7.3	23.5	9.8	27.1
Other	10.1	21.9	12.2	24.3	14.4	25.3

[a]Cisleithania: Excludes the Hungarian and Hungarian-dominated portion of the Habsburg Monarchy.

Source: Österreichisches Statistisches Handbuch 15, 1896, 8; 22, 1903, 20; 34, 1915, 16. *Österreichische Statistik* 33, 1894, 51; 66, 1904, issue 2, 66; New Series 3, 1916, issue 2, 2.

more than 1,000 workers, 8 were located in district 10 (Favoriten) and 7 in district 21 (Floridsdorf).[8] Of the 29 large factories established in Vienna before 1890, 12 had been previously located in the inner districts.[9]

While Banik-Schweitzer correctly argues that Vienna would have to be considered an industrial city before World War I, the evidence shows further that only the outer districts could be designated as primarily industrial, and even in these districts the work force remained a mixture of factory and artisanal labor during the entire period 1890–1938.[10] For example, Ottakring, with only one factory employing more than 1,000 in 1913 (the *K. K. Tabakfabrik*), retained its predominantly artisanal work force.[11] The outer districts were also the districts with the largest proportion of immigrant workers in their work forces. Although artisanal workers outnumbered factory workers, there can be no doubt, as Ehmer points out, that Vienna was a city of workers by 1900: more than one-half of those employed were designated as workers (*Arbeiter*) by the 1900 census report. A steady increase in the percentage of dependent (*unselbständige*) workers—in most cases factory workers—occurred during the 1890–1914 period: from 1900 to 1910 they increased from 66 to 70 percent of those gainfully employed.[12] As the map shows (Fig. 2), the number of Viennese districts with over 30 percent workers and day laborers had increased from 7 in 1890 to 9 in 1910.

By 1890, districts such as Favoriten had more factory laborers than artisanal workers. While only 2.3 percent of those gainfully

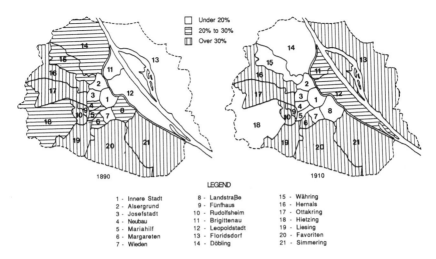

LEGEND

1 - Innere Stadt	8 - Landstraβe	15 - Währing
2 - Alsergrund	9 - Fünfhaus	16 - Hernals
3 - Josefstadt	10 - Rudolfsheim	17 - Ottakring
4 - Neubau	11 - Brigittenau	18 - Hietzing
5 - Mariahilf	12 - Leopoldstadt	19 - Liesing
6 - Margareten	13 - Floridsdorf	20 - Favoriten
7 - Wieden	14 - Döbling	21 - Simmering

FIG. 2. Portion of workers and day laborers in the population, Vienna. Top: 1890. Bottom: 1910. From Michael John, *Hausherrenmacht und Mieterelend, 1890–1923* (Vienna: Gesellschaftskritik, 1982), 10.

employed in Favoriten were listed as white-collar (*Angestellte*), compared to an average of 10 percent for districts 1–9, 34 percent were listed as workers (*Arbeiter*) and 3.6 percent as day laborers (*Taglohner*). The average for districts 1–9 was 22.2 percent workers and .009 percent day laborers.[13] From a total of 64,131 gainfully employed in Favoriten in 1900, 40,825 were listed as workers, 2,364 as day laborers, and only 13,996 as self-employed.[14] The inner districts had a much larger percentage of self-employed artisans. For example, about one-third of those employed in district 7 in 1900 were self-employed (13,626 of 36,106). By 1890, the iron and metal manufacturing, graphic, and transport industries had work forces that were overwhelmingly dependent laborers (10–11 to 1) compared with an overall Viennese average of 3.9 to 1.[15] These dependent laborers were divided into a small group of relatively well-paid skilled workers and a larger group of unskilled and usually low-paid workers.

The nature of Vienna's working population was influenced extensively by the economic transformation after 1870. The heavy influx of laborers from outside Vienna reached a peak in absolute numbers in the periods 1891–1900 (149,898) and 1906–10 (92,514).[16] Since most of these immigrants settled in the more industrialized outer districts, their populations grew at a much faster rate than the inner districts. While the inner districts were experiencing average growth rates of 20.5 percent between 1890 and 1900, the outer districts grew at a 26.5 percent rate. Favoriten, for example, grew from 84,813 in 1890 to 127,626 by 1900, while Vienna as a whole grew less rapidly, from 1,376,296 to 1,700,451.[17] The outer districts continued to grow at a rapid pace in the first decade of the twentieth century. Although the percentage growth was higher in the decades before 1900, the growth in absolute numbers was higher in the decade 1900–1910 (169,000 for the outer districts and outskirts [Vororte]).[18] But by the interwar period the working-class areas had become highly static communities; as a result of World War I and the economic decline that set in after the war, immigration from former areas of the Habsburg Monarchy dried up. Interwar immigrants came primarily from rural Austria.

The two generations represented in interviews I carried out among elderly residents of Vienna clearly depict the transformation of the working-class areas described above. Responses from 67 of those I interviewed, the generation of 1900–1920, showed that about 65 percent of their parents came from outside Vienna (87 of 134). The majority of them came from the Czech lands of Bohemia and Moravia (49 of 87). Sixteen of the total of 28 parents arriving in Favoriten, known as the Böhm (Bohemian) district by the Viennese, at the turn of the century were from Bohemia and Moravia.[19] About 45 percent of those living in Favoriten in 1900 (58,417 of 127,626) were born in the Czech lands. For Vienna as a whole, about 30 percent, both German- and Czech-speaking (518,333 of 1,674,957), had come from the Czech lands.[20] Glettler estimates that between 1856 and 1910 one-quarter of Vienna's inhabitants came directly from the Czech lands and another one-quarter were second- or third-generation Czechs.[21] Since about three-fourths of the Viennese Czechs were employed in industry or trade, compared with 46 percent of the German-speaking Viennese, they comprised a larger percentage of the work force than the German Austrians.[22] Viewed in an occupational manner, the Czechs comprised an ethnic majority rather than minority.

An analysis of males who married in Favoriten's St. Johann parish in 1910 and 1938 shows both the heavy influx of Czech-speaking inhabitants before World War I and the transition of the community from one with many immigrants to one that was almost unchanging. Only 27 of the first 212 grooms who lived in Favoriten and were married in St. Johann parish in 1910 were born in Favoriten, 36 were born in other parts of Vienna, and 149 (82 in the Czech lands) were born outside the city. Analysis of the 1938 marriage records shows a completely different demographic pattern: of all 212 grooms who lived and were married in St. Johann parish in 1938, almost half (102) were born in Favoriten, another 51 were born in other parts of Vienna, and only 60 were born outside Vienna (49 of these in other parts of Austria). But a large majority of the grooms' fathers was born outside Vienna; of the 102 grooms born in Favoriten, 44 of their fathers were born outside the Austrian lands (primarily in Bohemia and Moravia) and only 12 of the 102 were born in Favoriten.[23] Census analysis of all those living in Favoriten in 1934 reveals a similar picture; 62 percent of the 1934 inhabitants were born in Favoriten and only 20 percent were born outside the Austrian lands.[24]

In the last third of the nineteenth century, a persistent high birthrate combined with the large influx of laborers and insufficient housing made crowding in working-class areas inevitable. During the mid–nineteenth century (1840–70), immigration and an excess of births over deaths contributed rather equally to Vienna's population increase.[25] Due to a decline in the birthrate in the late nineteenth and early twentieth centuries, especially in the periods 1891–95 and 1906–15, immigration was primarily responsible for the population increase.[26] Although the working class began to limit the size of their families before World War I, the majority still had larger families than other social classes. For Vienna as a whole the birthrate dropped rapidly from 1871 to the 1930s. From a high of 40 births per 1,000 inhabitants in 1870, as depicted in Figure 3, Vienna's rate dropped to 24.18 in 1910, to 10 in 1930, and to only 5.4 per 1,000 in 1936.[27] But when the average number of births per thousand Viennese in 1910 was 24.18, the average for the working-class district of Favoriten was 27.13, compared with only 11.26 for the predominantly middle-class district of Josefstadt.[28] My own survey of working-class families reveals a similar pattern and points to the interwar period as the most important transition period for working-class families in the change from large to small families. While those I interviewed came from prewar families with an average of 5.18 children, their own interwar marriages produced an average of only 1.28 children.[29] A study of 1,320 female industrial workers in 1932 produced similar results; those under 45 had an average of only one child.[30] As Figure 4 shows, the percentage of the population 14 and under steadily declined during

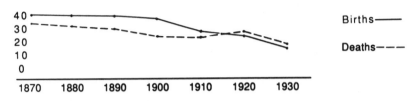

Fig. 3. Birthrate and mortality rate in Vienna, 1870–1936 (per 1,000 inhabitants). Adapted from Feldbauer, 40; Ehmer, 49, 55.

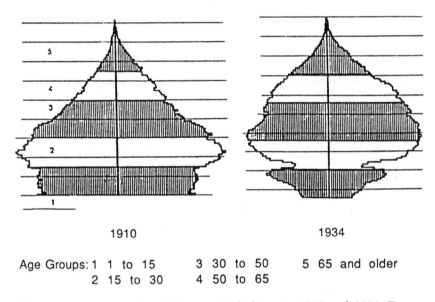

Age Groups: 1 1 to 15   3 30 to 50   5 65 and older
            2 15 to 30   4 50 to 65

Fig. 4. Age composition of Viennese inhabitants, 1910 and 1934. From Albert Kaufmann, "Demographische Struktur und Haushalts und Familienformen der Wiener Bevölkerung" (Dissertation: University of Vienna, 1966), 31.

the 1890–1939 period despite an increase in the percentage of the population that was marrying.

The comparison in Table 1.3 of two primarily working-class districts (10 and 16) with one socially mixed district (5) and one predominantly middle-class district (7) points out that the decline occurred more slowly in those districts with a larger labor population.

Since the declining mortality rate during the period 1870–1936 somewhat offset the declining birthrate, the population density remained high. From a high of about 35 per 1,000 in 1870, the

Table 1.3 Percentage of the Population Married and Under Age 14 in
Four Viennese Districts Between 1890 and 1939 (percent)

District		1890	1900	1910	1920	1939
10	(Married)	33.9	34.5	36.2	39.2	51.8
(Children under 14)		29–32	29–32	29–32	25–29	13–17
16	(Married)	31.1	33.8	35.7	39.4	52.0
(Children under 14)		29–32	29–32	25–29	17–21	9–13
5	(Married)	33.2	34.7	36.0	40.0	52.0
(Children under 14)		25–29	21–25	17–21	13–17	6.5–9
7	(Married)	31.2	32.5	34.5	38.8	49.0
(Children under 14)		17–21	17–21	13–17	9–13	6.5–9

Source: Renate Banik-Schweitzer and Gerhard Meissl, *Atlas der Stadt Wien*, 3.1, 3/1.

mortality rate had dropped to 13.4 per 1,000 by 1930.[31] It was
considerably higher for those under 10: in 1890, 1900, and 1910 the
mortality rate was 40.92, 45.17, and 37.24 per 1,000.[32] But the
mortality rate remained much higher in the working-class districts. In comparing the first district with Favoriten, one study
found that while the rate in the first district had declined to 11.6
per 1,000 by 1890, it remained near the 1870 level for Favoriten.[33]
Of the deaths occurring during the first year of life, the 1910 rate in
Favoriten was 5.56 per 1,000, compared with 3.31 for Josefstadt
and 4.32 for Vienna as a whole.[34] The major killer of children was
tuberculosis. In Vienna it was called the "proletarian disease." A
1900 study of the incidence of tuberculosis in Viennese city housing
showed that Favoriten, at 660 per 100,000, and Ottakring, at 580
per 100,000, far surpassed the inner district with its average of 326
per 100,000.[35] Tuberculosis continued to plague Viennese children
in the interwar period. Tests of 10,000 first-grade children during
the 1925–26 school year showed that 38.6 percent of the boys and
31.1 percent of the girls were tubercular.[36]

Despite a 350,000 drop in Vienna's population as a result of
World War I, other war-related and demographic factors prevented an easing of the housing situation. The number of living
units built from 1915 to 1920 fell 50,000 from the 1910–14 period.[37]
A little improvement came by the mid-1920s, when the city began
to build massive housing projects. Second, although the population declined, the percentage of those in the population between

age 30 and 60 increased and the number of households (*Wohn-parteien*) rose between 1910 and 1923 from 480,476 to 535,067.[38] Some of this increase was due to the return of civil servants and military personnel from the non-Austrian lands of the Dual Monarchy after the war. Also many of those who emigrated during and after the war had subletted rooms and their departure did not reduce the number of those seeking their own dwellings. The comparison of 1910 and 1923 census figures in Table 1.4 shows that the primary drop was in the 0–19 age group. In most cases the latter age group was not seeking housing while those age groups that had increased were. Therefore, the population decrease did not reduce the number of those seeking or holding apartments.

A final factor that influenced the housing situation after the war was an increased number of marriages. As a result of the growing inclination to marry, the many marriages postponed during the war and the still-high birthrate at the turn of the century, a large number of persons of marriageable age existed at the end of the war. Many had now reached their thirties, and as Table 1.5 shows, this group had declined little. Table 1.5 also shows that the number of marriages increased dramatically after the war. All of these factors resulted in an increase of 40,000 in the households between 1910 and 1923, despite a drop in the population of 167,759 during the same period.[39] Thus there was no relief from the overcrowding that began in the last third of the nineteenth century. However, as chapter 2 will argue, this overcrowding was not solely a negative experience for working-class children and their parents.

Economically, the period 1890–1938 can be divided into a gradually improving situation before World War I, the economic dislocation of the World War I period, and a stagnant or declining economy throughout the interwar period that arrested social development. In the 1890–1914 period, the slowly improving economic and demographic situation led to a relative stabilization of family life. Increasing wages made it possible for some husbands to support their families without a contribution from wives or children, and labor legislation and compulsory education freed most children from factory labor.[40] Reduced working hours provided laborers with more leisure time, and the declining size of workers' families provided relief for family budgets. But this favorable development was stopped by World War I and the interwar economic stagnation.

Politically, the period dealt with in this study can be divided into

Table 1.4   Changes in the age structure of Vienna between 1910 and 1923

Age Group	Increase	Decrease
0–9		132,229
10–19		48,916
20–29		62,191
30–39		17,057
40–49	43,439	
50–59	19,178	
60–69	10,088	
70–79		542
80 and above		1,836

Source: Rainer Bauböck, *Die Wohnungsverhältnisse im Sozialdemokratischen Wien, 1919–1934* (Salzburg: Wolfgang Neugebauer, 1979), 18.

Table 1.5   Marriages

Year	Number	Year	Number
1910	18,713	1914	22,294
1911	19,280	1919	26,182
1912	20,127	1920	31,164
1913	17,791	1921	29,274

Source: Statistisches Handbuch für die Republik Österreich, 1924, 14.

three parts: the period 1890–1914, World War I, and the interwar period. But overriding all these periods was continuing opposition among three political camps (*Lager*): the Social Democratic, the Catholic Christian Social, and the Pan-German nationalist. The Social Democratic Party (SDAP), with its primary strength among the workers in Vienna and other cities, had an important political and cultural influence on workers, especially during the period 1918–1934, when they controlled Vienna's city council. In the 1890–1914 period, the three camps were relatively independent. Although the SDAP had concentrated on improving conditions for workers in the prewar period, it maintained a theoretical belief in the ultimate demise of the capitalist system. While its Marxist rhetoric gained it support among workers and intellectuals, it bred opposition among the middle and upper classes. This dualist policy of reformism in practice and revolutionism in theory of the SDAP would prevent it from gaining support from any social groups other than workers. During the 1890s the Christian Socialist camp, under the direction of mayor Karl Lueger, provided the major opposition to the SDAP in Vienna. Lueger's many municipal reforms gained him widespread support among all but the working class.[41]

The high rents brought about by the private housing market led to the isolation of the poorer segments of the population in low-rent areas. Grouped together in the outer districts of Vienna were workers—lower-level white-collar workers and government workers—and a large casual labor force. Since economic conditions had improved until about 1906 for a large part of the labor force, the opposition to the government was not as intense as it could have been. Also, the SDAP did not capitalize on what discontent existed before the war, since most of their leaders believed in the parliamentary process and were therefore more intent upon improving conditions for workers within the existing political framework rather than overthrowing it. The SDAP remained loyal to the state in 1914, when they supported the Habsburg Monarchy against its enemies.

World War I would bring about extreme suffering for Vienna's laboring population. After the euphoria of the first few months of the war gave way to the reality of a war of attrition, opposition to the war began to grow. But workers' loyalty was retained through rent and price controls, which reduced some of the suffering brought on by the war and the lack of a revolutionary consciousness among most socialist leaders. When the Habsburg military forces collapsed in late 1918, a revolution of consensus developed among all political parties against a possible Leninist coup. The SDAP rejected a revolutionary course due to its basically democratic nature and its fear that a socialist takeover would bring about military opposition from the Western Allies, who feared that Leninist coups would break out all over Europe.

From 1918 to 1922, the SDAP and the Christian Socialists formed a governing coalition because they feared a communist uprising. This coalition collapsed in 1922, when Otto Bauer, fearing disunity in the party and defections to the communists, decided to take the party into opposition. The result was a growing antagonism between the SDAP and the forces of the right. Meetings of the national parliament were often disrupted by hostile altercations between the SDAP and the right. Meetings of the Vienna city council, where the SDAP had a clear majority, were also filled with acrimony and filibustering by the right. When the SDAP included a reference to a possible dictatorship to counter the forces of the right in its 1926 Linz party program, the antagonism between right and left became even more intense. The right was also antagonized by the continuing radical rhetoric of socialist leaders, their anti-Catholicism, and the city's housing program. The massive housing blocks of "Red Vienna" were perceived more as defensive fortifications because of the thick concrete walls and small windows of such apartment complexes as the Karl Marx Hof. The name alone was enough to raise the ire of the right. Many of the peasant supporters of the right, especially the pro-fascist *Heimwehr* (Home Guard), felt that Vienna workers were living much better than they were.

When the SDAP leadership failed to respond to the acquittal of several right-wing *Frontkämpfer* convicted of killing two workers in 1927, socialist rank-and-file members took matters into their own hands. When their demonstration was brutally put down by the police, the SDAP leadership belatedly called out its paramilitary organization (*Schutzbund*), but only to maintain order. The party refused to call for a general strike or to release the arms it had stored in the housing blocks. From this point on, the rank-and-file, and youth in general, began to dissociate themselves from the leadership of the SDAP. The leadership immersed itself in the party's cultural activities.

Politically, the party retained its parliamentary strategy despite being slowly weakened by attacks from the right. The defeats were viewed as only short-term setbacks by party theoreticians. Socialist control over Vienna came to an end in 1934, when the combined forces of the right used the Austrian army to put down worker resistance. The SDAP's belated call for a general strike in 1934 failed due to the economic situation (all were afraid of losing their jobs) and the demoralization that resulted from the SDAP's failure to counter the rightist offensive between 1927 and 1934. The authoritarian government under Dollfuss immediately stopped many of the programs of "Red Vienna." Caught between fascist Italy on the south and Nazi Germany to the north, the authoritarian government could maintain Austrian independence for only four years.

While in power in the interwar period, the SDAP's many political, cultural, and propaganda organizations tried to mold a new worker consciousness, or as they termed it, "new people" (*Neue Menschen*). But as both Vernon Lidtke and Richard Evans have argued in the case of Germany, a distinction must be made between "Social Democratic" culture and worker culture.[42] The cultural model that the SDAP tried to impose on the workers was more that of the dominant culture, and it was often rejected or only partially accepted by workers. Although Dieter Langewiesche's thesis that the SDAP "became a part of the dominant culture" may be somewhat exaggerated, since it rejected the dominant culture's religious views and the dominant social-political order, much of its cultural message and actions resembled bourgeois culture.[43] There were socialist folk dancers, chess players, animal raisers, workers' orchestras, and a multitude of other organizations that borrowed heavily from bourgeois culture.

Lidtke's conclusion that German Social Democrats "did not believe, for the most part, that there was much value in what workers already had" rings true for Austria as well.[44] As late as 1926, Otto Bauer spoke of the cultural aspirations of proletarian youth in high-cultural terms.[45] As chapter 6 will explain, many SDAP leaders stressed cleanliness, punctuality, sobriety, and sexual abstinence, as did the dominant culture. Those who participated in this cultural milieu lived in a predominantly SDAP world, albeit one that adopted many practices and attitudes of the dominant culture. They could engage in myriad political, social, and cultural activities arranged by the SDAP with very little contact with other cultural groups. Since the SDAP energetically opposed the influence of the Catholic church in society, children who became a part of this cultural milieu rejected organized religion and remained hostile toward the Catholic church throughout their lives. This was immediately apparent when interviewing elderly Viennese if they had been a part of the SDAP milieu. Their commentary was laced with references to class conflict and opposition to the Catholic church. Such comments as "The church is the greatest stupefying arena of all times" was a common attitude among the males caught up in the SDAP milieu.[46] Subsequent chapters will argue that the SDAP model became a major part of the cultural milieu of the upper stratum of workers and was accepted by only a minority of those in the middle stratum and by only a few of those in the lower stratum.

This short introduction to the economic, demographic, and political conditions of Vienna's laboring population points out the difficulty of reaching conclusions concerning working-class youth. Since Vienna's workers were not a monolithic laboring population such as that in a small mining community or even a primarily

industrial city, conclusions will necessarily be complex. Also, growing up in families with similar economic and social backgrounds
will not necessarily result in similar attitudes and behavior. As the
following analysis of the mentality and the social stratification
among workers will suggest, status was often not only an out-
growth of the objective economic and social conditions but also, as
E. P. Thompson has argued, a subjective understanding of one's
position in relation to others.[47]

In 1913 the socialist newspaper *Arbeiterzeitung* wrote that a street
name in the Kreta section of the mainly labor district Favoriten had
been changed by local wags to *Landesgerichsstrasse* (Superior Court
Street), "since in this street week after week entire bundles of criminal warrants were distributed in one house after another."[48] Some
former Favoriten residents used such descriptions as *Gesinde* and
Pöbel (rabble), *Schmarrn* (trash), *Raufer* (rowdies), *Gauner* (rogues),
Messerhelden (cutthroats), and *Proleten* (lumpenproletariat) to describe the Kreta inhabitants.[49] Still other former inhabitants of Favoriten viewed those living in the Kreta area as honest, hard-
working laborers who, though poverty stricken, could not be
equated with the law-breakers who lived in that area. Most differentiated between the term Proletariat, by which they meant honest
laborers, and *Proleten*, "those who aren't good for anything and
such."[50] They often identified the *Proleten* as those who drank themselves into destitution. In the words of the daughter of a bricklayer,
"The drunks, they were veritable *Proleten*. But we . . . we never felt
like the *Proleten*, but workers."[51] These responses reveal some of the
divisions within a predominantly working-class area that was often
separated as much by behavior as by material considerations. Examining these divisions within Vienna's largest working-class district,
Favoriten, and comparing Favoriten with other Viennese working-
class areas will provide a necessary background for later discussions of youth in the schools, at play, and at work.

According to former inhabitants, Favoriten was composed of
three distinct social and cultural areas prior to World War II. The
eastern part of the district, overlooked by the *Ankerbrotfabrik*
(which became the largest bread factory in the world in the 1920s),
was described by most of those I interviewed as the poorest part of
Favoriten in the pre–World War I period. Known as the Kreta to
most local inhabitants, it housed many of the unskilled workers
employed by the *Ankerbrotfabrik*, the nearby South Railway Sta-
tion (*Südbahnhof*), and the cable factory *Felten und Guilleaume*.

The Kreta's combination of smaller apartments, larger families, and sleeping space rented to *Bettgeher* (bed-renters) and subtenants resulted in overcrowded and often undesirable conditions for children. With few parks in the area, the children were forced to play in the narrow, dirty, and often dangerous streets. A 1912 report by Favoriten's city adviser complained about the rubbish and dust from the cable factory and rat-infested trash storage areas, which forced residents to keep their windows closed.[52] Behind these windows were a large part of Favoriten's unskilled, casual, and frequently unemployed laborers.

Still poorer were the immigrant brick workers who came to Vienna to take unskilled jobs in the Wienerberger Brick Works before World War I: about one-half of the brick workers in Favoriten at the turn of the century were from the Czech lands.[53] Housed often in the wooden barracks provided by the brick companies, but separated from the central core of the district by open fields, these factory workers had little contact with the more settled inhabitants of Favoriten. Many lived as bed-renters for years before they married: in 1910, 11.8 percent of the Czech-speaking inhabitants of Vienna, compared with only 3.2 percent of the German-speaking inhabitants, lived as bed-renters.[54] The son of a former worker at the Wienerberger Brick Works described the company housing as follows: "Four or six families lived in one large room, each in a specific part. There not only were children born but also, let's say, if you'll excuse me, produced."[55] A group that visited the Wienerberger worker housing in 1927 reported that every dwelling it saw consisted of only one room with no stoves or double windows.[56] Their children comprised the largest group that failed to complete elementary school (*Volksschule*); in 1906–7, 65 percent of those failing were Czech children.[57] The figures were undoubtedly much higher in Favoriten, since the least educated Czech-speaking inhabitants settled there; two-thirds of all students in the Czech-speaking *Volksschule* came from the homes of industrial workers.[58] Pressured by the brick-factory owners to begin work at age 12 or 14 or leave these one-room company dwellings, these youth never experienced a true adolescence. Czech-speaking children often had to withstand the taunts and barbs of the better-off children from Favoriten's central core. One former resident of Favoriten remembered how kids from the central core used to jeer, "You live in a barracks," at the children of the brick workers.[59]

By attributing certain undesirable characteristics to these two sections of Favoriten, inhabitants from the central core established their freedom from such behavior. As Standish Meacham found for England, "If an area was rough, everyone there was assumed to be rough as well."[60] When elderly former inhabitants of Favoriten's central core were asked to describe the Kreta dwellers, they almost always described them negatively. One former inhabitant, who described his parents as "almost in the middle class," despite the fact that his father, a skilled worker (upholsterer), drank himself to death, distanced his family from the "rogues" and "rowdies," the "uneducated" (*ungebildete*), and "the most primitive social group" who lived in the Kreta.[61] A former locksmith in Favoriten described the Kreta as "somewhat notorious, because the hoodlums were there" and "rowdyism" was endemic.[62]

Such social distancing was also apparent when workers were asked to describe their social standing. Many workers, including numerous unskilled workers, described themselves as socially "in the middle" in order to separate themselves from those at the bottom of society. For some the difference could be explained primarily in economic and occupational terms. After describing her husband as a worker who wrapped packages and delivered them to the post, a woman described her family as middle class, "because we weren't the very poor, you know."[63] A daughter of a carpenter answered similarly, "Well, I don't want to say rich, but probably more in the middle. Because I can't say poor either."[64] The daughter of a highly skilled artisan, a typesetter, described her family's social standing as somewhere in the middle because "we didn't belong to the rich (*höheren*), but we didn't belong to the poor either."[65] Here one notes the popular social perception that separated those at the top, normally referred to as the "better people" (*bessere Leute*) in Vienna, those in the middle, and those very poor at the bottom. Certain workers, such as brickyard, street, and seasonal workers, ranked low, since their jobs did not require extensive training, were low paying, and were associated with unpleasant working conditions. A trained auto mechanic who became a taxi driver out of economic necessity placed himself in the lower-middle class and pointed out that "we didn't associate with street pavers and street workers."[66] After describing her family as contented middle class (*zufriedener mittelstand*), the daughter of a carpenter characterized those socially below her family as those who could not manage their income, those who "live from day to day:

today fun and music, tomorrow we'll eat lard. It wasn't like that with us."[67] This comment indicated that one's social status depended not merely on income and occupation but also on behavior.

Within the better-off sections of a mainly labor district, including Favoriten's central core, inhabitants were divided by income, occupation, and, to a lesser degree, housing. At the top were a group of lesser officials (*Beamte*), most artisan masters, journeymen, and transport workers. They could earn less than the skilled factory workers, but they were separated from them by the higher social prestige of their work and the greater security of their positions. Lower-level officials and transport workers were laid off far less frequently than industrial workers, and they were not victimized by changing technologies or economic fluctuations as were laborers. Although many small artisan masters and journeymen lived close to the poverty level, their independent status and training placed them above factory workers. In the working-class areas, this upper group sometimes lived on the better streets and in the more desirable buildings but normally in the same buildings with manual laborers. When their sometimes low salaries forced them to live in the same buildings with laborers, they normally did not live on the ground floor, where passersby could see in, but on the first or second floors. In those buildings with a rear and front tract, they normally lived in the front.[68] Still, they were not superior to skilled workers in terms of income and not isolated from manual laborers, since they encountered them daily in the hallways and their children often played with the workers' children. The separation began with late childhood, when, at about 11, children from this group went to a secondary school—*gymnasium, realschule,* or *Gewerbeschule*—and manual laborers' children entered the upper-elementary school (*Bürgerschule*) or repeated some of the elementary (*Volksschule*) classes.

Austrian researchers often include lower-level white-collar workers and officials (*kleine Beamte*) in the same lower stratum (*Unterschicht*) as manual laborers or, as John wrote recently, "at least in a grey zone between a middle and lower stratum."[69] John also contends that concentration on manual laborers alone excludes this large group of workers who experienced conditions similar to manual laborers. These sometimes impoverished service-class workers were usually accepted by manual laborers as part of the larger "family" in the tenement houses that filled the predominantly working-class districts. There was resentment only toward those who tried to keep their distance from manual laborers. As a former female metal worker told me, "They were trash [*Schmarrn*] just like we were."[70] Female factory workers were often the lowest-paid factory workers and therefore more resentful of those with social pretensions.

Children growing up in artisanal families could experience quite different conditions, depending on their parents' position within the artisanal work force. As will be discussed more completely in chapter 5, occupational designations often disguised extreme differences in income and status. For example, in the Austrian putting-out system (*Verlag*) that was widespread in the late nineteenth and early twentieth centuries, a shoemaker-master might employ scores of small shop-masters who produced shoes or parts of shoes for him.[71] The small shop-masters might produce only a portion of a product for the larger master. Obviously, the income and living conditions of these artisan-masters would be very different. A 1901 study of tailors showed that about 15 percent earned above 2,600 kronen a year, while 33 percent earned 1,040 or less.[72] Shoemakers earned even less; in a 1906 study 70 percent of the masters and 94 percent of the journeymen earned 1,040 or less a year. By comparison, the study of 119 families (70 percent skilled workers) in 1912–14 revealed an average income of 1,945 kronen a year.[73] In the clothing industry a large number of women, called *Zwischenmeisterinnen*, worked on contract from larger masters. Their income was much higher than the two to five artisans they employed in their home or the many home-workers they hired. The cultural-social attitudes of the larger masters has been described as *kleinbürgerlich* by some, although detailed studies of their attitudes and practices have yet to appear.[74] As chapter 4 will indicate, artisans tended to put much more emphasis on secondary school than did skilled workers. The large numbers of artisans who continued to produce goods independently in competition with factories or who had switched to repair functions could normally not support a family on their own earnings. In order to compete with lower-cost factory goods, these numerous small-scale artisans exploited their workers and apprentices, as chapter 5 details. In these families the wife and often the children had to work as well. Their living conditions would have been similar to those of unskilled workers.

Among the nonartisanal workers a three-way division existed: a group of primarily skilled workers at the top, where normally only the father was gainfully employed; a poorer middle group in which the father had regular employment, but his low pay and periodic unemployment forced his wife and children to work full- or part-time and the family had to take in subtenants; and the very poor seasonal and day laborers at the bottom. As this work will argue throughout, these workers were divided by income, the prestige of their work, their housing, and their economic and social outlook.

At the top of the manual-laboring population was an aristocracy of skilled workers. Children growing up in such families experienced conditions similar to those among the better-off artisanal families. Prominent among the skilled workers were electrical and machine workers. Two recent studies of electrical workers have shown that their wages and work conditions were exceptionally good in comparison with other wage-earners. Some of these workers gained a 50-hour workweek in 1904 (Siemens-Schuckert workers), with no wage reduction, and a week's paid vacation after ten years of employment.[75] Only in the interwar period were most workers given a week's paid vacation, and in most cases employers managed to avoid granting it even then. These workers were highly organized—near 90 percent of the electrical workers in many firms—and highly active in the Social Democratic Party.[76] Although these workers still fit in a broad lower stratum of the population, only the fact that they are manual laborers fixes them socially below lower-level white-collar workers and independent workers.[77] Interestingly, many of these skilled workers wore fake white collars to work but removed them during the workday.[78] Wives of skilled workers tended to remain in the home, but their children normally attended trade rather than secondary schools during the period 1890–1938. They suffered less from unemployment, particularly in the pre-1914 period, when economic conditions were improving, and therefore suffered less from the instability that characterized the bottom two strata. Some researchers have concluded that it was only this stratum of the working population that adopted respectable behavior patterns.[79]

The second and largest group of workers included families where both the parents worked outside the home or the father worked outside the home and the wife worked in the home as a home-worker, usually for the textile or clothing trades. Sieder divides these groups apparently because he believes that children of parents who worked outside the home spent more time in the streets due to their parents' absence. However, this is really more a question of gender. Girls in both types of worker families did much of the housework and helped in the home-work (putting-out) industry, and boys in both worker milieus spent much time in the streets.[80]

. These families were distinguished from those in the lowest manual-labor stratum by their steadier employment (although they suffered from serious unemployment in the interwar period), their higher income, their more fixed residence in a working-class quarter, and their smaller families. The 21 individuals I interviewed from this group averaged 4.52 children per family compared with 5.94 for the 17 interviewees from the lowest stratum in the period before World War I.[81] Both my interviews and those of Viethen show that many families in this stratum lived in the same domicile for extended periods, and most moved only once or twice in their lives.[82] Many moved into the homes of their parents after their death and lived there until they moved to a retirement home in the post-1945 period. Perhaps best characterized as poor rather than truly impoverished, members of this group spent much of their time working and sleeping, with little time left for political and cultural activities. Except for a small portion who would become supporters of the SDAP, most of the children of this group would grow up apolitical. Although they may have had a subconscious feeling that life was unfair and that they were victims of economic and cultural oppression, they had insufficient time or knowledge to deal with it.

Education meant obtaining adequate training to provide them with their daily bread and to avoid misery, but not to achieve some exalted social or occupational level. Therefore, the children in this group left school as early as possible, especially in the pre–World War I period, in order to relieve family finances. Only the sons of families in this stratum would be able to obtain apprenticeships in any area other than the textile industry until the early 1920s, since they often required an initial payment to the master and always resulted in a period of little or no wages. Daughters were valued much less in this group than among skilled workers, since they often meant increased poverty for the family as a result of their reduced chances to find meaningful employment. The smaller families of the interwar period would bring some change in this attitude, since girls would experience an increasingly better chance to find work during the postwar period. The children in this group could expect limited nurturing in the home, since both parents were often forced to work.

Although wives often worked in the home as cottage-industry

workers, they had little time for child care. Because families in this stratum often depended on their older children to help run the household, children often took the role of ersatz parents. Fathers in this group tended to avoid excessive drink but did visit taverns periodically. The children in this group had more difficulty in school because of language problems: the non-German-speaking because of their lack of knowledge of German and the German-speaking because of their heavy dialect and lack of knowledge of "book" German. Their parents had neither the time nor the education to give them much aid with their schoolwork. Few of their homes contained any books or had parents who were sympathetic to education beyond the minimum requirements.

This group encountered periodic hardship due to unemployment of the parents, or sickness or death of a parent, but usually managed because they were able to budget their resources and sometimes received aid during hard times from their neighbors or relatives, who often lived nearby. They sometimes managed through letting out space for a bed-renter (*Bettgeher*) during the night, and, as a result, they could often rent a larger dwelling and have use of it except when it was occupied by the bed-renter, usually from 9 P.M. to 5 or 6 A.M. Their lives were marked by more security than those in the lowest stratum, especially in the period before World War I, when economic conditions were improving—less so in the interwar period, when all workers were subject to unemployment on a massive scale—and they were clearly separated from those in the lower strata by their more permanent housing, their relationships, and their desire to lead an orderly, respectable existence.

A third group of truly impoverished, primarily first-generation Viennese inhabitants, along with some seasonal workers, made up the lowest stratum. Pulled to Vienna's factories and construction projects from Bohemia, Moravia, Silesia, Italy, Hungary, and the Austrian provinces, these casual laborers encountered serious hardships. Children of those who tended to stay in Vienna, primarily the immigrants from the Austrian lands of Bohemia, Moravia, and Silesia, encountered serious language obstacles in the schools and were often rejected by the German-speaking inhabitants of the working-class districts. A few had it easier as a result of contact with relatives or friends who had made the trip earlier and had achieved some economic stability. The grouping together in ethnic neighborhoods often made it possible for persons from this group to exist.

Their pay was low and often interrupted by unemployment, and they were not as apt to receive material and psychological support from their neighbors and relatives because of their lack of fixed domiciles. They often had their own ethnic organizations, including political and leisure-time groups and schools and were therefore further separated from the social groups immediately above them. As the commentary from former inhabitants of Favoriten has shown, this lower stratum was separated from other segments of laborers by more than just distance. Socially and culturally, this group comes closest to that much-disparaged "lumpenproletariat" described by Marxists.

There were economic and social differences within this lower stratum. The seasonal workers, who came primarily from Italy and Hungary, were the most impoverished, ill-housed, and socially rejected segment of this lower stratum. But conditions were also damaging for those who would make Vienna their permanent residence. Since many of the adults came to Vienna alone and did not marry until they could set up households, their low income made it necessary for them to become bed-renters and spend much of their time in neighborhood taverns with fellow workers. Although some may have drunk very little, all were assumed to be heavy drinkers by the more settled inhabitants of a district. Once married, these first-generation Viennese tended to have more children than the earlier residents. Those 17 that I interviewed from this group came from families with an average of 5.94 children during the pre–World War I period. In three of the five cases where three or fewer children resulted from the marriage, the father had either died young or deserted the family. In two of the three families with eleven children, six had died young.[83]

These families often came into conflict with the Habsburg authorities and the Social Democratic city administration in the interwar years concerning the health and care of their children. Social Democratic child-observation centers sometimes took their children from them—3,324 were taken in 1926—because their homes did not meet the socialist leaders' *bürgerliche* ideal of cleanliness or orderliness.[84] Children from this lower stratum, both those non-German-speaking and those who spoke Viennese dialect, experienced extreme difficulty in adjusting to the schools because of their language handicaps. In some cases separate schools for ethnic minorities made the transition easier, but it extended the period of

adaptation to the Viennese environment. The chapters on schooling and work will show how difficult the period of adaptation was
for these ethnic minorities.

Sometimes cutting across these material and occupational considerations in determining one's social status in a primarily manual-
labor area was a worker's possession of some industry, sobriety, self-
control, knowledge, and cultivation. After describing her father (a
typesetter forced to operate a small transport business because of
the unhealthy air associated with typesetting) as an educated
worker (*gebildete Arbeiter*) and her family as *mittelstand*, a woman
explained that family members had obtained cultivation (*Bildung*)
at home.[85] To separate his family from those below them, a son of a
baker's assistant (*Bäckergehilfe*) described his family as *mittelstand*
and those at the bottom as "afraid of work" (*arbeitsscheue*), as "drinking up all they earned," and as poorly clothed.[86] His further remarks
that "they made themselves Proleten" indicate again that social
position was often determined more by behavior than by job or
income.[87] The daughter of a trained blacksmith remarked that her
family's social position "was not by the lower class" because her
father was cultured (*gebildet*).[88] The son of a small-scale independent
artisan distanced his family from casual laborers by pointing out
that "in our building all the men had something to do and none of
the wives worked."[89] He separated his family further from the
poorer laborers by explaining, "We didn't have any bed-renters in
our entire house."[90]

Lower-level white-collar workers, who often earned less than
skilled laborers, stressed cultivation and education in determining
one's social position. The daughter of a lower level white-collar
worker (*Hilfsbeamte* in a government ministry), whom she described as a needy wretch (*Hungerleider*) because of his small income, described the family's social position as "lower-middle class
or middle-middle class because my father was a very intelligent
man."[91] For many, then, social position was not just a matter of
income but a matter of behavior. Of course, it was much more
likely that one would behave "respectably" if one were the product
of *gebildete* parents and a better neighborhood.

This division of the working population into "rough" and "respectable" segments should not be confused with any desire on the
part of the latter group to adopt a middle-class lifestyle. Rather
than viewing this quest for respectability as a *kleinbürgerlich* goal,
it should be seen as a means and not an end. Respectability was a

defense against anomie, dehumanization, and disintegration of personality. The desire to present a respectable image normally entailed a visible defense against those charges that workers were dirty, lazy, cultureless, sexually promiscuous, and financially incapable. Since I first presented this respectability thesis in 1982, several Austrian researchers have tentatively reached similar conclusions.[92] But one believes that only the upper stratum of skilled workers exhibited any sort of respectable behavior.[93]

I will argue throughout this work that at least some aspects of respectable behavior penetrated to all but the lowest stratum of workers. Evidence for such behavior exists not only in my oral interviews but in those of the Institute for Economic and Social History and in many contemporary accounts of working-class behavior. This is not to argue that workers always exhibited respectable behavior or that they behaved in a manner that the bourgeoisie believed to be respectable. For example, workers' leisure-time activities, when they had time for them, might well include what the bourgeoisie would consider an excessive amount of drinking in a local *Gasthaus* by the father, an excess of cohabitation before marriage, and too much unsupervised playing of children in the streets.

As the criteria discussed in this chapter indicate, it is no simple matter to determine where a particular laboring family fits in society. While economic and occupational criteria may point to a particular rung on the ladder, behavior patterns may contradict any neat categorization. Still, there was normally a close relationship between one's economic/occupational position and behavior.

2

Life on the Hallway (*am Gang*)

*Oh, that was a rent barracks, door on door, and then three or four
parties for each toilet, and then the water supply on the corner [on the
hallway].*[1]

—*Daughter of a shoe-factory worker*

*Six parties used our toilet. Can you imagine that in the morning people
were lined up in front of the toilet. They banged on the door and cried
out 'What is going on' so that you would come out.... One thing for
sure, through those apartments was, for example, let's say, the feeling
of togetherness, was much better than today. Because people ... met
each other by the water faucets and while waiting in front of the toilets
always became involved in conversation. And each one helped the
other.*[2]

—*Son of a carpenter with a small shop*

Although conditions improved slightly between 1900 and 1910, Vienna remained one of the most densely crowded cities in Europe
during the period 1890–1914. Since the figures in Table 2.1 include
the entire population, they are necessarily misleading concerning
working-class crowding, but they do give some general indication of
Viennese conditions in comparison to the conditions elsewhere. In
order to meet the demand for housing, huge apartment buildings,
called *Zinskaserne* (rent barracks) by the Viennese, were constructed
throughout the city by private investors. Normally crowded and
overpriced, the *Zinskaserne* were singled out by reformers as the

Table 2.1   Average Household Size, 1880–1933

Year	Vienna	Berlin	Munich	Germany
1880	5.0	4.5	4.3	4.6
1890	4.7	4.3	4.4	4.6
1900	4.4	4.0	4.3	4.5
1910	4.1	3.6	4.2	4.4
1933	2.9	2.7	3.3	3.6

Source: Adapted from William H. Hubbard, *Familiengeschichte: Materialien zur deutschen Familie seit dem Ende des 18. Jahrhunderts* (Munich, 1983), 125.

major reason for physical and psychological problems among the working class. They continued to house most laboring families in the interwar period. A 1930 study calculated that a quarter of all "poverty experiences" and suicides could be attributed to the poor living conditions in the *Zinskaserne*.[3] Another found the *Zinskaserne* to have an especially deleterious influence on working-class girls.[4] All contemporary critics agreed that the major problem with the *Zinskaserne* was overcrowding and its consequences: lack of privacy, poor and often psychologically damaging sleeping conditions, repeated conflicts brought about by crowding, high mortality rates, and the forced sharing of utilities on a common hallway.

To overcome this crowding, the Social Democratic-controlled city council launched a major building program in the interwar period. They reduced rents to such levels that private investors were driven out of the housing market. Although this effort has been much lauded by socialists, recent investigations have pointed out how little this program did, no matter how well meaning, in alleviating the housing crisis.[5] But the SDAP was interested in more than merely providing housing for the poor. In their drive to create "new people," socialist leaders hoped to mold a new worker consciousness through a multitude of cooperative projects in the new housing projects, such as common kitchens, day-care centers, kindergartens, and numerous evening events. Although World War I provides a clear break in terms of the mentality underlying housing construction, the situation inherited by "Red Vienna" in the interwar period and the limited resources available curtailed what could be done to eliminate the housing shortage. How serious, then, was the housing problem, and how was it dealt with by youth and their families?

There can be little doubt that the working-class areas experienced severe overcrowding prior to World War I because of the small size of the apartments and the large families that were common among the lower classes. The typical working-class family lived in a one-room/kitchen (*Zimmer/Küche*) or *Zimmer/Küche/ Kabinett* (cabinet) apartment. The cabinet was often listed as half a room by census officials since it was so small. It normally had one or no windows while the room (*Zimmer*) usually had two windows. In 1890 the average-size dwelling in Favoriten was 2.2 rooms compared to 5.4 rooms for the upper-class first district, 3.6 rooms for the predominantly middle-class fourth district, and an average 3.4 rooms for all the socially mixed nine inner districts.[6] Conditions improved only slightly during the next two decades. In 1913, 76 percent of the 540,990 dwellings (*Wohnungen*) in Vienna were two rooms or fewer. Most of these small dwellings were located in workers' districts; 96 percent of the dwellings in the working-class district of Ottakring were listed as two rooms or fewer compared with only 46 percent in the fourth district (Wieden).[7]

The working-class family typically spent most of its time in the kitchen, since it was often the largest room and contained the only source of heat, the kitchen stove. As a former inhabitant of Ottakring remembered, "Even when we had visitors—our visitors were mostly relatives on my grandmother's side—we sat in the kitchen."[8]

Not only were the dwellings small in the working-class districts, they also housed more people. Although the average number of persons per household in Vienna declined between 1880 and 1910, laborers' housing remained crowded because of their larger families and smaller dwellings. A comparison of the number of persons per room shows a great disparity between districts. In comparison to a 1910 Viennese average of 1.36 persons per room (*Bestandteile*), Favoriten averaged 1.87, and the third, fifth, and sixth districts averaged 1.26, 1.23, and 1.05, respectively.[9] Only a slight easing of the crowding occurred during the period 1890–1914: in Favoriten the decline was from 1.95 to 1.82 persons per room and in Ottakring from 1.78 to 1.63.[10] This decline was primarily the result of the decline in family size and a reduced taking-in of subtenants and bed-renters. But these figures are misleading in that they include all inhabitants of a predominantly labor district. A study of 119 working-class families carried out by the Austrian Trade Ministry from 1912 through 1914 indicates even greater crowding among the families of laborers: 5.25 persons per dwelling and 4.61 persons per room.[11] This last figure is undoubtedly more accurate, since it excludes most of the upper strata of inhabitants in Favoriten, such as small-shop owners, lower-level service workers, and artisan masters. But it is still somewhat misleading, since it excluded the lower stratum of workers who would have had larger families and smaller quarters in the prewar period. In my sample, the 17 families comprising the lowest stratum averaged 5.94 children per family compared with 4.52 for the 21 families in the middle stratum and 4.00 for those families in the highest stratum.[12]

Subtenants [*Untermieter*] and bed-renters [*Bettgeher*] were common in Vienna. While a subtenant had use of a room day and night, a bed-renter could use a bed only during the night. In 1890, 10.12 percent of Favoriten's population was categorized as bed-renters.[13] In the 1912–14 survey of working-class families, one-third of the families subleased part of their dwelling.[14] Gulich calculated that 17 percent of those living in small apartments in 1914 took in bed-renters.[15] A decline in the portion of dwellings taking in subtenants and bed-renters, from 39 to 26.5 percent between 1880 and 1910, obviously relieved but did not resolve the situation.[16] Recent immigrants to the city often lived as bed-renters until they earned enough money to be able to live as a subtenant or rent their own dwelling. As discussed in chapter 1, most of the bed-renters in Vienna were from the Czech-speaking lands.[17]

Normally bed-renters could spend only the time needed for sleeping in the dwellings. The son of a woman who took in ironing remembered, "Many in our house had a bed-renter. They could come only at seven in the evening. The bed was opened up then, and they had to leave at seven in the morning. Where they were during the day and what they did concerned no one."[18] Subletting, especially bed-renting, was not a totally negative phenomenon. By renting a bed at night a family could possibly avoid eviction or afford a bigger dwelling that they had the use of during the day. Such a strategy could markedly improve the family situation and might mean that the wife or children would not have to work. Josef Mooser found that this half-open proletarian family was a stigmatizing mark for bourgeois observers in Germany, "but for workers [it was] a means to overcome poverty."[19]

The sharing of common facilities on the hallway produced potentially explosive situations. There must have been much of the "pounding on the toilet doors," since many working-class families had to share them with at least four other families. A comparison of the number of bathrooms and toilets in some typical working-

Table 2.2   Dwellings with Bath and Toilet, 1910 (percent)

District	Bath	Toilet
1	33.5	67
2	9.1	36.4
3	9.3	31.4
4	19.1	50.2
5	3.5	19.2
6	15.6	41.6
7	13.4	40.8
8	16.2	46.5
9	14.4	47.8
10	0.8	3.6
11	1.3	4.6
12	2.7	8.6
13	9.5	20.2
14	1.3	6.4
15	2.0	11.5
16	0.9	4.7
17	1.5	7.4
18	9.2	26.5
19	14.0	29.3
20	1.2	10.3
21	1.6	6.3
Vienna	7.1	22.0

Source: Michael John, *Wohnverhältnisse sozialer Unterschichten im Wien Kaiser Franz Josephs* (Vienna: Europa, 1984), 247.

class districts to those in socially higher districts indicates that sharing facilities was a common working-class problem. As Table 2.2 shows, the worker districts such as 10, 11, 16, 20, and 21 had the greatest shortages in 1910. Although only in the first and fourth districts did more than half the dwellings contain a toilet, only a third had baths, even in the first district. The absence of toilets in the apartments in the *Zinskaserne* was potentially more damaging, since there were more occasions for conflict.

Another way to illustrate the overcrowding is to examine the number of children who had to share a bed or were without a bed entirely. Of those involved in the 1912–14 study of working-class families, 58 percent had to share beds.[20] Since this group was comprised primarily of those in the upper two labor strata, the average for all families would have been much worse. Some of those I interviewed vividly remembered the prewar crowding. Recalling her prewar experiences, a woman from a lower-stratum family of eleven children compared their sleeping arrangements to that of a hospital, where, she remarked, "We had a table-bed in the kitchen that served as a table during the day. The table was opened up [at night] and two boys had to lie there."[21] Another remembered a one-room/kitchen apartment for nine people, where "we slept like rabbits."[22] She also puzzled over how her parents could have had sexual intercourse given the cramped sleeping quarters. A carpenter's helper's daughter recalled, "We had a room/kitchen dwelling and a sleeper. After my father was inducted into the military, all of us slept in my parents' bed, all nine of us."[23]

An additional dilemma faced primarily by the lowest group of workers, and to those in the middle stratum when unemployment or sickness struck, was repeated dwelling changes brought about by eviction by their landlords, or by their search for better conditions or lower rents. In 1914, 129,062 eviction notices were issued, with three-fourths of them demanding vacation within the legal minimum of two weeks. Of these, 12,669 were in Favoriten and 13,411 in Ottakring.[24] Landlords often moved families out in order to raise rents. As a former resident of Ottakring who had been abandoned by his father told me, "We moved often. Yes, that was the way it was then. When you got the apartment clean, the landlord evicted you, since he could ask the next tenant to pay a gulden or a krone more."[25] Another recounted how his family moved often in the mainly labor district of Brigittenau before World War I in order to get a cheaper dwelling or escape bad conditions.[26] Still another former inhabitant of Brigittenau and son of an unskilled worker remembered, "When the rent was a few kronen cheaper, one moved to the cheaper dwelling."[27] His parents lived in three different dwellings in Brigittenau while he was growing up.

Families could also move to higher floors, the ground floor, or cellar apartments, where rents were a bit lower. As the son of a woman who took in washing told me, "In the house where we first lived, mother moved to the third floor because it was a few groschen cheaper."[28] A common reason for eviction among the lowest strata was too many children. Poor families sometimes had to send one or two of their children to sleep with nearby relatives and instruct them never to group together due to landlords' limit on the number of children permitted in a dwelling. An interviewee of Viethen remembered, "There were seven children [in our family] and the landlord permitted only six. . . . We had to register one of my sisters elsewhere; she was registered with our aunt."[29]

Dwelling changes occurred much less among those in the first two strata. The survey of 119 prewar families, primarily skilled workers, shows that only 17 percent (21 families) moved every two years or less.[30] Those I interviewed, especially those from the two upper strata, moved infrequently. Ten of the seventy children moved into their parents' dwelling and lived there until after World War II or until retirement. Most moved two or three times in their life—this was also true of those interviewed by Viethen—and most of these moves were not the result of evictions but the desire for some minor improvement in housing.[31] Evictions occurred normally among the upper two strata when unemployment or death struck the family.

As rents rose in the inner city in the latter half of the nineteenth century, workers were driven to the lower-rent outer districts (*Vororte*). Few workers could have afforded the average 338 kronen per room of the first district in 1900 or even the 203 kronen per room of the fourth district. Only Favoriten's 137 kronen or the other outer districts' average of 143 kronen was affordable.[32] But some found it difficult to pay even these lower rents. A common conception among those I interviewed was that their rent took about a week of their fathers' monthly wages. John found this to be the rule of thumb as well among those interviewed by the Institute for Economic and Social History.[33] Other sources indicate that the average was probably somewhat lower for the better-off families. With heating and lighting included, the 119 families in the 1912– 14 survey of working-class families paid about 18 percent of their income on housing.[34] However, with an average income of 1,945 kronen, the families in the survey were somewhat above the average among working-class families. The seventeen casual laborers' (*Hilfsarbeiter*) families in the survey paid 20.1 percent of their income on rent and heating.[35] The only way to avoid excessive rents was to move to a smaller dwelling, a basement dwelling, or a less expensive district. But families hardly ever moved to another district because they had no contacts in other districts to aid them in getting an apartment, they desired to stay near friends and relatives, they disliked change, and they often became attached to the district in which they had been reared.

As chapter 1 argued, the peculiar demographic effects of World War I and the lack of any significant housing construction during the war resulted in even greater housing shortages after the war. Although the socialist city administration was able to build 61,000 dwellings in about a decade (10 percent of the total number of housing units available), recent studies have shown that a much larger number was needed to meet the housing shortage.[36] With private investors driven out of the housing market by high real-estate taxes and rent control, the only building was done by the city. Rents were reduced from about 14 to 25 percent of income in the prewar period, depending on a family's income and size of dwelling, to somewhere between 3 to 6 percent of income in the interwar period.[37] Two interwar surveys of housing indicate that the typical worker dwelling continued to consist of only two rooms, as Table 2.3 shows. Most of this was due to workers' continued residence in the prewar *Zinskaserne*, but some was due to the SDAP's desire to build as many dwellings as possible to meet the housing shortage and to prevent workers from taking in tenants and to build political support for the party. They therefore kept apartments small (only units of 414, 520, and 630 square feet were available), did not provide bathrooms, and even kept kitchens small in some units in order to force families to cook cooperatively in common kitchens. By 1934, after the building program, only 1.8 percent of dwellings in Favoriten and Ottakring had bathrooms, and only 22.3 percent in Favoriten and 15.6 percent in Ottakring had toilets.[38] The small size and inadequate number of dwellings continued to be reflected in the number of youth sharing beds. An examination of 275 elementary school (*Volksschule*) students in Ottakring in 1928 revealed that only 73 had their own beds, 190 (about 70 percent) had to share beds, and 12 had no beds at all.[39]

Relief from the crowding came more rapidly in the 1930s as a result of the depression. Unemployment and reduced wages forced many families to limit births: by 1934 the average number of persons per family had dropped to about 3.10 from the 4.23 in 1910.[40] Working-class families contributed significantly to this decline. Ironically, children growing up in the lowest labor stratum would produce a smaller average number of children in the interwar period than the offspring of the two higher social milieus: their marriages produced only .73 children compared with .89 children from those in the middle and 1.06 for those coming from the highest stratum.[41] Those offspring of the highest stratum had received superior occupational training and were therefore better able to afford slightly larger families despite the poor economic conditions.

The subletting problem had also improved by the 1930s. Although Favoriten still had 5,084 subtenants and 219 bed-renters in

Table 2.3   Size of Dwellings of Worker Families (percent)

Number of Rooms	Home-workers (1928)	Industry Workers (1932)
1	17.1	15.1
2	46.6	55.1
3	26.8	26.5
4 or more	3.5	3.2

Source: Dieter Langewiesche, "Politische Orientierung und soziales Verhalten: Familien und Wohnverhältnisse von Arbeitern in 'roten' Wien der Ersten Republik," in Lutz Niethammer, ed., *Wohnen im Wandel* (Wuppertal: Peter Hammer, 1979), 177.

1934, this was an improvement over 1890, when 10 percent of Favoriten's population consisted of bed-renters.[42] Although the number and size of housing units was still far from what was needed, the smaller number of subtenants had reduced the number of "half-open" families significantly. With subtenants removed from most workers' homes by the 1930s, the SDAP strategy to promote the small nuclear family that they believed would bring about an orderly family existence seemed to be succeeding.[43] Since relatives would not be able to live-in in the small dwellings, wives would be forced to remain in the home to care for children and cook.

Although the enormous economic instability of the interwar period could suddenly plunge even the best-situated worker family into economic despair, it was the families in the lower two strata, especially the lowest one, who were most liable to be unemployed or subjected to the worst living conditions. Dwellings changes among the upper two strata were less common. Most of those interviewed by Viethen and by me moved only once or twice in their life.[44] Of course, less movement occurred during the interwar period due to official rules against evicting tenants without giving them adequate notice. Before World War I poor tenants could be evicted within two weeks after having been given notice.

Did such crowding and its consequences lead to despair and the disintegration of family life, as has often been assumed, or did other factors intervene to ameliorate the poor conditions? A recent study of Vienna claims that "the single room-kitchen dwellings in the Viennese rent-barracks were overcrowded and the exclusive living together of children and parents, a requirement for the establishment of a conclusive family life, was realized by only a minority."[45] Ehmer considered the taking in of subtenants especially deleterious in these "half-open" families. But recently a number of researchers have suggested that the despair often associated with working-class existence has been exaggerated. Jackson and Meacham have argued that although conditions were difficult for the working class it was not a despairing situation for most. Jackson maintains that his evidence for Duisburg, Germany, suggests that "onerous housing conditions did not automatically produce alienated, hostile people. On the contrary, evidence is accumulating which points to more social stability, and less disintegration, among city dwellers. Family life flourished in the city and was one of the basic means by which individuals managed the urban experience."[46] Meacham believes that "middle class observers suggest a despair which most [laboring families] appear to have kept at bay."[47]

My research indicates that much of the Viennese working class was also not as despairing as has often been assumed. Researchers have concentrated on that lower stratum of day laborers and seasonal workers, for whom conditions were debilitating, but have neglected that vast mass of workers for whom conditions, although periodically unstable, were less destructive and family attitudes more constructive. As Dieter Langewiesche recently wrote concerning Eugen von Philippovich's dismal account of worker housing before the war, "He painted, despite all the differences in his evidence, a unitary picture of misery."[48] It is probable, as Sandgruber argues, that the housing and living conditions of that lowest stratum were better in Vienna than in the rural and small urban areas of the Habsburg Monarchy.[49]

Although residents of working-class districts tended to exaggerate the extent of community solidarity as a result of comparing their youth with modern-day youth, oral interviews and autobiographies suggest that a feeling of community togetherness compensated somewhat for the difficult living conditions. Those I interviewed repeatedly spoke positively about community (*Hausgemeinschaft*) and solidarity (*Zusammengehörigkeitsgefühl*) to describe the working-class areas they lived in during the early twentieth century. As one said, "When it was necessary we helped each other. We were like a family."[50] Another remarked, "It was a community. Not like today where everyone lives for himself."[51] An unskilled laborer recalling the interwar period responded, "It was always a large family, therefore somewhat, a community. The feeling of togetherness was better then."[52] A former resident of the Kreta in Favoriten remarked, "So, at that time, today it is no longer the case, my wife can confirm it, then the neighbors were exceptional, one helped the other. It was all one family. Everyone knew each other, everyone helped each other, it was a family."[53] Such cohesiveness was primarily the result of families' having to share facilities on a common hallway and having to help each other in times of need.

The hallway (*Gang*) was the center of community activity. It was in the hallway, while women gathered water at the *Bassena* (water outlet), that they heard the latest gossip or discussed the plight of another tenant. Everyone knew each other's problems and triumphs. And as one told me, no one needed to ask, "Where do you come from? Who are you? and so on. Then all were one hand and soul."[54] Another pointed out how helpful neighbors were to each other then and how different conditions were today: "Completely different than today. Then neighborhood help was a matter of course. Due to the fact that the water and toilets were on the hallway, the inhabitants knew each other better and were more willing to help each other. Not like today, today everyone is in his apartment, locks himself in and doesn't know his neighbors."[55] Most spoke of the inhabitants who lived along one hallway as a family. As one so aptly described the relationship, "Everyone was together."[56] This relationship could sometimes stretch to an entire building. As a former inhabitant of the Brigittenau described it, "The entire house was together. Why? Because we met by the stairways."[57]

A common view was that the vanishing of common utilities on the hallway led to a fading of the communal relationship. Although all I spoke with praised the city housing constructed in the 1920s, they noted that moving the water and toilets inside the apartments had destroyed that special relationship enjoyed by workers in the old *Zinskaserne*. One said that "in the main one was more isolated. . . . Earlier the women met and talked on the hallway. That they have now stopped."[58] Another preferred the old *Zinskaserne* apartment to the new city dwellings they occupied later because "there was always a child, and the workers played music on the streets or in the building."[59] John found a similar sentiment expressed by those interviewed by the Institute. As a woman told him, "We all banded together in contrast to the city housing, where they shut the door and don't come out willingly."[60] When comparing the old *Zinskaserne* to the socialist housing constructed in the interwar period or the housing constructed after 1945, they almost

all believed that people were now more isolated and less neigh-
borly. Most agreed that people now locked themselves away from
others.

While conflicts between residents undoubtedly occurred, they
were often of short duration. According to one former resident of
the *Arbeitergasse* (Workers Street) in the fifth district, "Many got
along well together, then they had a falling-out, then they made up.
Life was very full then."[61] This comment points to an essential
difference between working-class and middle-class culture. The
necessary mingling brought about by their living conditions added
a dimension, in many cases a richness, that was not present in the
higher social groups. Normally the richer the apartment building,
the larger the apartments and the fewer the contacts. As the daughter of a shoemaker recounted, "It depends on the size of the dwellings. If one had a room-kitchen-cabinet apartment, one went out
less often in the hallway and had less contact. If one had a smaller
apartment, then there were more apartments on a floor."[62] This
popular conception is supported by a study of children and poverty
in the interwar period by Hildegard Hetzer that claimed that "the
influence of the neighborhood would lessen as the social situation
improved."[63] Recent social research tends to confirm these conclusions. Those with greater financial means tend to reach beyond
their local area for intimate ties while those with limited means
are constrained to a place. As sociologist Claude Fischer concludes,
"Relations constrained within a group or place become dense, mul-
tiplex, frequent and functionally important, and thereby become
more communal than others."[64] Workers' restraint to place and
economic needs forced them to turn to each other.

Socialist publications in the interwar period stressed how inhabitants of the city apartment buildings [*Gemeindebau*] had supported each other during the trying economic conditions of the
interwar period, but they failed to mention that this had long been
common practice. As we have seen, social relationships became
more distant in the better housing provided by the city. A common
characteristic of life in the old *Zinskaserne* was support and help
from neighbors. Only a few I interviewed failed to mention this aid.
As one said, "When it was necessary, when the wife was sick perhaps, then we stuck together. We helped out."[65] After the birth of
children, other women often helped with the cooking and the care
of children. As a woman who sewed in her home told me, "My
mother immediately cooked a good soup with the fine noodles for

those who had recently given birth."[66] They also often loaned clothes to those who had interviews and took up collections for those who could not pay their rent, but not if they had not economized.[67] Neighborhood help was not a result of socialist efforts to bring about political unity. As a former sign painter explained, "No, no, that was universal. If one was a Social Democrat or a Christian Socialist, that was entirely beside the point. People helped each other and it didn't have anything to do with the party."[68]

In areas where the working-class population was not in a majority, the close, almost familial relationships typical of the working-class areas did not develop due to the lack of contact with others of a similar social strata. In predominantly bourgeois districts, workers were often forced by high rents to live in cellars or attic apartments or in the cheaper rear-tract dwellings of an apartment building. As Figure 5 shows, cellar living-quarters predominated in the high-rent districts of Hietzing and Döbling. The rear-tract apartments were restricted primarily to the middle-class-dominated districts, such as the third and eighth districts. In these areas anyone from the working class was relatively isolated and often alienated. Those who served as building caretakers (*Hausbesorger*) in middle-class-dominated districts experienced a heightened sense of isolation. Their contacts with middle-class tenants were infrequent and seldom more than perfunctory. As a building caretaker's daughter in the eighth district recalled, "No, it didn't go well. . . . No one looked after us. . . . They were friendly, but we had no contact with them."[69] A trained mechanic remembered being ostracized by inhabitants of a building in Hietzing where he and his wife worked as house caretakers: to them, he recalled, "You were only a worker and you had to see that the dirt was cleaned up, otherwise nothing."[70] While any worker would find it difficult to gain acceptance in a bourgeois district, the cellar dwellers in a predominantly working-class district, who were invariably from the lowest stratum, experienced social ostracism. The daughter of a skilled worker recalled that there were people who lived in cellars in the Columbusgasse, "but I didn't have anything to do with them."[71] As discussed in chapter 1, this social distancing enhanced the respondents' feelings of respectability.

A common practice in the *Zinskaserne* of the pre–World War I period was house or hallway dances and balls. They ranged from

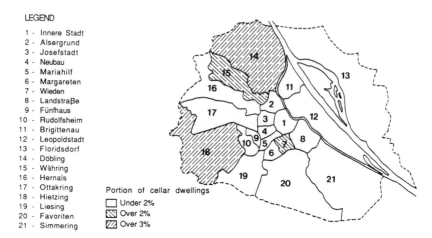

FIG. 5. Cellar apartments by district before World War I. From Michael John, *Wohnverhältnisse sozialer Unterschichten im Wien Kaiser Franz Josephs* (Vienna: Europa, 1984), 154.

dancing to harmonicas to "schrammel" music in the hallway to whole house celebrations. As a former resident of Ottakring remembered, "House musicians came and played harmonicas and guitars while inhabitants danced in the hallways."[72] Several spoke of the musicians playing in the courtyards while the tenants threw down money and danced in the hallways.[73] These dances were especially widespread during Fasching according to those I interviewed. But they were also common on birthdays, name-days (*Namenstag*), and Sundays. The daughter of a carpenter remembered that such celebrations occurred every Sunday in her building: "Can you imagine, the room on the second floor was cleaned out every Sunday, everyone in the house visited us with chairs and set up two cabinets and stretched a curtain between them and they put on a theater. All the kids were there, . . . the children brought chairs with them, they came from the entire house, and from the opposite house."[74]

As the previous examples of social interaction indicate, the relationship among women was especially close. As one woman said, "The women understood each other much better. They helped each other out and the children played together."[75] The constant need to share resources or provide physical support brought women together into what John Gillis has described in the British context as a matrifocal network.[76] Mothers served as financial managers, house caretakers, doctor and nurse, and the homes' primary representative to the outside world. Viethen found that mothers were primarily responsible for family behavior.[77] While fathers might have ultimate authority in the family, it was the mother who dealt with family concerns on an everyday basis. It was the mother who had to meet with authorities when children ran afoul of the law or when they had trouble in school or in the neighborhood. Through their constant contacts with other women, women knew where to turn when their family encountered difficulty. Having normally already provided aid to other families, they could expect aid in return. Since fathers spent long hours at work, they did not have these neighborhood contacts. The father traditionally gave the mother most of his pay and let her manage the finances. As in some other countries, the wife was referred to as the finance minister since she managed the family budget.[78] When she was unable to make do, blame was heaped on her shoulders rather than on her husband's meager earnings.

Family contacts outside the neighborhood tended to be with relatives, except for those few who were active in unions or politics. Relatives normally lived as close as possible to each other. Of the 70 persons I interviewed, 36 settled in the same district as their parents and 5 in an adjoining district.[79] This confirms Tilly and Scott's speculation that the working-class young settled near their parents in the early twentieth century as well as later in the century.[80] Often the primary reason for the grouping of relatives was the fact that those seeking housing could more easily find apartments in areas where they were known or where they had relatives.[81] Another factor was the security and aid that nearby relatives provided. Grandparents often looked after children when both parents worked. In some cases families moved near or in with grandparents in order to have supervision for their children. Also, it was better to have grandparents as subtenants to share costs rather than strangers. Perhaps the best example of relatives living near each other that I encountered was from Brigittenau. A former resident told me that her relatives lived in five of the seven houses on the street and that all but one of her children lived near her.[82] As a child, she spent most of her time with her grandparents, since "my grandmother lived on exactly the same street."[83] Trips to other districts were infrequent and normally related to one's place of work being located in another district.

Families often became emotionally tied to a district. A former inhabitant of the working-class district of Simmering (eleventh district) told me his family moved to the seventh district when he was about ten years old but moved back after only nine months because "we couldn't forget Simmering. The freedom. It was different there, there [seventh district] it was all built up. Yes, yes, dyed-in-the-wool Simmeringers, we didn't want to leave."[84] In some cases, inhabitants identified with only a particular section of a district. In describing his boyhood in Ottakring, Karl Ziak wrote, "Strictly speaking, I wasn't an Ottakringer but a Neulerchenfelder boy. This difference can be understood only by those who know the history of the sixteenth district."[85] Even after the Neulerchenfeld's incorporation into Ottakring in 1890, Ziak claimed, "In their hearts they remained Neulerchenfelders. They were called that also and crossed reluctantly the Reinhartgasse [today the extended Habergasse] and the Habichergasse, which had constituted the border against the usurpers."[86] As will be discussed in chapter 3, such attachments often developed from youths' defense of their district or area against "foreign" youth groups.

In addition to this sense of belonging, working-class families were able to find satisfaction in small successes in coping with their environment. Rada hints at this when she writes, "In a large number of dwellings in the old apartment houses, the inhabitants prized tidiness, hardly felt the cramped quarters, and were proud when they could display a good tablecloth or a new oilcloth on the table."[87] This characteristic of working-class behavior, described by one student of working-class culture as "making fundamentally punishing conditions more habitable," explains the often excessive house-cleaning typical of working-class homes.[88] Almost all those I interviewed stressed their mothers' obsession with cleanliness and tidiness.[89] It demonstrated a control over one's meager resources and thereby separated families from those who had no self-discipline or control. The psychological satisfaction of a tidy house was so overpowering that socialist leaders encountered stout resistance from working-class women when they tried to convince them to spend less time on housecleaning. Such attitudes were less an attempt to emulate bourgeois practices than to distance themselves from the slovenly masses at the bottom of the social ladder. As Hoggart found for Britain, "Cleanliness, thrift and self-respect are not attempts to imitate the middle class but arise more from a concern not to drop down, not to succumb to the environment."[90] A woman from Favoriten described with great admiration and respect how the wife of an unemployed man with five children kept her dwelling spotless (*tadellos rein*) and her family nourished through her own hard work and sacrifice.[91]

Although socialist party leaders, predominantly middle-class professionals, opposed obsessive cleanliness and tidiness, they associated slovenliness and uncleanliness with apathy and fatalism and sought to exorcise them from working-class mentality. In an article in the socialist women's magazine *Die Frau*, a female party member wrote, "In a neglected, untidy dwelling neither husband nor children feel motivated to take care [and] we want to educate our members to be clean and tidy and a well-kept dwelling is the prerequisite for that."[92] They recognized that the inclination to give up was most likely among the unemployed and those at the very bottom of the social ladder. In a letter to the *Arbeiterzeitung*, a socialist welfare worker tried to encourage even unemployed workers to keep tidiness the watchword by pointing out that "not all the unemployed live in dirt and disorder, and those who have an earned income are not always the cleanest and most economical."[93] When the socialists took over the Viennese city administration in the 1920s, these welfare workers clashed constantly with the poor lower stratum of workers. They often removed children from homes that they considered to be unclean or psychologically damaging. This clash, as chapter 7 will explain, depicts the vast chasm separating the leadership of the socialist party and that small impoverished segment of workers at the very bottom of working-class society.

As chapter 3 will elaborate, children growing up in these closed communities with few contacts outside their districts knew no other lifestyle. As the daughter of a painter recalled, "I never thought that it could be otherwise, I never felt that I was poor," even though she remembered not having shoes.[94] Another remarked, "In the building . . . everyone lived the same lifestyle, therefore, it didn't occur to us that others lived differently."[95] Ignorance of better conditions elsewhere was fostered by the limited mobility of most working-class youth and the absence of the modern communications network. Few working-class homes had a radio until the 1930s. Life was played out in the neighborhood or at most the district, and only those workers living in predominantly middle-class districts realized that life could be better. This does not mean that misery did not exist. Obviously, the lower stratum of workers had been plagued by low wages, frequent unemployment, and overfilled dwellings in the prewar period. But by the interwar period much of the overcrowding in Vienna had disappeared. While dwellings continued to average about two rooms a family, the number of occupants had declined to an average of only three persons, including the lowest stratum of workers.

With a majority of working-class homes consisting of only parents and one child by the 1930s, the realization of a family-centered life was now possible. However, since the post-1929 economic depression had forced many families to limit births or abort fetuses, the familial desire to provide better for fewer children was not the primary motivation in all cases. But the reduction in births and resort to abortion were in the main a result of an impetus to remove want and crowding from the lives of children. The decline in births had begun even before World War I, and a common sentiment among interviewees was that their children should have a better material life than they had experienced. By examining more closely the daily life of working-class children, chapter 3 will look beyond the housing question in order to provide further insights into the lives of working-class youth.

3

Everyday Life (*Alltag*)

The proletarian child: How it was conceived and born; poorly fed; degenerated parents; father poisoned by alcohol; mother weakened by excessive work, household duties and births; no relief during pregnancy; unhealthy and crowded dwelling.[1]
— *Notes of socialist party leader Marianne Pollak for a 1922 lecture*

The most wonderful thing was, we children had a glorious freedom. For we had water, the so-called ponds, on the Laaerberg. There were woods, then the ponds, meadows, we had everything.[2]
— *Son of a galvanizer and a cleaning woman*

Vienna, particularly in the pre–World War I period, produced many of the conditions that the cultural-deprivation school found most destructive of the working-class condition: the massive influx of workers, excessively crowded housing, large families, and the absence of a social net to deal with poverty conditions. Such conditions should have produced those destructive consequences described by socialist leaders such as Marianne Pollak.

Since it has been established that many working-class families lived in crowded conditions in the prewar period, and to a lesser extent in the 1920s, did such conditions bring about family disintegration among all workers and their families? To what extent did youth experience physical and psychological deprivation result in poor health, early death, antisocial behavior, and criminality. Or, can an equally good case be made that adversity, assuming it is not totally debilitating, brings about cohesiveness and strengthens the family? As noted in chapter 2, Johnson has argued from English evidence that one of the fundamental aspects of working-class culture is successfully dealing with adversity.[3] Certainly the post-1945 period has shown that material abundance does not automatically bring about happy and well-adjusted youth. Although the family per se is not the primary topic of this study, it will be necessary to explore at length the family conditions and attitudes that shaped child rearing and youth's attitudes before proceeding to a discussion of youth culture.

Although the topics discussed in this chapter will encompass three historically distinct periods (the prewar, war, and interwar periods), these periods are not as distinct in terms of youth and family behavior as economic and political affairs might lead one to expect. Social conditions certainly improved in the interwar period due to the decline in immigration and the birthrate—resulting in less crowding and a more settled population—and a widened social net provided by the socialist administration of Vienna. Even further reductions in the birthrate and crowding resulted from the severe economic problems accompanying the economic depression following 1929.

While these changes certainly brought significant alterations among the working class as a whole, there were some more stratum-specific behavior patterns and attitudes that remained consistent over time. For example, the tendency for lower-stratum workers to spend more of their income on drink and less time on family affairs changed very slowly. As discussed below, youth games and leisure activities were marked by their class and stratum-specific continuity throughout the entire 1890–1938 period. While such novelties as the radio and cinema began to transform youth activities in the interwar period, they influenced the upper levels of the working class more simply because of the costs involved. As some historians have suggested, discerning group variation may be as significant as establishing change over time.[4]

One of the most prevalent attitudes concerning youth and the family is that a utilitarian perspective toward children and high child-mortality rates among working-class youth in the nineteenth century made it impossible for parents to provide the necessary affection to offspring. This lack of emotional attachment in the working-class home allegedly robbed the child of the care, warmth, and consideration that were necessary for a full development of the child's potential. A recent study of Viennese working-class women cites a lack of complete *"Häuslichkeit"* (domesticity) and affection in the working-class home as late as the early twentieth century.[5] To Ehmer, the close family relationship inherent in *Häuslichkeit* was hindered by the crowding brought about by the presence of strangers in the household. Ehmer's evidence comes primarily from studies by Rada and Hetzer of interwar working-class youth.[6] Rada wrote about the absence of "an unselfish love with social feeling" [von selbstloser Liebe, von sozialem Gefühl] and opined that everyone thought only of themselves.[7] Hetzer agreed that there was a suppression of an "intensiven Gefühlserlebnisse" among working-class youth.[8] Neither, however, ever provided adequate evidence to support their views.

While it may be impossible to prove definitively because of the lack of evidence concerning emotional states, the evidence I have gathered from Viennese workers who lived in working-class districts during the pre-1914 period indicates that the affection issue is more a matter of what social stratum one belonged to. While it is no doubt true that most working-class youth were not harbored, showered with affection, or esteemed, as was the case in many middle-class homes, only a few had negative memories of parents, and they came invariably from the lowest stratum.[9] Only 2 of the 70 persons I interviewed spoke bitterly about their family experiences. One, a casual laborer in Favoriten in the interwar period, was the daughter of a peasant family who was forced to go into domestic service and leave home at the age of 12.[10] The other case resulted from a broken home and hostility between the new stepmother and the children.[11] Among those interviewed by Viethen, two had negative attitudes about their home environment. One came from a family with seven children and a mother who worked as a cleaning woman. Since her mother boarded her out, she remembered that there "was no mother love, no proper [love]."[12] The other, also from a family of seven children, remembered going without shoes in the winter and thinking as a child, "I will not have so many children. . . . Because then a mother had really nothing and the children also nothing. . . . No one concerned themselves about us."[13] In addition to these few respondents who specifically recalled the absence of affection, chapter 6 argues that most children in the lower stratum failed to get the attention they deserved for their successes in school.

Against these negative responses came a majority who spoke positively about their childhood experiences. The daughter of a small-scale shoemaker remembered, "We had poverty as youth, but it was a wonderful youth, not as it is today."[14] Another who was often left alone while her mother worked said, "It was a happy childhood even though I had to help with all the housework."[15] One respondent remarked that "we had a wonderful youth. Today's youth no longer have that."[16] It eventually became apparent that many respondents' remarks were partially a result of a collective memory conditioned by their negative attitude concerning post-1945 youth behavior. In rejecting present youth behavior, they exaggerated their own positive youth experiences and forgot their more trying times. But, social milieu also played an important role in conditioning the respondents' attitudes. It was primarily in the larger families typical of the lower working-class stratum and part of the middle stratum that children could not get enough attention and love. But the declining fertility rate common to all strata before World War I (described in chapter 1) indicates that parents may have been adopting a new strategy in order to better provide for their children. Once parents realized that most of their children would live to adulthood and that more children did not lead to higher family income in the age of compulsory education and child labor laws, adequate attention could be exercised only by limiting births. A closer examination of family strategies and the home environment will shed further light on this question.

The reduction in the number of children born to working-class families was less the result of any growing hostility toward children, as charged by a socialist critic in the interwar period, but a conscious desire in the face of material scarcity to provide better care and lavish more attention on a few children.[17] After experiencing the material deprivation brought about by the typically large families of the period before World War I, some parents decided to limit the size of their families. The dismal wartime and postwar economic conditions encouraged families even more in this family-planning strategy. The fact that the post–World War I period brought with it a working-class family strategy of only one or two children—apparently differing from England, where this occurred only after World War II, according to Gillis—meant parents could spend more time with each child and would have less need to make choices about which children would receive advanced training.[18] In trying to explain his wife's resort to abortion, a former unskilled laborer sounded a common refrain among those I interviewed: "Stay at home? Nobody could do that. I had to resort to abortion. There were so many of us in the apartment with nothing to eat, always unemployed. How could we have brought a child into the world?"[19] Another said, "I love children and I wanted to have children, but my husband said the times were too bad. And by the time things improved, I was too old. Because at 36 or 37 years of age one should not have any children. When they reached 20, I would look like a grandmother."[20] In addition to this concern for their offspring, some working-class families found it necessary to limit the size of their families because of the crowded housing conditions. Because of the apartment shortage, many newlyweds had to live with their parents for extended periods. Of the 70 persons I interviewed, 12 lived as subtenants with their parents after marriage. In many cases they lived with them until their parents' death, at which point they received the apartment. Some were unable to obtain apartments in any other way.

Although the size of families began to decline in the last two decades before 1900, the generation that began about 1910 was the first that severely restricted the size of their families (see chapter 1). The high incidence of abortion indicates that families were trying to limit the size of their families and were therefore involved in at least a primitive form of family planning. The officially recorded arrests for abortion, according to all who have commented upon them, account for only a small percentage of those actually performed.[21] Since abortions were illegal, only those abortions that led to the illness or death of the mother became known to the authorities. Several of the persons I interviewed spoke of their mothers' abortions—one calculated that his mother must have had three—and the mid-wives (*Hebamme*) who carried them out.[22] Of course, there were also a large number carried out by the pregnant women who could not afford a midwife. One socialist critic attributed abortions almost totally to an intentional adoption of a "bourgeois ethic"; in his words, "the striving at the cost of unborn children to rise into a higher class."[23] Some of the reasons he cited—the striving of women for independence and emancipation from motherhood, a compulsion (*Zwang*) for work outside the home, lack of responsibility, and reduced authority of the husband—are contradicted by most existing evidence.

As chapter 5 explains, most of the working-class mothers in a survey of 1,300 industrial workers in 1932 would have quit work if their husbands had earned enough to support the family.[24] In this survey, work appears to be a family necessity. There was, however, a generational difference: single and younger women, those reaching their maturity in the interwar period, had a greater desire to continue work. But women had few occupational possibilities that would lead to independence and emancipation from motherhood. Most of the jobs held by working-class women in the interwar period were grueling factory positions or unimportant clerking duties that were ill-paid and roundly disliked. Again, it seems that a much stronger case for limiting births can be made for the poor economic conditions of the interwar period, the housing shortage, and a decision to avoid the worst aspects of working-class existence they had experienced as children. Many I spoke to wanted to have more children but found it impossible due to late marriages (see chapter 6) and crowding that forced many couples to live as subtenants for extended periods. It does not appear to be the result of the reduced authority of the husband, since many of the males I spoke with shared responsibility for the decision to limit the size of their families.[25] The fact that the lowest stratum had even fewer children than the upper two strata in the interwar period also indicates that the purely economic considerations were paramount.[26] It seems unlikely that unskilled and often unemployed laborers would reduce their number of offspring merely for social reasons.

Much responsibility for the poor home environment has been attributed to capitalism's removal of the mother from the home. Although this theory has been rejected by many, it continues to receive support. A recent Austrian study maintains that inadequate nourishment in the home resulted less from the limited budget of the typical worker family than from the little time that working mothers had to carry out household chores. This author also accepts the stereotypical image of the working mother as a poor housekeeper and cook.[27] The evidence provided for this view is the establishment of household-schools and mother-advising centers for working mothers. Although some working-class mothers would have benefited from such schools, assuming they would attend them, their creation is much more a result of the bourgeois attitude, common even to socialist leaders, that lack of knowledge rather than funds was most damaging to laborers' families. The examination of family consumption below will argue that lack of funds was the most critical element when undernourishment existed.

A related claim that the majority of working-class homes were characterized by their untidiness and uncleanliness as late as the interwar period is also more a petit-bourgeois perception of the working-class condition than an accurate description of conditions.[28] As discussed in chapter 2, an untidy home was an exception among the working class. Only in a portion of lower stratum homes did lack of funds, work, and excessive crowding make it impossible to maintain tidiness and cleanliness. The drive for cleanliness cut across stratum lines. A common theme in my interviews and those of Viethen and the Institute for Economic and Social History is the mother's ability to run a tidy, well-organized home despite the crowding and often meager finances. Failure to do so was viewed as the exception and was attributed to laziness, excessive drinking, and similar character failures.[29] Even socialist leaders, who thought that orderliness and cleanliness were necessary in the home, thought that working mothers spent too much time on cleaning and caring for their homes.

Many believe that a patriarchal, authoritarian, unfeeling discipline characterized most working-class homes in the nineteenth and early twentieth centuries. Two interwar socialist observers, Otto Rühle and Felix Otto Kanitz, maintained that the typical worker family was dominated by a tyrannical father who demanded unquestioning obedience from both wife and children.[30] As Kanitz argued, "The authority of the strongest ruled in the proletarian family."[31] Recent accounts based on oral history provide some support for Kanitz's position.[32] One argues that evidence showing that children had to be home when the father returned from work, that the father's supper always had to be ready when he arrived home, and that he meted out punishment when he returned home attests to the father's unquestioned authority.[33]

Although some working-class homes were dominated by a patriarchal authoritarianism, my evidence suggests that the first four decades of the twentieth century either witnessed some modification of this practice or it had never been widespread among the upper reaches of the working class. The dominant impression of my interviews and those of Viethen was not that of a harsh, authoritarian father.[34] Since most of our interviewees came from the upper two strata of workers, where one might expect change to first appear, there was little evidence of the authoritarian pose. It is also very difficult to determine how much the wife's attitudes and actions were shaped by her husband. While she was often responsible for the daily running of the household, it is likely that the husband normally set the standards for the home. Elizabeth Roberts's model, based upon English evidence, that the rigid application of the patriarchal model "distorts the true picture" and overlooks the "power and achievement of women" is not totally at odds with the authoritarianism argument."[35]

In many working-class homes the mother—through her presence, her handling of family finances, and her moral authority—took the place of the father as the authority figure.[36] In most cases the father was at work or sleeping and the household was run by the mother. This is not to contend that the father did not have final authority in the typical working-class home, but to argue that industrialization had removed the father from the home for most of the day and left him too tired at night to exercise his authority as completely as he might have liked.[37] Most of those I questioned remembered their mothers or older siblings as the authority figures in the home. Although existing evidence cannot fully resolve this question, my evidence suggests that the patriarchal argument hinges on what working-class milieu one is describing. Only in the lowest working-class strata was there a strong patriarchalism by the interwar period. When authors such as Kanitz and Rühle write about a typical proletarian authoritarianism, they are referring to the lowest working-class stratum.

Working-class children had little to look forward to according to most students of working-class history. If they lived past their first year, they faced a dismal life characterized by physical and intellectual retardation that could not but lead to despair and debility. In the Viennese case socialist critics were united in their dismay at the working-class condition. A group of socialist writers—Victor Adler, Hildegard Hetzer, Käthe Leichter, Charlotte and Karl Bühler, Paul Lazarsfeld, Fritz Predan, Fritz Kanitz, and many others—sought to improve conditions by exaggerating the material and social disadvantages experienced by working-class youth. In numerous books and essays, often based on surveys of working-class youth, they attempted to show how working-class children developed at a slower pace than their middle-class counterparts. The reasons, they argued, were inadequate and less nourishing food, poor housing, and the lack of stimulation and encouragement in the home. Now, sixty years after most of their work appeared, their conclusions are still the major bases of most studies on the subject. A large number of these studies has provided indispensable information for any study of this period, especially those studies of groups of children at school or of the attitudes of large numbers of youth, but many are flawed by the necessity to prove that conditions were excessively damaging for the entire working class.

What were the conditions, then, according to these studies, and how did they influence the growth and development of working-class children? A 1922 Viennese study found that school children of poor people (*armer Leute*) weighed three kilograms less and were 7.5 centimeters shorter than children from middle-class families.[38] Hildegard Hetzer's 1929 study of children and poverty, *Kindheit und Armut*, argued that 56 percent of the minimal family needs were not met in the proletarian family compared with only 10 percent in the middle-class family. She further contended that proletarian children dropped behind middle-class children in physical and intellectual development because they were undernourished. She based much of her conclusions upon a 1925 study of 800 Viennese 6- to 13-year-olds, which found that 52 percent of day laborers' children and 39 percent of skilled workers' children compared with only 23 percent of middle-class children weighed too little.[39] According to Hetzer, this undernourishment, combined with a lack of care and a scarcity of light and clean air in the home, resulted in working-class children beginning to talk six months later than middle-class children.[40]

A survey of 616 Viennese children in 1926 by the Seminar for Socialist Education found that 70 percent of the children were healthy and 30 percent were either sick or suffering from "organ weaknesses."[41] The survey does not explain the nature of these organ weaknesses. But the health conditions seem to have had little influence on their intellectual development. From 575 cases, the survey calculated that 87 percent were judged normal, 6 percent gifted, and only 7 percent intellectually underdeveloped. Rada's study paints a slightly less dismal picture of working-class nourishment. Of the working-class school girls she studied, 60 percent weighed near the normal weight and the other 40 percent averaged only three kilograms below normal according to the school doctor.[42] But many told her that they did not eat any breakfast, ate only *Schmalzbrot* (bread spread with lard) or dry rolls at the *Gabelfrühstuck* (mid-morning snack), and seldom ate meat; 80 percent ate meat at most three times a week and some only on Sunday.[43] But Rada later points out that some of the lack of nourishment was not due to the shortage of food but to the girls' habit of eating only those things they liked and substituting *Schmalzbrot* for those things they did not like.[44] Hetzer attributed the better condition of Rada's subjects to the location of their housing on the outskirts of the city, where more vegetables were available in the gardens.[45] In most cases physical condition resulted from the number of children in the family: those with the largest number of children, normally those families of unskilled workers and day laborers in the lowest stratum, were the most undernourished.

Undernourishment undoubtedly contributed to the higher mortality rate among the lowest stratum of workers. When the higher mortality rates of the working-class districts discussed in chapter 1 are subjected to a closer scrutiny than census data permit, the primary responsibility of the lowest stratum for the excessive mortality rate becomes clear. Among my interviewees, two of the three families from the lowest stratum with 11 children lost 6 of their children and the other family lost 4.[46] Of the three families in this stratum with 3 or fewer children, the father died young in two cases and deserted the family in the other case. There were large families in the highest stratum, but few children died in this stratum due to the better nourishment and conditions.

Except for Rada's brief discussion of this subject, these studies tell us little about how families dealt with scarcity. Did families accept their lot apathetically, collapse in despair, or meet the challenge with resourcefulness and thereby limit the impact of scarcity? If all of these responses occurred, what special family or individual characteristics determined which course they would take? Oral-history evidence permits us to look at the way families and individuals responded to scarcity. Although varied, there were certain common responses to the problem of shortage regardless of the level of laborers. Those common denominators were almost always to divide up (*"einteilen, einteilen, einteilen"* one told me), to economize (*wirtschaften*), and to utilize fully what could be bought. Those who followed these guidelines, with the exception of the truly destitute, managed to "make do" on meager incomes.

A major consumption rule was that families hardly ever splurged, with the exception of a holiday, Sunday, or special family occasion. For example, meat consumption was strictly regulated. With the exception of the father, who might eat meat almost every day, meat as a separate dish was eaten normally only on Sunday. As the son of an unskilled worker told me, "We kids didn't get any meat in order that father could have his fill."[47] The son of a bag maker responded similarly, "There was often meat only on Sunday. And in many families, ours as well, the meat belonged to my father. We got the soup because he was the breadwinner and needed strength."[48] If meat was eaten more than once a week, it would more than likely be horse meat. Beef and pork would be eaten only on Sunday, with sometimes a goose on holidays. Most remembered eating horse meat, but few remembered it favorably. One who did preferred it to other meats: "It was our favorite."[49] No matter what meat was purchased, the usual practice was to stretch it by making most of it into soup.

So what did most children of working-class parents eat? The answer is soup, various types of noodles, vegetables, and bread. Breakfast was normally bread with weak coffee. This was followed by a morning snack of *Schmalzbrot*. As the son of a shoemaker, who claimed his family lived from week to week, said, "We were reared on larded bread."[50] Reformers lamented the excessive consumption of *Schmalzbrot* among the working class. While no doubt heavily laden with fat, it nevertheless provided necessary calories and was common Viennese fare even among the middle class. Lunch was almost always a noodle dish or soup, bread, a vegetable, and an inexpensive pastry or fruit for dessert. As the daughter of a better-off shoe-factory foreman said, "We had a lot of vegetables and soup."[51] The daughter of a typesetter recounted that "we ate soup for years since it was cheaper."[52] Soup was obviously one of the least expensive ways to stretch the small amounts of meat that could be bought. In the evening a few of the better-off families had sausage, but most had either soup or *Schmalzbrot*.[53]

Working-class perceptions of their childhood fare were far different from the undifferentiated scarcity described by socialist leaders. A shoemaker's son told me, "Well, we didn't eat badly. Food was not so expensive and one had merely to be frugal."[54] The daughter of a furniture-factory worker and one of eleven children thought that she "got what the body required."[55] There was little of the dismay that fills the pages of socialist publications in the early twentieth century concerning the working-class condition. In fact, only one of the 70 I spoke with thought she had been undernourished. And in this case, factors other than the supply of food were responsible. The daughter of a mail carrier in Favoriten complained that her mother, who had divorced her father, gave her brothers more food than she received.[56] This may have been true since it fits with the common working-class assumption that males

FIG. 6. This prewar working-class family eating depicts several traditional practices. The father has the responsibility of dividing the meat and the children wait obediently. Note also the cramped quarters. A bed is situated in the right background and a small kitchen in the upper-left corner. (Courtesy Bildarchive, Austrian National Library, Vienna)

need more nourishment and women and children should sacrifice to this end. In general, those I interviewed were proud that they had been able to "make do" on their families' low income, and this included managing the food supply. It was not so much the quantity or quality of the meat that became a mark of family respectability, as Meacham believes was true of English workers, but how that meat could be utilized to meet family needs without resorting to borrowing, indebtedness, or charity.[57] Undoubtedly, scarcity existed among most working-class families, especially among those in the lowest stratum. With an average of nearly six children in the prewar period and an ill-paid and often unemployed father, families in the lowest stratum must have experienced continual shortages. But the view that all working-class families suffered equally from undernourishment results from an inattention to economic-social divisions among laboring families.

Naturally, working-class children had far fewer personal possessions than middle-class children. The son of a carpenter told me,

"When a child had a tricycle, he was looked up to."[58] Few working-class children had more than one pair of shoes. Forced to go to an orphanage at the age of six when his father died, he remembered that "we each had one pair of shoes and they were ripped. When we were able to buy something, we went to the *Dorotheum* [pawn shop] and bought used clothing."[59] The son of a galvanizer recounted that a neighboring family of a ditch digger with twelve children, obviously lower stratum, could not even provide their children with shoes: "They didn't even have shoes in the winter. Directly across from the apartment house stood the school. Before school began, they stood barefooted on newspapers. When school began, they ran fast across the street and into the school since it was heated." He went on to point out that "all of these children became respectable."[60] Again, dealing resolutely with scarcity in the working-class environment was essential if one did not want to lose the respect of other inhabitants. For most working-class families it was not how much one had but rather how one dealt with scarcity that was important.

As discussed in chapter 2, crowded housing was not a totally negative experience for the working-class family. Against the indisputable health and educational disadvantages of cramped quarters, the crowded tenement houses provided plenty of other children for playing and often brought parents together to care cooperatively for the children. The common feeling among inhabitants of the *Zinskaserne* that they were one large family was partially a result of children's playing together in the hallways and courtyards. Wives often looked after the children of the next-door neighbor and sometimes cooked for them when their parents were unable to.[61] As the son of a bakery worker remembered, "Every family had from two to four children in our building . . . and the doors were open on the hallway. The children bumped into each other . . . for example, at *Jausezeit*, someone's mother cut bread, spread lard on it and gave every kid a piece. The next day another mother did the same."[62] Many I spoke with remembered how they came to know many of the other occupants of their building through the children.[63] Often, the economically better-off or those with jobs in the food industry shared some of their food with their neighbors. The daughter of an Anker Bread Factory worker remembered how the neighborhood children used to always drop by for bread, which her family was amply supplied with.[64]

This sense of community often extended beyond the hallway to the streets. But a sharp division existed between those working-class families who restricted the amount of time their children could play in the streets and those who did not. It became a mark of respectability among some working-class families, as well as a precaution against injury, to keep their children, especially daughters, out of the streets. A woman reared in Favoriten remembered that "my mother paid very close attention to me. She was very strict. When I slipped away, I went into a park and fooled around like the devil."[65] The daughter of a furrier worker who was reared by her grandfather, a railway worker, recalled, "Everything had its rules. I couldn't play with the street kids. The parents of the street kids were not so proper; they lived down below in the cellars."[66] This division between those who played in the streets and those who did not reflects somewhat that division between the respectable upper stratum and the remainder of working-class society discussed in chapter 1. Normally the children from the upper reaches of the working class, especially the daughters, were supervised while playing in the streets, or they played in the apartment courtyards or parks. Except for the lowest stratum, parents usually refused to let their daughters go into the streets at night alone once they had reached puberty.[67]

But most working-class boys did spend much time in the streets. As the son of a plasterer in Ottakring recalled, "After school, we did our lessons and then we were in the streets."[68] The daughter of a locksmith in Favoriten remembered the mothers being happy when the children were outside, since it provided some relief from the noise in the crowded living quarters. She told me, "They were happy when the children, all sixty children in the building . . . were outside."[69] Although playing in the streets was against the law, it normally was not enforced by the police. This plasterer's son remembered a policeman who did try to keep kids out of the street: "We said, ow, the lightning flash is coming, because it was like lightning flashing when the sun shone on his helmet, it glittered."[70] Some working-class children tended from an early age to play outside the family circle due to their parents' absence at work and the more communal nature of working-class housing. Hetzer found that a 3- to 5-year-old working-class child spent 16 percent of his time with his play group. Thus they were bound to be more influenced than middle-class children by their peer group.[71] By the time working-class children reached school age they had a much greater independence than the children of higher social classes, who were "ängstlich kontrolliert" according to Hetzer.[72] A recent study points out that in the bourgeois family any "spontaneous and unplanned meetings with other children were strongly discouraged."[73]

Children's play activities best exemplify the importance of group variation and continuity rather than change over time. Through all the difficult times of World War I and the depression, children's play changed very little within a particular social stratum. The major changes resulted from the fewer possible playmates brought about by the demographic transition described in chapter 1 and the emergence of a multifaceted Social Democratic youth program that kept some children occupied in more structured activities in the interwar period. The enormous number of possible playmates available in the prewar *Zinskaserne* simply did not exist in the thirties. Games such as soccer, which had been played in the streets by large numbers of children at the turn of the century, were played on a reduced scale in the thirties. Most youth in a working-class district took advantage of SDAP-sponsored activities, although their parents never became avid party supporters. Some youth could now swim in SDAP-built baths rather than swimming in the ponds in the outlying districts, or they could take part in SDAP-sponsored hikes or myriad other activities. But it remained the practice for lower-stratum children to spend much more time in the streets than others and to play the same games they had played prior to World War I. Also, more lower-stratum youth had the opportunity for play in the interwar period due to the reduced use of child labor in the more mechanized plants. The emergence of the cinema began to have an impact on leisure among the upper reaches of the working class, as discussed in chapter 6, but it was too expensive for most lower-stratum youth.

Youth games reflected children's social milieu. In Favoriten, many games were the direct product of the crowded conditions and the streets. One game, called corner spying (*Eckengucken*) in Favoriten, required that one player run around an apartment building while another followed peering around corners and upon catching sight of the one being sought yelled "Is schon wer!" (Here he is).[74] *Strawsack* was another favorite street game. Players first stood on a sewer cover in the middle of a street crossing, counted off, and then hopped away on one leg. A catcher waited until one player put down both feet and yelled "strawsack," after which the latter became the catcher. Players were permitted to hop only on the sidewalk or along the curb.[75] One game, robber and policeman

(*Räuber und Pole*), characterized children's attitudes toward the police. All wanted to be robbers rather than the policeman. When a robber was caught, the policeman hit him three times and yelled "police hit" after each time.[76] Another game that was tied closely to working-class areas was *Drei Handwerksburschen* (three handicraft workers). In this game three children split off from a fourth youth and chose an occupation. After choosing they had to tell the first letter of the occupation and then describe it through movement while the others guessed what it was.[77] But the game most often played in the streets was soccer. It was played with a homemade ball (*Fetzenlabrl*) constructed from one of their mother's stockings and anything they could find to stuff inside it that had some bounce. A favorite game was opening one shop door after the other and then watching the shop owners come out to search for the perpetrators.[78]

As the children grew older, street games became more violent. Loosely organized youth groups often established dominion over a certain street or area and drove non-neighborhood children away. Through a number of interviews with former inhabitants, it is possible to reconstruct how youth groups operated. From an early age youth marked off their turf and exercised control over it. To a certain extent it was merely a way of preserving the streets around their apartment buildings as their playgrounds. Not only were all sorts of games played in the streets, but it was also the place where the majority of personal relationships developed and were played out. One of the severest punishments parents could impose was to refuse to permit their children to go into the streets. When 60 interwar, primarily proletarian, higher-elementary-school children were asked what the worst punishments of their life had been, many cited not being permitted to play in the streets.[79] Rada found that 42 percent of the 120 12- to 13-year-old girls she observed found their enjoyment in the streets.[80] This percentage probably dropped considerably during the subsequent years as these girls would soon be experiencing puberty.

In Favoriten, competition took place between youth from different streets and areas. Three former inhabitants independently described the antagonists as the youth groups around the houses on the *Triesterstrasse*, known as the *Weber* from a man who built housing there, against groups in the vicinity of the Gasthaus *Müller* on the corner of the *Herz*- and *Davidgasse*.[81] As the son of a paperhanger described it, "We were the *Müller*, because our *Gasthaus* was nearby and it was called *Müller*, around the corner from the school . . . and the others were the *Weber*. . . . He built houses, large and many, and they are still called *Weber* houses; they are on the *Triesterstrasse/Quellenstrasse*. And that (kids from these houses) was, the Weber, right, and we fought against them."[82] In the inter-war period these areas were separated by fields rather than filled with apartment buildings, as they are today. There was also antagonism between adjacent streets. One former "nonfighter" recalled having to avoid the *Siccardsburggasse* because of a "clique that was downright dangerous," that "contested one's passing through."[83] A former "fighter" remembers battles between the *Herzgasse, Favoritenstrasse*, and *Senefeldergasse*.[84] Battles between the *Müller* and the *Weber* reminded some of those I interviewed of the conflict among youth groups they had seen in the American film *West Side Story*.[85] Although the battles did not reach the gravity of those depicted in the film, since the major weapons were stones rather than knives or guns and the youth groups lacked the organized leadership typical of the contemporary gangs, the potential for more serious violence existed.

During World War I, when conditions were dire and mothers and fathers were in the factories, the youth groups sometimes became more violent. They would beg from passersby and when dissatisfied would take money or food by force.[86] Police and educators often exaggerated the violence and criminality of these *Platten* (bands). A *Bürgerschule* teacher wrote in 1910 that every boys' school on the periphery of Vienna had a group of the "*Plattenbrüder*" that "hang out on busy corners, bother passersby without regard for their age or sex with the grossest, most provocative intimidations, accompanied not unseldom by theft."[87] A similar response by a Boy Scout leader in 1925 warned that "on every street corner, before almost every house door, bands of greasy youth can be seen standing around, cigarettes in their mouths, hands in their pockets, bothering girls who pass by, exchanging smutty jokes, and concocting plans for minor robberies."[88] A close examination of their violations indicates that fear of these groups may have been excessive. The *Bürgerschule* teacher, for example, explains that most violations were thefts of objects of minimal worth, such as fruit, and that injuries from the scuffles were minor.[89] The Boy Scout leader was most concerned with the disorderly appearance of the boys and what they might do rather than actual crimes. He was afraid that their "wild" growing up would be a "severe threat to the internal order of the country."[90] While this "larking about" could sometimes lead to more serious crimes—and it did during World War I, when dire need drove youth to steal food and money—such excesses were not typical.[91] It was the "Schlagen und Raufen" scuffling between street kids and minor theft that was more typical.[92] However, there were a few more dangerous individuals in the streets. A 1927 report in *Das Kleine Blatt* pointed out that some dangerous cutthroats (*Messerhelden*) in Favoriten were feared by both the *Plattenbrüder* and the police.[93]

Youth rivalry sometimes extended to competition between districts. One former inhabitant of the Kreta in Favoriten remembered fights against boys from the neighboring district of Simmering after soccer games on the fields of the *Laaerberg* (Laaer mountain), which were used by inhabitants of both districts. As he said, "We always played and scuffled there. We had a ball."[94] This competition was typical of other districts as well. As a former resident of the fourteenth district remembered, "People would say we were *Sechshauser*, and those on the other side, they were *Fünfhauser*, right. Yes, so, we were district rivals. Often, one could not even go into that district. . . . They waited for you and then beat you up."[95] He also remembered that battles were waged between street rivals within the district as well. The son of an unskilled laborer from the Brigittenau recounted, "We went into the ninth district and picked fights, . . . ten from the Brigittenau and ten from Alsersgrund, and then it was hot and heavy."[96]

The most compelling explanation for youths' sometimes violent street activity is that the streets provided a place where youth were not dominated, except for the occasional policeman, where they were in control. Here they could give free reign to their innermost feelings, to a spontaneity that was not permitted in their cramped working-class quarters where the authority of their parents was normally unquestioned.[97] They were also not subject to societal divisions in the streets, since the major requirement for participation was not one's social background but one's willingness to share in the common youth street culture.[98] Their identification with the local area gave them a basis for collective action. Former Favoriten residents remembered identifying with a prominent tavern (*Müller*) and housing area (*Weber*) in their neighborhood.[99] That youth sometimes resorted to violence points to the greater emphasis on masculinity within working-class culture. Conquering an opponent is much more important than one's ability to articulate. The stronger members of the youth groups were invariably the most respected.

Fortunately, many working-class children did not have to depend solely on the streets. As a result of being pushed to the edge of the city by high inner-city rents, most of the working-class districts contained large undeveloped areas that could be used for games and wandering. Rada calculated that 50 percent of the 120 children she studied spent their free time in the spring and summer evenings in the meadows in their districts.[100] Children from Favoriten and Simmering had the Laaerberg and Wienerberg. Those from Ottakring had the military exercise area called the Schmelz, and Floridsdorf youth had the Danube flood plain. One called the *Laaerberg* area in Favoriten "our paradise" and recalled that in the afternoon they often "had three or four hours of deviling around there."[101] Another remembered the "wonderful freedom" of the Laaerberg, where one could run in the woods, meadows, and along the ponds surrounding the excavations for clay for the brick factories.[102] A mother recalled that she often took her children there with other mothers: "The children, a sack with the afternoon snack (*Jause*), we went out to the Laaerberg, to Inzersdorf, to the meadows and the *Ziegelteich* [ponds formed from where the clay was extracted to make bricks] . . . that was our stomping grounds. The kids went swimming there and we played cards."[103]

Anton Proksch remembered that "three housing blocks away were already the meadows and fields and we went there with our mother often when the weather was good."[104] Looking back at his boyhood in Favoriten, one man stressed the freedom of the open spaces there: "It was for us—me and my brother—an Eldorado for playing and swimming in the summer . . . and we in a certain sense were given free reign by our parents."[105] Another pointed to this same freedom when he explained about all the things one could do in the undeveloped areas of Favoriten, such as "dig holes in the meadows, play Indians and trappers, shoot birds, play soccer, steal vegetables from the surrounding gardens . . ."[106] While the police would characterize shooting birds and stealing vegetables as "criminal activity," working-class youth would view it as "getting their kicks" but hardly criminal. Karl Ziak recalls a rhyme that boys recited to accompany the military trumpeter on the military exercise grounds: tattatra, stole an apple, tattatra, a pear, tattatra, ate it, tattatra, mmmm.[107] Similar to the streets around their dwellings, these open spaces permitted youth to obtain a measure of independence that was normally not possible at home.[108]

While there is no denying that difficult conditions existed in Vienna's working-class districts in the early twentieth century, it is also difficult to deny that a relative stability, rather than disintegration, characterized life for most of the working class there. While World War I and the depression brought hard economic times, the smaller families typical of all strata in the interwar period reduced the economic suffering. Of course, those children of often-unemployed lower-stratum workers experienced the greatest want. No doubt their desperate conditions forced them to reduce their number of offspring below that of the other two stratum during the interwar period. The prewar crowding and resultant lack of attention experienced by lower-stratum children undoubtedly influenced them as parents in the interwar period to limit family size. With fewer children and with the help of neighbors and relatives, these families managed to scrape by during the depression. Youth play had changed somewhat by the interwar period due to the many activities provided by the SDAP and the fewer children competing for facilities, including park and street space. It was possible in the interwar period for the children of lower-stratum parents to experience greater affection since they had fewer siblings competing for their parents' attention.

4

Schooling

It was a special luxury at that time when anyone in this group let their children study—so to speak. By study one meant really only a Matura.[1]

—*Son of a trolley car conductor*

I was really good. But we were poor people who didn't have the opportunity to learn . . . couldn't study then.[2]

—*Daughter of a bricklayer*

According to these former inhabitants of working-class areas, real "learning" implied something more than their attendance at the compulsory elementary school. To them it meant study beyond the basic minimum level of instruction that most of them had received in the *Volksschule* (elementary school) and *Bürgerschule/Hauptschule* (upper-elementary school). European working-class children's failure to advance beyond the elementary school before 1914 has been attributed to family considerations, to youth attitudes toward family and society, and to the class-based nature of educational systems. Studies have explained the high attrition rate among students from working-class homes as resulting from the elitist educational systems characteristic of European governments before World War II. Since authorities, it is argued, viewed schooling for the working class merely as a means to keep youth off the streets and out of the job market, little attention was given

to bringing about real improvement in the schools. Schools became, in effect, detention centers rather than learning centers.[3]

Working-class family attitudes toward the schools were both
practical and psychological. While many parents were apparently
hostile because schools reduced family income by preventing
their children from working, some viewed schools as possibly
erecting intellectual barriers between parents and children and
thereby stripping parents of their rightful role as educators of
their children.[4] Most of those parents who were not outright hostile still did not believe that schools equipped their children for
the real world of work or suited the working-class environment.[5]
Such studies have explained the high attrition rate among students from working-class homes as resulting from the essentially
middle-class status and career-oriented values characteristic of
the schools.[6] Youths' attitudes toward the schools have been explained as either outright hostility, as indifference, or as a desire
for learning that was thwarted by family needs. Those who adopt
the hostility thesis argue that youth viewed schools as part of the
dominant culture and therefore opposed, sometimes violently, the
acceptance of their value system.[7] Others fail to see any group or
class solidarity in resistance to the schools and therefore reject
this class interpretation.[8] What, then, were the reasons for Viennese working-class acceptance or rejection of schooling, and to
what extent did their attitudes change between 1900 and 1940?

In Vienna, working-class opposition to schooling began with the
preschools. Not one of the 70 persons I interviewed, all but four
born before World War I, attended a kindergarten.[9] Ludwig Battista, a ministerial adviser for education and author of several studies on the Austrian schools, determined that as late as the 1930s
only one-seventh of eligible children attended a kindergarten.[10]
Only 19.4 percent of the women workers with children studied by
Leichter sent their children to the free city kindergartens or socialist *Kinderhorte* (day-care centers with some instruction), even
though their children were given preference for the existing openings.[11] Since many of these mothers were members of labor unions
and the socialist party, and therefore presumably were more aware
of the purpose of the *Horte,* and since many were in need of some
sort of child care (17 percent of the children were left at home
without any supervision), the response of all working-class mothers must have been even less enthusiastic.[12] This study led two
students of the working-class experience to claim that the working

class viewed preschools only as a necessary evil, which they would utilize only when home supervision of children was impossible. The reasons they offer for this attitude—that parents believed preschools were not places where children could obtain a desirable collective education but were only places of supervision—describe the motivation only of those who were politically involved.[13]

Avoidance of preschools was tied closely to workers' lives. Writing in the socialist magazine *Die Unzufriedene* in 1929, Gerda Kautsky determined that working-class parents opposed kindergartens because, in the parents' opinion, they increased the possibility of infectious disease, exposed their children to bad influences, and robbed mothers of the responsibility of educating their own children.[14] Kautsky rejected the first argument because she did not believe it possible to protect children from disease unless they were kept at home constantly. This reason may have been an excuse that concealed other, more important reasons for avoiding preschools, as Kautsky argues, but it is consistent with the working-class desire to avoid sickness and should not be dismissed as a reason among some working-class families. As a mother of three recounted, "No, my kids didn't go to kindergarten. My husband said 'no, they'll only bring sickness home.' " Leichter's study of 1,320 working mothers also found that fear of sickness was an often-cited reason for keeping children at home.[15] Any additional sickness in the family could spread to other wage-earning family members and result in reduced income and hard times. Therefore, what may have appeared to Kautsky to be irrational seemed logical to them.

Kautsky was astonished that proletarian mothers could claim that their children might be influenced by "bad elements" in the preschools. She attributed this attitude to the parents' "bourgeois consciousness" and dismissed it as a valid reason. But, as noted earlier, the more respectable working-class families might well have sought to keep their children from associating with children from less reputable areas and families. They would no doubt only postpone the inevitable encounters with such children, as Kautsky argues, but by the time they reached the *Volksschule* at age six they would have been better able to avoid "contamination" due to their greater maturity and the family values they learned at home prior to elementary school.

This brings us to the reason that Kautsky found to be decisive: proletarian mothers feared that preschools, by taking over much of the education and training of children, would deprive mothers of their most significant responsibility and their reason for being. Kautsky recognized an attitude that much subsequent research has shown was common to all classes in Central Europe: a reverence for private family virtues over public (communal for socialists) values.[16] The typical "respectable" proletarian family, as discussed earlier, valued nurturing in the home nearly as much as the bourgeoisie. Despite the most industrious efforts of Vienna's socialist administration in the 1920s to instill public virtues in the working class—common kitchens were the most glaring failure—most working-class families continued to shun public organizations and functions other than those in their immediate neighborhood. As we will see, these attitudes continued to influence working-class attitudes toward education well into the twentieth century.

There were also many other reasons that led working-class families to avoid kindergartens. First, few existed in working-class areas until the interwar period. Factory owners set up kindergartens in the working-class districts in the late nineteenth century, but they were few in number and understaffed and could not truly meet workers' needs. It was therefore difficult to take children to them even if the parents had desired to send them.[17] Second, the operating times of most kindergartens, from 8 A.M. to 4 P.M., did not fit the daily schedule of most working-class families. Only with the inception of *Volkskindergärten* (people's kindergartens) in the 1920s, with their starting time of 7 A.M. and closing time of 6 P.M., could parents take their children to them before work and pick them up after work.

The *Volkskindergärten* removed another obstacle by providing a free breakfast and lunch at a minimal price.[18] Third, since most working-class parents were not as influenced by the middle-class attitude that kindergarten attendance would help their children get ahead, they first turned to relatives to care for their children. As a former resident of Favoriten recalled, "When one had no other way out, when one had no private supervisors for the children, neighbors, relatives, etc., then one put the children in the kindergarten."[19] Finally, pre-schools were just not a part of the dominant working-class subculture, especially in the prewar period. Many working-class parents did not even consider sending their children to a kindergarten. As a former resident of Favoriten told me, "Kindergartens were not typical with us. There was a kindergarten, but the only kids who could go there were those kids whose parents had work or money."[20] Only a few socialist leaders—not proletarian mothers as Rigler argues—demanded the easing of working-class burdens through the establishment of kindergartens, community kitchens, and laundries.[21] Even in the interwar period, mothers continued to leave their children with relatives or friends or in the care of older daughters who had been kept home from school.

While most working-class parents resisted the schools, government and private agencies worked to institutionalize youth in order to provide "in industry and trade a morally predisposed, efficient, intellectually and physically sound generation and to protect against *errors* [italics mine] in the interest of the state and society," according to Josef Meixner, president of the Imperial Federation of Youth Defense (*Jugendwehren*) and Boy Centers (*Knabenhorte*) of Austria. Meixner headed the Department for Welfare Work for Industrial Employed Youth in the Ministry for Public Affairs. An alleged 86 percent increase in crime among 10- to 14-year-olds between 1880 and 1905, cited in Meixner's article, provided much of the impetus for the private and government actions to control youth.[22] Although much of the crime attributed to youth could have resulted from a broadened interpretation of criminal activity, fear of an uncontrolled street culture with possible damaging social and military consequences lurked in the hearts of the authorities. Military leaders warned about the lack of discipline and physical fitness among street youth and the consequences this could have for military preparedness.

Government and private organizations promoted youth activites such as the *Pfadfinder* (Boy Scouts) and *Horte* in order to get youth off the streets and instill discipline and respect for authority. In order to channel "the stormy impulse of wild but good-hearted boys in an ordered way," the *Horte* were to instill duty, obedience, and good manners.[23] Private military *Horte* provided uniforms and marching bands to curb the feared excesses of street youth. In addition to the 369 *Jugendhorte*, funded by the Austrian Ministry for Public Works, numerous military, municipal, and church *Horte* had emerged by 1910 to, as Meixner phrased it, prevent the "growing brutalization and degeneration of school-aged youth."[24]

Socialist party leaders tried to counter the street milieu as resolutely as did the government. Convinced that traditional working-class culture was responsible for the educational deficiencies of the lower classes, the predominantly middle-class SDAP leadership sought to fashion a new working-class consciousness by reforming youth behavior. By creating "new beings" (*Neue Menschen*), social- ists hoped to bridge the social-cultural gap between the bourgeoi- sie and laboring strata. But the intellectual-cultural gap between SDAP leadership and most workers severely hindered attempts to transform working-class behavior. For example, the socialist *Horte* established to care for children after elementary school hours were only partially successful in their mission to keep working-class children off the streets and provide them with some supplemental education to help keep underprivileged children abreast of the privileged. The socialist educator Fritz Kolb wrote in the magazine *The Socialist Education* that "the most capable, most intelligent children did not visit our *Horte*, at least not continually. Most chil- dren preferred the streets, because our offerings in the *Horte* were not appealing because we were coercive *Horte* (*Zwangshorte*)."[25] One of the Institute interviewees remembers the *Horte* set up by the socialist *Kinderfreunde* negatively, since "there I couldn't climb a tree," so he chose to return to a street youth group, where he was known by and knew everyone.[26] Eventually the SDAP set up a youth organization (*Roten Falkans*) modeled on the bourgeois Boy Scouts (*Pfadfinder*) in order to appeal to adolescents. As will be discussed in chapter 6, the *Red Falcons* were not as appealing as the SDAP had hoped. Almost without fail, the streets were more appealing than organized and supervised activities.

Government efforts to enforce compulsory education to the age of 14 often foundered because of the elitist nature of the educational system. The elementary and secondary school system of nineteenth- and early twentieth-century Vienna was a typical European two- tiered system with eight years of compulsory elementary school for children of the lower classes and twelve or thirteen years of elemen- tary and secondary school for the upper classes. Before 1927, the Austrian requirement for cities included a five-year elementary school (*Volksschule*) and a three-year higher-elementary school (*Bürgerschule*) (Fig. 7). Austrian rural students attended an eight- year elementary school. The *Bürgerschule* stressed the needs of in- dustry, agriculture, and the home and prepared students for the vocational schools or work that would follow. It included instruc- tion in industrial arts and did not require foreign languages. For the upper classes, seven or eight years of secondary school (*Mittelschule*) followed the *Volksschule*. Since there was no provision prior to 1927 for passage from the *Bürgerschule* to a *Mittelschule* (*Gymnasium*, *Realschule*, *Realgymnasium*), working-class youth were cut off from

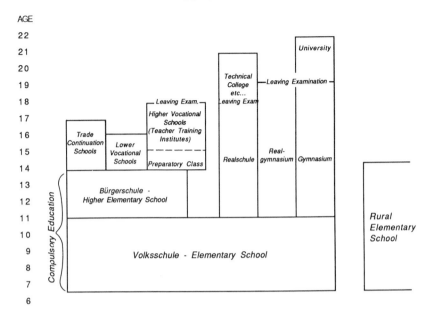

FIG. 7. The Austrian educational system before the 1927 reform. From May Hollis Siegl, *Reform of Elementary Education in Austria* (New York, n.p., 1933), 20.

both the secondary schools and the university. Many could hope only for a placement in a vocational school upon completion of the *Bürgerschule*. Only three of the seventy persons I interviewed followed a course of study other than the minimum eight-year *Volksschule/Bürgerschule*. Of these three exceptions, one completed the *Mittelschule* as an adult following World War II, one attended but never completed the *Mittelschule*, and one completed study in a teachers' training institute for elementary school teachers.[27] The one who attended the *Mittelschule*, in this case a *Realgymnasium*, could complete only the first four of the necessary eight years since her mother told her, "You can't stay at home that long, you must choose something else."[28]

For the few working-class youth who might pass the entrance examinations for the *Mittelschulen* upon completion of the *Volksschule*, the fees were the next and often insurmountable obstacle. Parents would not only have to wait years for any possible financial help from their children but would also find it necessary to sacrifice already meager funds for what most considered to be unnecessary schooling. For in the working-class world, obtaining a position in a vocational school or an apprenticeship in a trade were notable achievements. So both the financial and social obstacles to advancement to higher education were formidable and continue to exist for much of the working class even today.[29]

These obstacles continued to hinder youths' school attendance and performance, particularly in the prewar period. While compulsory-attendance laws forced working-class children to remain in school until age 14, they could not be forced to attend school regularly and often could not remain at the appropriate grade level. Before 1914 most children from working-class homes failed to finish the *Bürgerschule*. A 1909 survey of 11,803 Viennese girls aged 13 and 14 showed that 24 percent (2,816) had not yet reached the *Bürgerschule*, about 40 percent (4,467) were only in the first *Bürgerschule* class, and nearly 25 percent (2,924) were still one year behind their grade level.[30] The failure rate for boys was not much better. From a total of 10,721 boys aged 13 and 14, about 20 percent (2,045) had not yet completed the *Volksschule*.[31] Since the typical working-class child left school at the legal school-leaving age of 14, most of the 10,207 students who had not reached the third *Bürgerschule* class would never finish. Because few children from middle-class families attended the *Bürgerschule*, the vast majority of these students were from working-class families. For the working-class districts of Favoriten, Ottakring, and Floridsdorf, the 1910 failure rate was between 12.7 and 14.5 of every 100 *Volksschule* students, while the non-working-class districts had failure rates of less than 10 percent. The primarily middle-class fourth district had a failure rate of only 3.8 percent.[32] As a former student during the prewar period told me, "No, no *Bürgerschule* ... six *Volksschule* classes. I was kept back twice."[33] Another responded, "*Volksschule* and two *Bürgerschule* classes, because I left during the third class."[34] It is likely that the failure rate would have been even higher had not teachers been instructed to pass students on to the next class in order to conceal the high failure rate before World War I.[35]

World War I reversed some of the gains made in educating working-class children. Since many schools were used as hospitals during the war, some students simply had no schools near their homes to attend. The absence of husbands forced many children to work in order to support the family. Wartime school attendance records indicate the extent of the reversal. While 42 percent of all boys and 49 percent of all girls had reached the third *Bürgerschule* class during the 1906–14 period, only 40 percent of boys and 47 percent of girls reached the same class during the 1914–20 period.[36] The fact that many husbands did not return from the war meant that the war would continue to influence family life long into the interwar period. As chapter 5 shows, the high wartime earnings of workers in the metal and munitions factories tempted youth to begin work as soon as possible and forego further schooling or trade school training.

The urge for youth from the lower two strata to begin earning money as soon as possible and to reject schooling was still a powerful force in the interwar period. Vienna's Occupational Advisement Office reported that from a total of 4,433 youth that it advised in 1922, 3,900 left school before it ended, or, in all likelihood, when they reached age 14 during the school year.[37] While the postwar economic conditions were no doubt responsible for many youths' having to leave school, the lure of an early income in a factory compared to long and ill-paid apprenticeships or schooling that seemed to working-class parents to lead nowhere led youth to continue to choose factory work rather than extended schooling. In 1927 a popular socialist daily, *Das Kleine Blatt*, wrote of the thousands of working-class parents who were eagerly awaiting their children's fourteenth birthday so that they could begin to support themselves.[38] Working-class parents had to be warned by the Viennese Occupational Office in 1928 not to take their children out of school the day they reached 14 because of the shortage of jobs.[39] In the 1931 study of 1,320 female industrial workers carried out by Käthe Leichter, 56.5 percent went directly from elementary school to work.[40] One of Rada's 13-year-old female students told her, "If I could only quit now. I could go to work and earn my own bread. . . . If only the year [school year] were over."[41]

Attitudes toward schooling beyond that absolute minimum were similar elsewhere in Europe. Rowntree reported that in York, England, in 1936 "working-class children usually leave school at 14 and go to work, most of them in factories."[42] But the percentage of working-class youth staying in school until age 14 and being at grade level had improved slightly by the interwar period. *Volksschule* students forced to repeat a class had declined to only 5.99 percent of all Viennese pupils by 1924.[43] A survey of 380 *Ledergalanterie* apprentices in 1927 showed that 372 had finished the *Volksschule* and 205 the *Bürgerschule*. Another 90 had finished two

classes of the *Bürgerschule*.[44] Pressure from school administrators
and socialist functionaries, job scarcity, and a growing acceptance
that schooling was important were primarily responsible for this
slight improvement.

Working-class interest in the more academic secondary schools
(*Gymnasium, Realgymnasium,* and *Realschulen*) was limited
throughout the period 1900–1940. Except for the few upper-
stratum parents who began to see these *Mittelschulen* as a step to
advanced white-collar positions, most could not be convinced
that their children would benefit from them. This was especially
true of the elite secondary school, the *Gymnasium,* with its emphasis on classical language, literature, and preparation for university education. The eight years required to complete the *Mittelschule* would keep children in school until age 18, an age when
most laboring families expected their children to be supporting
themselves. With its population of 141,363 in 1920, Favoriten had
only one *Mittelschule,* while the first district with only 43,322
inhabitants had four. The ratio of one *Mittelschule* for each
141,363 inhabitants in Favoriten compared unfavorably to a Viennese average of one for every 44,927 inhabitants.[45] In the early
twenties, 370 of 1,000 *Volksschule* students in the first district
entered the *Mittelschule,* compared to only 31 of 1,000 in Favoriten.[46] In addition, almost all the secondary students in the
working-class districts came from the upper strata.

The working-class author Karl Ziak remembers that few of his
classmates in Ottakring's sole *Realschule* before World War I were
the children of workers.[47] The records of students who attended
this *Realschule* support Ziak's claim. Only 6 of the 115 students
entering the *Realschule* on *Schuhmeierplatz* in 1909 were the sons of
workers. Much more heavily represented were the sons of artisans;
17 were sons of masters or journeymen.[48] Little change occurred in
the interwar period. Only 3 of 66 students entering in 1928, and not
one of the 42 boys entering in 1935, were from skilled-worker
homes. Again, artisans' sons were more heavily represented; 5 of
the 42 were sons of masters or journeymen.[49] Since *Mittelschule*
attendance was a requirement for entering a university, few children of workers attended a university. A 1908 survey of 868 university students (*Hochschulen*) revealed that only 1.7 percent came
from workers' homes.[50]

Socialist attempts to replace the *Mittelschule* and *Volksschule*
with one unity school (*Einheitsschule*), stressing both the practical

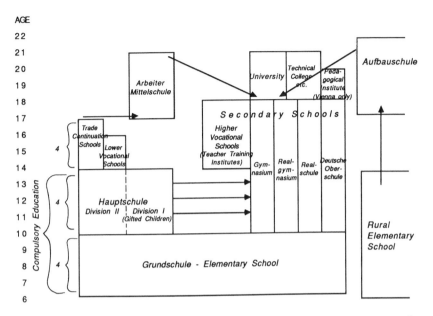

AGE

FIG. 8. The Austrian educational system after the 1927 reform. From Ludwig Battista, *Die österreichische Volksschule* (Vienna: Österreichischer Bundesverlag, 1937), 140.

and the academic, never succeeded. But a compromise between the socialists and the other major party, the Christian Socialists, resulted in a two-tracked, four-year *Hauptschule*, which replaced the *Bürgerschule* after 1927 (Fig. 8). It was different from the *Bürgerschule* in that it either instructed children in basic skills or gave gifted students the opportunity to continue studies in a four-year *Mittelschule*. Students in the "fast track" of the *Hauptschule* had the possibility of passing each year to the *Untermittelschule* without passing entrance examinations, if they achieved a "good" rating and had completed the necessary foreign language the previous year in the *Hauptschule*. Upon completion of the *Hauptschule*, students could go on to a vocational school, a *Mittelschule*, or take special language classes to prepare them for the last four years of a *Mittelschule*. Although few working-class youth could take advantage of the *Mittelschule* option because of the poor economic times that followed, it was now possible to move on to the secondary school at some time other than at the end of the *Volksschule*. The other part of the compromise, the introduction of some industrial arts (*Handfertigkeitsunterricht*) in the *Untermittelschule*, was praised by socialists as the means by which "head" and "hand" workers would be brought together.[51] However, these reforms were only partially implemented and were reversed in all areas outside Vienna by constitutional amendment in 1929 and in Vienna in 1934, when Austria fell to the authoritarian regime established by Engelbert Dollfuss.[52]

In opposition to these attempts to institutionalize youth was the indifference, and in some cases hostility, of most working-class youth and parents toward the schools. Oral interviews reveal that few respondents could remember much, especially anything positive, about their school experience.[53] Certainly very few remembered it as being an especially pleasant experience. Children could speak only when spoken to by the teacher and had to sit upright with their hands on the desk and pencil at the ready. Peukert's description of the German schools during the Weimar Republic as places of detention more than learning centers rings true for many of the Vienna schools as well.[54] It is little wonder that most yearned to escape to the streets and their own less oppressive world. Alfred Molnar wrote in his autobiographical study, *Unstet und Flüchtig*, that he skipped school ten days during the first half-year of the 1911–12 school year so that he could play with his peers.[55] Parents were especially opposed before World War I to learning other than the basic reading, writing, and arithmetic. They did not consider education useful unless it had some occupational importance. Wenzel Holek's mother told him, "Those who learn and study a lot will go crazy, will end up in an insane asylum."[56] Adelheid Popp, an Austrian socialist leader and former factory worker, wrote that her parents thought that three years of school was enough and those who had not learned anything by the time they were ten would learn nothing after that.[57] Humphries argues that the English "saw it as an imposition with little relevance or application to the world of the working-class child."[58]

Even those with outstanding elementary school grades knew that they would not be able to attend a secondary school. As the son of a mason and agricultural worker related, "I had very good report cards in the *Hauptschule* and *Volksschule*. I was always an excellent student. But it was not possible for me then, although the teacher offered it to me . . . I should study further, attend the *Gymnasium*. But it was naturally not possible since my father was only a mason by training and we had a very simple household. I had two brothers, my mother was in the home, and we had to live from my father's income alone."[59] Family considerations continued to take precedence over individual goals far into the twentieth century. This attitude was not unique to Austria. Elizabeth Roberts found family considerations to be dominant among the English working class throughout the entire period 1890–1940. As she wrote, "The children learned early to subjugate personal ambition to their parents and to care, on a daily basis, for the needs of other members of the family."[60]

Working-class parents preferred to get their children into an apprenticeship so that they could either aid the family financially or at least cease to be a financial burden. This traditional attitude predominated among all workers before World War I but began to subside among the two upper strata of workers in the interwar period. While children of middle-class families could concentrate on schoolwork, working-class children often had to divide their time between education and work. Many elementary school students worked before and after school and on weekends. A 1913 report from the Austrian Labor Statistical Office showed that large numbers of Austrian school children were employed while still in school and had been employed at a very early age. One-third (148,368) of the school children surveyed were gainfully employed, and three-fourths of them had begun work before the age of 9. Over one-third worked more than three hours a day during the winter months and 42.9 percent worked on Sundays and holidays.[61] Another survey of 80,859 Austrian school children in 1908 had similar results: 23,016, or 28.5 percent, were gainfully employed.[62] Figures for other European countries paint a similar picture. Bray calculated that 25 percent of all London school children were employed after school hours as late as 1910.[63]

These official statistics do not, however, tell the whole story. Children who worked for their parents or at odd jobs before and after school were often not listed in official statistics. Such work depended again on the sex of the children and family needs. Many women I questioned told of early morning work that forced them to rise early and arrive at school already tired. This work normally involved various cleaning and shopping tasks for better-off families. In addition, girls were often kept at home to care for younger brothers or sisters when their mothers had to shop or do part-time work. During the school year 1898–99, girls missed school an average of 28.5 days and boys 22.9 days.[64] The interwar period brought little improvement for young women. A 1931 study found that 45 percent of the working-class girls were kept home from school regularly and 12 percent of them missed school 25 percent of the time.[65] A woman who grew up in the prewar period remembered, "We had to look after the children and do odd jobs, and I didn't do well in school as a result."[66] Nor do official statistics report that many young girls were responsible for much of the care of their homes. Rada's study of working-class girls during the interwar period calculated that 17 percent of them were responsible for all their own housecleaning.[67] Since the oldest daughters served as housekeepers and babysitters, younger sisters had more educational and occupational opportunity.

Working-class parents' lack of concern about "advanced education" for their children could change to open hostility toward subjects and activities they considered to be culturally and psychologically damaging, impractical, or time-consuming. As studies for England and Germany have found, working-class parents feared that advanced learning would separate their children from the family and, in effect, the child would be lost to the family.[68] Children would be educated "out of their estate [Stände]."[69] One former resident of Favoriten recalled his mother telling him not to waste his time reading poetry. When he attempted to read poetry to her, she angrily responded that he should stop such "nonsense."[70] Another remembers not being permitted to read newspapers until she was fourteen.[71] The socialist leader Anna Maier wrote that "when a comrade loaned me the Arbeiterinnenzeitung, I had to hide it, for at home I wouldn't dare read it in front of my mother."[72] Rada found that 56 percent of her students were forbidden to read newspapers.[73] One told Rada, "I most like to read about legal trials, especially murder trials, and the weather. My father forbade that I read the newspaper, but I found the time to do it."[74] Some of the parents' objection was certainly that knowledge of destructive behavior might promote similar behavior among their children, but, more important, such time could be better spent helping with housework, working in part-time jobs to aid the family economy, or learning some skill that would be more "useful" later in life. Essentially the family came first, and parents opposed too much independence and anything that would enhance it.[75] Reading introduces independent ideas and reduces the parents' control over their children.

Adverse conditions in the schools and at home could also hinder

Fig. 9. It is apparent that this *Volksschule* classroom for girls was in a middle-class area because of the elaborate hairstyling and the hats hanging from the railing. (Courtesy Bildarchive, Austrian National Library, Vienna)

learning. Excessive class sizes in schools in the working-class districts made it impossible for children to receive individual attention. Compared to Vienna's first district, where the average class size was 40.6 pupils in 1909, class size in Favoriten, Simmering, Ottakring, and Brigittenau averaged 53.4, 55.8, 57.3, and 53.3.[76] Classes with more than 70 students were not uncommon in the working-class districts. In 1911, 95 classrooms in Vienna exceeded 70 students, and another 365 had more than 65.[77] This situation was aggravated by conditions in the typical working-class home. While middle-class students had better-educated parents and favorable home conditions that might overcome the shortcomings of the schools, children of lower-stratum parents were beset with scores of problems at home. Parents with little "book" learning, insufficient time away from work, and reduced energy levels due to long working hours could offer their children little aid with their schoolwork. Even the smaller families of the interwar period provided little relief. Rada found 40 percent of the children in her study could get no help from family members due to time and work impediments. From the remaining 60 percent, only 10 percent actually received any meaningful aid because of a lack of time and knowledge by other family members and the children's reluctance to admit they needed help.[78]

FIG. 10. In a coed *Volksschule* classroom, the girls sat on one side and the boys on the other. The short haircuts on both boys and girls and the absence of hats indicate that this school was in a working-class area. (Courtesy Bildarchive, Austrian National Library, Vienna)

A common obstacle encountered in school by working-class children was the necessity to learn "book" or formal German. Since few Viennese youth ever left the working-class areas, where only Viennese dialect was spoken, they seldom encountered anyone speaking "book" German. It was almost as if they had to learn another language. A woman who had moved to Ottakring from the first district during her youth told me, "I came out here and the children laughed at me. For the school it was wonderful [knowing formal German] . . . my friends . . . they all had difficulty in school because they didn't speak formal German at home. They couldn't. They had to learn it first. For me it was second nature."[79] But outside the school, and especially in the streets, dialect held sway. Rada related how one of her students who tried to speak formal German was embarrassed by her brother when he sarcastically responded, "Look at the goose, she wants to act high-born [*will nobel tun*]."[80] A woman who grew up in Favoriten recalled that "we spoke 'book' German when we went walking . . . it was a lot of fun.

FIG. 11. A typical *Volksschule* building built in the prewar period. This building is still standing on the Quellenstrasse in Favoriten (District 10).

We were refined girls then."[81] It was therefore difficult outside the schools to speak "book" German even if one knew it.

Rada further noted that her students disliked subjects such as history because they were embarrassed to recite in class since they knew little "book" German.[82] In order to overcome this language barrier, a few schools used the Viennese dialect to instruct pupils in language classes.[83] The objective was to make use of the home environment to introduce students gradually to "book" German. A survey of 90 female *Bürgerschule* students in the interwar period showed that gymnastics (19 percent), drawing (18 percent), and German (17 percent) were the favorite subjects. Religion, geometry, and foreign language were not selected by any of the students as their favorite.[84]

When workers' attitudes are combined with problems in the schools and the physical inadequacies of the typical working-class home, there can be little doubt why few working-class youth reached the secondary schools. Chief among the home problems was the cramped living quarters, the absence of any place to study,

FIG. 12. A *Volksschule* class with 55 pupils was not uncommon in the prewar period. (Courtesy Bildarchive, Austrian National Library, Vienna)

and the never-ending darkness of the rooms. The small living quarters made it impossible for children to have a separate place to study or even put down their books. Since the small, primarily one-room/kitchen apartments were crowded with beds and people, children often had to study in doorways and on tables that could only be used for short periods of time between meals. One woman remembered the children in a family of six who had to study on the floor of their apartment. Her father let one of the children study in their apartment in order to escape the crowding.[85] Rada's study of working-class girls calculated that only 3 of the 90 children she observed had a desk, and they were not from the "proletariat" but from the more substantial working-class families.[86]

A common complaint of those I interviewed was the darkness of their dwellings. Before the city housing units of the interwar period were built, working-class apartments commonly had one small window per room that often opened onto the wall of another building. Since working-class homes possessed few lamps, children grew up in a dimly lit world. Some of the *Wohnküche* apartments described in chapter 1 had no windows at all or at most one window.[87] A man who grew up in housing provided for brick workers in Favoriten remembered, "We had to burn lights day and night. Despite that, the dwelling was rather expensive. Every window opened onto a wall."[88] Although the municipal housing of the interwar period destroyed some of the cohesiveness engendered by the cramped prewar housing, it did receive praise from those I interviewed because of the larger number of windows and increased light. The apartments were also arranged so that none of the windows was obstructed by other buildings.

While it was difficult for all working-class children to succeed at school, girls found it even more difficult than boys to obtain advanced schooling or training. As late as 1928, *Die Unzufriedene* reported that one could still expect working-class mothers to say that it did not make any difference if girls attended secondary school, but for boys their entire existence depended on it.[89] One study of Austrian women rightly contends that women were viewed as financial liabilities in the age of compulsory education and child-labor laws and as soon as possible were forced into gainful employment.[90] Of the 45 women I interviewed, 32 began work at age 14 or earlier, another 11 went to a trade school for two to three years, one went to a teachers' training institute, and one attended but never finished secondary school.[91] A woman recalled that her mother, a housecleaner, expected her to work as a day laborer because she was expecting money right away.[92] As we have seen, older daughters were often taken out of school to do housework and tend children. One woman, the oldest in the family, remembers her mother simply saying, " 'I'm taking you out of school because I need you at home,' because I was the oldest."[93] During the school year 1898–99, girls missed school an average of 28.5 days and boys 22.9 days.[94]

The interwar period brought only limited improvement for young women. A 1931 study found that 45 percent of working-class girls were kept home from school regularly.[95] This lack of concern for girls' education often led to a family's disregard for their performance in school. The daughter of a painter who hoped to bring attention to herself as a result of her bad grades was sorely disappointed when she did not. After receiving a "5", the lowest possible grade, in drawing because of what she described as idle chattering in class, she remembered, "I was glad and thought now they'll hopefully be upset. Nothing, no one was upset, not even my siblings. No one was concerned about me."[96] One of Viethen's interviewees remarked, "Nobody asked if you had homework or if you had learned something. Or what you were doing in school. Nobody asked. . . . We never received a present or reward [for good grades]. Who would trouble themselves? Mother was sick . . . father . . . nobody asked if I had a lesson or not. And I always received high grades."[97] Of the 19 women interviewed by Viethen, only one set of parents, inspired by the socialist desire for self-improvement, encouraged their daughter to pursue her studies.[98] Some working-class families openly resented their daughters' love for school, since they viewed it as an excuse to avoid work.[99]

Such conditions and attitudes made it difficult for a girl to attend secondary school. Until the interwar period even bourgeois girls seldom would have attended a secondary school. As late as 1900 only one private *gymnasium* for girls existed in the entire city.[100] Bourgeois girls attended girls' lycees, where they obtained "culture" but not the right to go on to a university or gain any practical knowledge. Käthe Leichter wrote, "They were reserved for those circles who could send their daughter to a school for six years that imparted only refinement."[101] While difficult even for a bourgeois girl, attendance at a secondary school for a proletarian girl was impossible in the prewar period. As already noted, most did not even finish the advanced elementary school, the *Bürgerschule.*

Similar attitudes prevailed in England before World War I. Dyhouse found that English working-class parents felt that "schooling was encouraging the wrong kind of aspirations in girls, and undermining their attachment to home and appreciation of domestic duties."[102] Tilly and Scott found that intense parental opposition to advanced schooling for French girls had to be overcome as late as the period immediately preceding World War I. Their contention that "in the twentieth century a daughter's work continued to be shaped by her family's needs" is supported by the Viennese evidence.[103]

While some working-class families began to view advanced schooling as desirable for their children, including in a few cases their daughters, few had the money for school fees or books. Faced with these realities, parents chose to obtain occupational training rather than secondary school for their children. Only a few of those I interviewed, the generation of 1900–1920, had any advanced training that would have prepared them for anything other than blue-collar jobs. But success in the working class was measured more in terms of the occupational training one could obtain. Here again, important differences existed among the strata. Compared to 17 of 31 in the upper strata who attended trade school, only 7 of 21 in the middle stratum and 3 of 17 in the lowest stratum received any schooling after the *Bürgerschule*.[104] One of the upper-stratum respondents proudly stated that he and all eight of his siblings had attended a trade school.[105]

Their children, the generation of 1920–40, began to have greater opportunities as a result of the increase in white-collar jobs, smaller families, and a willingness among working-class parents to permit their children to pursue advanced education. When one woman I interviewed wanted to convince me that her children had greater occupational possibilities than she had had, she explained that her daughter had pursued a sales apprenticeship and her son had failed his secondary school exam.[106] In other words, even to have reached the secondary school examination was an unusual achievement in a working-class family. Another remembered that his father had tears in his eyes when he completed his *gymnasium* studies in night school after World War II.[107] But educational possibilities for girls remained limited. As late as the 1929–30 school year, in Favoriten only 165 girls (probably including few daughters from the lowest two strata) attended a secondary school.[108] The fact that only 8 of the 165 were in the final year of a secondary school further indicates that few were actually finishing school and that the larger numbers were a recent phenomenon. By comparison, the much less populated first district had 722 female secondary students with 48 in the final year, and the fourth district had 779 female students with 65 in the final year.[109] Of the 55 students attending the girls' *Realschule* class in Ottakring in 1935–36, only 6 were the daughters of skilled workers; the remainder were the daughters of artisans or the bourgeoisie.[110]

Youth's job aspirations in the interwar period confirm this reluctance to break with traditional job and educational possibilities. The 1922 study of the occupational desires of 2,700 males in their final year of school showed that only 7 percent desired schooling other than vocational schooling leading to blue-collar jobs.[111] Although girls found that their educational goals often had to be sacrificed to family and financial considerations in the interwar period, the 1931 report of the Occupational Office reported that girls desired advanced education more than anything except tailoring.[112] This was a change from the early 1920s, when few listed advanced education as a goal. So, while the traditional working-class assumption that children's formal education was over at age

14 was beginning to break down by the late 1920s, the poor economic conditions of the interwar period made it impossible for most workers to seek advanced learning for their children, especially their daughters.

If attendance at a secondary school is used as one of the measures of working-class acceptance of schooling, most of the Viennese working class did not meet the test before World War I, nor did the lowest stratum meet it even in the interwar period. More difficult to answer is the precise nature of working-class youth's opposition to the schools. Some contend that their hostility toward the schools represents a "class-cultural struggle over the form of social relationships that were to prevail in the schools."[113] To them, acts of opposition in the schools, be it truancy, misbehavior, or assaults on teachers, represent the opposition of the subordinate culture to the dominant culture. Students' disenchantment could also result in "dissociation" rather than a contracultural rebellion.[114] In either case youth's actions represent an opposition to the dominant culture represented by the schools, since they tend to "reproduce the social tensions and contradictions inherent in the societies that produce them."[115] Many students found school boring and meaningless and sought to avoid it or refused to comply with school rules when they were forced to attend. The result was a harsh discipline imposed by the teachers and student and parent opposition in return. But the main response in Viennese working-class areas was not violent resistance but a stoic acceptance that resulted from the deference to authority learned in the typical working-class home or brought with them from the countryside.[116] A survey of school punishment carried out in 1922 showed that most working-class boys meekly accepted penalties handed down by their superiors. The survey revealed that a higher percentage of working-class boys than bourgeois boys agreed that school spankings were necessary.[117] In the sense that the schools represented a different social milieu from that of most of the working class, youth's opposition, whether direct in the form of action or indirect in the form of noncompliance, represented a form of class opposition.

In general, the much smaller working-class families typical of the interwar period made it possible for a few skilled workers' children from the upper stratum to continue their studies. In comparison with other European countries in the interwar period, Austria experienced a similar paradox: an increased public debate and institutional action to provide more educational opportunity on the one hand and a minor improvement in the actual school experience of the lower classes on the other hand.[118] While the typical one-child family of the post-1925 period made it possible in those families that were not victims of unemployment or sickness to let their children pursue vocational training or advanced education in a secondary school, financial matters and some parents' continuing opposition to advanced schooling limited change. Tilly and Scott's contention that children were expected to be family wage earners despite the increased educational and occupational possibilities remained true for girls and most boys throughout the interwar period. Although the portion of family income supplied by youth declined in the working-class household budget study of 1925–34 compared with that of 1912–14, it can be explained primarily by the greatly reduced number of children per family that could contribute to family income among the families studied in the 1925–34 study.[119] As discussed in chapter 1, the average number of children declined from about five in the prewar period to less than two in the interwar period. Therefore, while youth had greater job and educational possibilities in theory, they were still constrained by traditional family considerations and, more important, the poor economic conditions of the interwar period.

5

Work

The first money that I earned was 8 gulden a month, a month! Yes, and I had to give that to my parents.[1]
—*Daughter of an unskilled factory worker*

Father said, 'Let the boy study. Girls, promise me,' he said in the hospital. . . . All of us wanted to learn something, but it was not possible. [Only three of the seven children in this family received occupational training beyond the upper-elementary school][2]
—*Daughter of a typesetter*

I had to learn dressmaking. I didn't want to, but I had to. My father said, 'you can always, when you have learned something, you can always switch over.'[3]
—*Daughter of a blacksmith who worked as a transport and construction worker*

In these quotes from persons recalling their youth in Viennese working-class areas in the early twentieth century are summed up many dominant attitudes and practices of youth as their formal schooling ended and they sought and began work. Throughout the period 1890–1938, job choice continued to be conditioned overwhelmingly by gender, youth were still expected to contribute much of their earnings to the family, and work began at an early age. Although change was beginning to transform work roles as the

factory system was gradually supplanting artisanal forms of production, as white-collar work expanded, and as employment in
domestic service declined, strong family pressures, economic conditions, and the persistence of the outwork industry locked many
youth, especially women, into traditional occupations. In the large
working-class families of the pre–World War I period, most young
women had to subordinate their occupational desires to those of
their brothers. An important demographic factor that began to
improve job opportunities was the decline in the size of working-
class families and, as a result, increased opportunity for youth to
obtain occupational training. But, as we will see, traditional attitudes and economic realities in the interwar period limited daughters' occupational training to certain female trades such as textiles,
sewing, and dressmaking. This chapter will consider when work
began for working-class youth, youth's occupational choices and
desires, their actual work experience, and their role in the family
after beginning work.

The period 1890–1938 was an important transitional period for
the Austrian economy and, in some regards, also for youth. For
males the transition was primarily from one type of skilled labor to
another and from artisanal to factory labor, but for females the
change was much greater. In some industries women moved from
early-industrial to high-industrial conditions. For the first time,
women growing up during World War I and the interwar period
were employed in factories in large numbers. In addition, traditional forms of women's work, such as domestic service, declined
dramatically during and after the war. Finally, a continuing shift
from artisanal to factory production with a concomitant deskilling
of work and the growth of the service sector further transformed
youth's possibilities.

While small industrial enterprises (up to 20 employees) still predominated as late as 1902 in Vienna, the transition to larger firms
had been underway since about 1890 (described in chapter 1) and
was beginning to dominate production in the outer districts.[4] Those
industries experiencing the most rapid growth were the machine,
electrical, textile, and clothing industries. Not only the size of the
firms but also the nature of the work force changed. The number of
self-employed workers declined (in most cases a result of the decline
in small artisanal shops for men and washing and cleaning jobs for
women). From 1910 to 1923, the percentage of independent female
workers declined from 13.81 percent of those gainfully employed to

only 9.45 percent.[5] Males were less influenced by this transition, since they often converted their small shops to repair and installation functions or contracted to sell their products to larger distributors.[6] The new and expanding electric and machine industries were set up on a large-scale mass-production basis and used primarily unskilled and therefore less costly labor. As a result of this deskilling, the percentage of female labor jumped from 12.6 to 25.2 percent of the laborers in the electric industry from 1902 to 1913.[7] A good example of this transition was the electric-light manufacturing industry, where, during the 1920s, 4,000 predominantly skilled workers were replaced by only 1,600 unskilled workers, but with an output equivalent to that of 6,000 skilled workers in the prewar period.[8] Apprenticeships became unnecessary in such factories where unskilled workers could be put to work within hours. But many factory workers continued to be hired as apprentices, since owners could pay them less. The concentration of manufacturing and distribution of products under larger firms (*Verlag system*) also resulted in a division of labor and the continued use of apprentices. Since small shops contracted to supply larger firms with only one part of a product, for example, the soles of shoes, shop owners could hire apprentices rather than more skilled artisans, since workers did not need to have the skills to produce an entire product.

For women, the early twentieth century was an important transition period not so much in terms of the percentage of women working but in the kind of work desired and performed by them. From 1890 to 1934, the number of women employed in industry grew from 118,760 to 141,671, but as a percentage of the work force the change was only from 28.41 to 32.35 percent.[9] However, the structure of women's work, and therefore girls' job possibilities, changed markedly. First, a gradual shift occurred from *Heimarbeit* (cottage industry) to factory labor. As late as 1902, about one-third of the female labor force in Austria was listed as *Heimarbeiter* (201,303 of 660,077); the percentage was only about 25 for Vienna (30,605 of 123,943).[10] But by the interwar period, the number of women working in large factories and in formerly male-dominated jobs had grown rapidly. Nowhere was this transformation more evident than in the metal industry. Described by one investigator in 1900 as the womanless industry, the metal industry had a female union membership of about 20 percent by the 1920s.[11] The actual increase was from 14 to 22,000 women from 1893 to 1924; during the same period the number of male workers increased from 4,607 to 104,000. De-

spite laws that prevented married women from working during the
depression years, female employment continued to increase as employers sought cheaper labor. In 1929, the metal industry's demand
for female unskilled labor began to outstrip that for men: for every
100 men seeking work in 1929 only 13 openings existed, but for every
100 women 20 openings were available.[12]

An equally important structural change was that a higher percentage of working women compared with men were employed in
large factories. In 1926 about three-fourths of employed women
worked in factories with more than 100 employees and 65 percent
worked in factories with more than 1,000 workers.[13] In the metal
industry, 9,294 of 11,540 employed women in 1928 worked in factories with more than 100 workers.[14] Leichter's survey of 1,320 female workers found that 62 percent worked in factories with more
than 100 employees.[15] The changed structure of work was apparent
in the shoe industry, where, for example, most males worked in
firms with fewer than 50 employees, while 2,023 of 4,043 women
employees, overwhelmingly young and single, worked in firms
with between 100 and 500 employees.[16] The perpetuation of small
predominantly male-operated shoe shops was made possible primarily by cobblers' agreements to supply larger distributors.[17]

Naturally, such a transformation in women's work could not have
occurred without sizeable structural changes in work traditionally
dominated by women. As shown in Table 5.1, employment as domestic servants declined rapidly between 1910 and the interwar period
as a result of the postwar economic decline of households that had
previously hired domestic servants. Women were also pulled by
higher wages toward industry, white-collar and public-service areas, and, in some cases, improved working conditions. From 1910 to
1934, the number of workers employed as *Angestellte* (white-collar)
increased from 140,633 to 242,220, or from about 12 to 25 percent of
the work force, and the number of women white-collar workers
increased from 24 to 37 percent of the total women employed.[18] The
growth of female employment in public service and the professions
showed a marked increase as well: from 20.98 percent of all employed in 1910 to 35.03 percent in 1934.[19] Of course, middle-class
women profited primary by the increased employment in this latter
area, since few working-class women had sufficient training to fill
these positions. Also, women from working-class homes often
lacked the clothing and necessary freedom from family concerns to
fill such jobs.

Table 5.1 Women's Employment in Vienna

	1910	1934
Domestic Service	99,157	49,155
Industry	145,033	172,504
Service (white collar)	34,072	90,570
Trade, Transport, and Finance	63,523	82,725
Public Service and the Professions	23,656	40,525

Source: Edith Rigler, *Frauenleitbild und Frauenarbeit in Österreich: Vom ausgehenden 19 Jahrhundert bis zum Zweiten Weltkrieg* (Vienna: Verlag für Geschichte und Politik, 1976), 123.

Given this work transformation, how did youth make their job decisions and how significant were gender and generational differences in the early twentieth century? While it is possible to make generalizations concerning work choices, marked differences existed between cities and different levels of the working class. In Vienna, where wages were lower than German cities, youth had a greater tendency to choose hairdressing and restaurant work, since tips augmented their income.[20] Socially, children of lower-stratum workers tended to follow more in their father's footsteps and to limit their choice of occupations.[21] Among the lower social stratum, parents could not afford to send their children to trade school or pay apprenticeship fees. In addition, parents often had to feed and house their offspring while they served their apprenticeship. Among the upper stratum of workers, children had a much greater knowledge of work possibilities and more financial resources to endure a long apprenticeship or attend a trade school. With these qualifications in mind, it is possible to pursue some generalizations concerning working-class children.

John Gillis's comment in *Youth and History* that about 1900 "in almost every western country the concept of adolescence was democratized, offered to, or rather required of, all the teenaged" is, in regard to work, a premature assessment for Vienna's working-class teenagers.[22] While a slow transformation was under way in the period before World War I, only a few working-class youth were able to enjoy that exemption from work that Gillis described as one of the adolescent conditions. Gillis partially acknowledged this himself when he stated that "only ten percent of [English] working-class boys born 1910–29 were staying beyond the primary grades," and presumably all others were forced to enter the adult world of work with its obligations."[23] Before World War I, most Viennese working-class children began work at the legal school-leaving age of 14 or even earlier on a part-time basis. A survey of Austrian school children carried out in 1908 by the Imperial and Royal Trade Ministry found that 17.8 percent of the 6- to 8-year-olds, 35.6 percent of the 9- to 10-year-olds, and 40.7 percent of the 11- to 12-year-olds worked on a regular basis.[24] These figures exclude many of those who worked at home in the putting-out industry and most of those involved in odd jobs before and after school. A Viennese Chamber of Commerce study of 119 primarily upper/middle-strata working-class households from 1912 to 1914 showed that all 42 children over age 14 in those households worked full-time.[25] Therefore, few Viennese working-class youth before 1914 meet one of Gillis's conditions for adolescence, i.e., exemption from work. They were, in effect, young adults with little opportunity to engage in an adolescent culture. There are again significant differences depending upon the particular stratum, as will be discussed below and in chapter 6.

Youths' choice of jobs tended to diverge increasingly from their parents' occupations as the artisanal work force declined and factory production became dominant. With fewer artisanal shops to pass on to offspring, there would naturally be some change. The normal late nineteenth-century pattern was for youth to take up occupations similar to their parents' or to accept occupations and trade schools recommended by their parents. At the turn of the century in the machine and electrical industry, sons tended to be employed in the same branch as their fathers but seldom in the same factory or shop.[26] While most males continued to learn a trade through apprenticeships, a large number were no longer working as true apprentices, since the artisan shops were losing workers to the factories at the end of the century. As a result, many were forced to work at unskilled factory and transport jobs, or they were taken on as apprentices by small masters but used as unskilled laborers. Increasingly, unskilled labor designations such as day laborer (*Taglöhner*) and helper (*Hilfsarbeiter*) comprised a larger percentage of Vienna's work force. Of the 102 parents of men married in Favoriten's St. Johann parish in 1938, 42 were listed as *Taglöhner* or *Hilfsarbeiter*.[27] Since the sons' average marriage age was 29, most of the fathers would have been born before 1890 and have entered the job market in the period when the rapid industrialization was well under way.

For married women, piecework in the home became the dominant trend in the last three decades before World War I. Most employed married women worked in the outwork sector. In 1910, 107 of the first 212 brides in St. Johann parish listed *Handarbeiterin* (in most cases, needlework in the home) as their occupation.[28] This abundant, cheap supply of labor made it possible for masters both large and small, especially those in the textile and clothing industries, to continue the cottage-industry system well into the twentieth century. Such practices were not restricted to Austria. A survey of 1,350 home-workers in Germany in 1912 revealed that 73 percent were married, widowed, or divorced.[29] With few exceptions (10 of 69), the mothers of those I interviewed remained housewives who in some cases cleaned outside the home or took in sewing on a part-time basis. Of the exceptions, two worked outside the home only after their husbands' deaths, two worked with their husbands in their shops, two cooked in restaurants, two were domestic servants, one worked in construction, and one was an embroiderer. Before marriage, many of these women came to Vienna as domestics. As one told me, "My mother came from Lower Austria, also the oldest daughter of a peasant family . . . and then it was common that girls from a small farm had to become maids in the city. My mother went to Vienna and became a cook."[30] Of 212 brides in St. Johann parish in 1910, 42 were cooks or maids.[31]

Young girls growing up in the prewar period were, in most cases, bound to the household. They were needed for child care, for help with their mothers' piecework, and for household duties. The possibility of learning a trade or attending advanced schooling was reserved for only a small minority. About 29 percent of my female interviewees (13 of 45) had some occupational schooling, but most were forced to learn some form of needlework.[32] Only three of the nineteen working women interviewed by Viethen were able to learn a trade and two of these were unhappy with the trade their parents forced them to learn.[33] The remaining sixteen took whatever casual employment existed in the neighborhood once they reached the school-leaving age. In 1906, only 7,596 of the 43,300 vocational school (*gewerbliche Fortbildungsschule*) students in Vienna were female.[34] Also a large portion (82 percent) of these girls continued to live with their parents, while only 44 percent of the boys remained in their parents' home.[35] Since vocational school was a long-term financial liability for parents, occupational training was often reserved for sons.

After 1910, boys' occupational choices continued to be influenced by their fathers' occupation and by local circumstance, but the high pay of jobs in the machine, metal, and electrical industries during the war led many youths to reject traditional artisanal training for apprenticeships in higher-paying factory jobs where they could begin earning a wage immediately. Meager knowledge of many occupations, especially about the white-collar jobs pursued by the middle class and the upper strata of the working class, restricted their job possibilities to primarily manual-labor jobs. A study of 973 Viennese 12- to 14-year-old boys' occupational choices in the 1920s determined that 29.7 percent chose a job that resembled their fathers' and 8 percent took over their fathers' work.[36] Another 23 percent chose an occupation because it promised to provide economic advantages. Immediately after the war, young men choosing apprenticeships in the electrical and metal industries because their older brothers or fathers had earned high wages in those industries during the war found them overcrowded. Of 2,700 males seeking advice in Vienna's Occupational Advising Office from 1 May to 31 December 1922, 68 percent wanted to take up apprenticeships in a factory or workshop and only 7 percent desired advanced technical schooling or schooling that would have prepared them for jobs as white-collar workers.[37] But about half cited interest, appeal, or goal fulfillment as influential in their choice.[38] About half of those who chose an occupation because they saw it leading to some goal cited independence as a major part of this goal.[39] The lure of artisanal independence remained strong among most males. But, as in other parts of Europe, family tradition and local circumstances played a major role in job choice in the early 1920s.[40]

However, significant differences existed among the various working-class strata. A 1923 survey of youths' occupational choices showed that 922 males who had finished the third *Bürgerschulklasse* would not take up an apprenticeship in low-prestige occupations such as chimney sweep, mason, glassmaker, rug maker, barber, painter, bookbinder, shoemaker, or glove maker. This upper group desired apprenticeships in the more prestigious but overcrowded mechanical and electrical industries. Most of those who had finished only the *Volksschule* (18 percent) selected apprenticeships in the low-paying shoe industry.[41] In 1925 the most popular occupations remained the same, even though few job possibilities

existed in these areas: 491 boys sought apprenticeships as electrical technicians, but only 53 openings existed; 842 desired apprenticeships in some form of mechanics, but only 253 were available.
The more traditional artisanal trades such as sheet-metal working,
decorating, and bookbinding lost their attractiveness: respectively,
only 40, 46, and 30 youths desired apprenticeships in these occupations compared to 231, 101, and 123 openings.[42] As one who had
lived through that period remembered, "Before the war, before the
year 1914, the printers were elite earners, big earners. . . . After the
war the metal workers became number one and the printers were
knocked below, right."[43]

Although many youths did not find a position in the trade for
which they were trained, due to the poor economic conditions during the interwar period, most males went to a trade school or
learned a trade as an apprentice. In most cases, working-class families could afford to send only their sons to trade school. A father's
plea to his daughters to "let the boys learn" was typical during the
period 1910–1925. In interview after interview, women related how
their brothers received occupational training while they received
none or were forced to take apprenticeships in traditionally female
occupations. The 1923 census revealed that although women comprised almost one-half of the Viennese labor force (200,000 of
444,968), they comprised only about one-quarter of the apprentices.
Moreover, 10,620 of the total of 13,245 female apprentices were in
the traditionally female-dominated clothing industry.[44] Even those
girls who gained an apprenticeship often worked as unskilled laborers in areas other than that in which they had been apprenticed.

The transitional nature of the period after 1910 is further indicated by the increasing incidence of wives' employment outside
the home; the 1912–14 study of 114 Viennese working-class households found that 18 wives worked solely at their household duties
and 46 worked outside the home compared with about an equal
number (50) who worked at the more traditional *Heimarbeit*.[45] The
occupations of those I interviewed—most beginning full-time work
after 1910—differed even more than the 1912–14 study from the
primarily household duties and part-time artisanal work of their
mothers. From a total of 45, 7 worked as sales assistants, 13 worked
as unskilled laborers in factories, 6 became dressmakers, 10 were
housewives, 2 were milliners, 2 were domestic servants, and 4 pursued one of the following occupations: nurse, teacher, hotel direc-

tor, and waitress.[46] The need to replace men who were at war or unemployed speeded up a transformation that was already under way before the war.

Girls' occupational choices began to shift from jobs traditionally performed by women to service and factory work in the period 1910–34. From 1922 to 1932 a traditional female occupation, dressmaking (*Schneiderin*), dropped from first to fourth among occupations most often selected by girls of school-leaving age (13–14). But, as is apparent in Table 5.2, it remained among those occupations most often selected by girls. Of the 45 women I interviewed, 6 pursued dressmaking as an occupation and two sewed in their home. As late as 123, the Viennese Occupational Office lamented girls' one-sided preference for certain occupations, especially dressmaking, and attempted to change the attitudes of girls and their parents through a concerted propaganda campaign.[47] It was often not a daughter's "choice" but parents' pressure to pursue tailoring, since they thought it would give their daughter security and prepare her for marriage. The woman quoted at the beginning of the chapter wanted to become an office worker, but her father forced her to learn dressmaking.[48] Another woman told me that her father simply told her, "You will become a dressmaker."[49] When I asked a lower-stratum woman who worked as a maid in the 1920s if her parents had asked her about her occupational goals, she gave a typical response, "No, then people said, you must leave home and feed yourself."[50] Rada related that two fourteen-year-old girls who lived with their grandmother refused to return to their father when they reached fourteen because, in their opinion, "now he wants us since we are fourteen and can now earn money."[51] Another influential reason children from the lower stratum began work early was to escape crowded and sometimes oppressive conditions in the home, as the comment from the young woman who wished to earn her own money indicates.

But white-collar jobs were fast winning over the more traditional occupations in the interwar period. By the early 1930s, sales assistant (*Verkaufspraktikantin*) had become the most desired occupation, followed by hairdressing and office assistant (*Büropraktikantin*). While this change in occupational choice reflected the growing employment in these occupations, the number desiring them often exceeded the number of apprenticeships available. In 1931, the number choosing sales, hairdressing, and dressmaking was 887, 632, and 312, respectively, but the number of open ap-

Table 5.2 Occupational Choices of Girls
Leaving School in 1922 and 1932

1922	1932
1. Dressmaking	1. Sales Assistant
2. Trade School	2. Hair Dresser
3. Advanced schooling	3. Office Assistant
4. Sales Assistant	4. Dressmaking

Source: Die Frau, August 1933, 17. *Arbeiterzeitung,*
14 February 1923, 8.

prenticeships was 554, 29, and 477.[52] Other traditional female occupations such as millinery declined rapidly; only 95 chose it despite the existence of 298 apprenticeships.[53] Many girls expressed a desire to continue their studies (697) in 1931 but realized the futility of such a course (both a lack of money and educational background) and opted for something less. As a result, it was possible to hear a young girl say, "If I can't be a teacher, I'll perhaps be a maid in a large house."[54]

One reason that girls continued to select dressmaking was the security that it offered. An interwar study of 12- to 14-year-old German and Austrian *Volksschule* students found that while boys ranked independence as the major motive for their occupational choice, girls placed security at the top (36.8 percent), with independence somewhat less influential (29.2 percent).[55] This group represents the upper reaches of the working class, since many children of the lower stratum did not seek advice from the occupational advisement offices from where the data were taken. Also, since security was an important motive of many parents when they pressured their daughters to be dressmakers, it may represent more the parents' desires rather than their daughters'. Even if girls failed to get full-time positions as dressmakers, parents assumed they could always pursue it at home on a part-time basis as *Heimarbeiter.*

Factory work for girls in the interwar period was still considered to be a last resort among many working-class parents, since work conditions were often poor, work strenuous, and the social consequences perceived to be damaging. But in comparison to *Heimarbeit,* factory work was better-paying, normally involved less actual hours, and often gave young workers companionship and more independence than they would have had had they worked with their parents at home. Many working-class families found it necessary to send their daughters to work in factories, since they could not afford apprenticeship fees and their families needed the extra income. Women normally worked in these factories until they married.

A report by the Viennese Worker Health Insurance Office in 1928 showed that women 14 to 20, followed by those 21 to 30, were most often employed in factories and shops. Those aged 31 to 40 were employed only about half as often as those aged 21 to 30.[56] Many small factories and shops did not observe the 44-hour workweek limitation for women and children, and women often needed to increase their pay through a longer workweek.[57] Many laboring families still considered factory work as unfeminine. The daughter of a man who cared for a doctor's horses recalled that her father told her, ". . . a factory girl. No good will come of it."[58] Adelheid Popp, who began work in a factory at the age of ten, wrote, "I tried to dress well. When I went to church on Sunday, I didn't want anyone to recognize me as a factory worker. I was ashamed of it."[59] What some parents desired was clean, less strenuous work offering some training that could be used later in married life. Many families thought factory work would damage their daughters' chance for a profitable marriage. Leichter's study of 1,320 female industrial workers found that 85 percent (95.3 percent of the married women and 68.1 of the single women) would have remained at home if their husbands or fathers had earned enough to support them.[60]

There is little doubt that factory work was low-paying and physically taxing. But how it stacked up to other possible work for youth is another and more important question. Certainly unskilled female workers in factories were ill-paid—less than half the male wages—and therefore forced to accept grueling piecework as the only way to make a decent wage. A 1929 study of 170,293 Viennese laborers revealed that 45 percent of the women, but only 20 percent of the men, toiled at piecework. Nevertheless, women's pay was still only about half that of the men in the study.[61] The feverish pace that was necessary in order to justify piecework rather than straight wages was obviously extremely tiring. But all *Heimarbeit* was piecework without the pay, possible companionship, and independence that factory work might provide. As a recent study concluded, the lower pay in artisanal work meant that artisan masters could "offer only phrases in place of hard cash."[62] A trade magazine, *Die Gewerbliche Fortbildungsschule*, reported even before World War I that "parents without means seek a trade for their children, but youth themselves prefer the unencumbered life as a factory worker to the discipline of an apprenticeship."[63] Meissl found that many girls perceived factory work as liberating in the sense that they achieved warm relationships with their co-workers and more strictly delimited working hours.[64]

When married women worked outside the home, they undoubtedly added another duty to their previously taxing duties as housekeepers and child-rearers. Since men seldom helped at home, the arduous nature of women's work would have led few married women to look favorably upon this additional burden. While youths were increasingly inclined to prefer work outside the home to house work because it provided some financial independence, a still large 65 percent of the girls between age 16 and 20 questioned by Leichter in 1931 chose household over other work.[65] However, there is a clear difference in the responses from married and single women. About one-third of the single women responded that they would not give up their work if their father or husband had earned enough to support them, while only about 5 percent of married women responded similarly. Clearly, the generation coming of age in the interwar period began to consider work as a more permanent part of their lives.

Nor did apprenticeships offer youths an attractive alternative to household duties. They no longer provided the training and care they had offered in the nineteenth century. Factories, with their increasing specialization, no longer needed workers with extensive apprenticeship training. Indeed, they preferred young unskilled workers who would not be as bored by the monotonous mass-production techniques of the factory. In order to compete with factories producing cheaper goods, small masters employed large numbers of apprentices at low wages or some for only their room and board.[66] In many cases, masters used apprentices for unskilled tasks such as cleaning, delivery, shopping, and child care and never provided proper occupational training. As a female sewing apprentice at that time remembered, "I learned very little about my job at first. The first half-year I learned to shop, deliver, and perform all shop routines. . . . You couldn't call it instruction. . . . I bungled my way through until I was set free and then became a pieceworker like all the others."[67]

Robyn Dasey found that apprenticeship training in Berlin "was often as brief as two to six weeks, cost 10–12 Marks, and was followed by up to six weeks on 3–4 Marks weekly. The least reputable workshops doing low-grade work collected the fee, used this free labor as long as possible in peak season and then simply sacked the girl."[68] Meacham called a similar English practice "improving" or "following up." English youth would agree to long-term contracts with firms (5 to 7 years) in order to gain training at a minimal salary. In reality, they learned very little and finished their training with no well-developed skills.[69]

The Viennese Industrial Inspector's annual report in 1924 singled out apprentice misuse as a major abuse.[70] In many cases apprentices were that in name only. A 21-year-old apprentice in the pearl industry complained that she was hired as an apprentice but used as an unskilled worker, since her *"Lehrfrau"* used her as "babysitter and errand girl" [*Kindermädchen and Laufmädchen*].[71] As a former female worker in a tailor shop during World War I told me, "So, I didn't receive very much as an apprentice. They exploited us . . . we had to do everything."[72] In addition, many youths were not working in the occupations for which they had been trained but as unskilled labor in other jobs. A 1926 survey by the Viennese Chamber of Labor revealed that from every 100 male and female workers, 62.40 of the former but only 35.14 of the latter were skilled. But about one-half of the skilled female workers (16.30 of the 35.14) were not working in the occupations in which they had been trained but as unskilled laborers in factories.[73] Those youths with apprenticeship training who were working as unskilled laborers did not consider their work to be an occupation. Surveys of Berlin and Viennese unskilled laborers in the 1920s often obtained an answer of "none" when asked to name their occupation.[74] Parents were often responsible for their children's exploitation. The Apprentice Protection Office reported in 1919 that parents often forced their children into apprenticeships under masters they had been warned about.[75] These parents were apparently operating under the old assumption that an apprenticeship was necessary for a meaningful job.

Nor did the expanding service sector offer youth, especially women, the kind of satisfaction that might have kept them at work. In most cases, white-collar jobs were low-paying and demanded long working hours. Few ever obtained a leadership position in such work. The 1930 study of 1,320 female industrial workers found that only about two percent reached supervisory positions (*Vorarbeiter*) and then only in those few female-dominated industries such as dressmaking.[76] Another 1931 survey of 643 female service workers in industry discovered that about one-half were clerks, designated "Mädchen für alles" (girl Friday) in Austria, who were responsible for all the menial office tasks. Two-thirds of them claimed that they had no chance for promotion.[77] Many worked in small offices where little possibility for advancement existed. A study of 14,474 firms in 1930 by the Viennese Employee Bureau showed that 5,962 had only one employee and another 2,583 only two employees.[78]

In addition, the status of most clerking positions declined as employers increasingly employed untrained help in order to cut costs. Hiring girls fresh out of school was one means to this end. A typical advertisement in 1930 read "Clerk for afternoons, attractive, cultivated woman under 28 years of age."[79] Most working-class parents encouraged their daughters to take such positions, since the parents could avoid the expense of sending them to trade schools or into an apprenticeship. In many cases office work was short-term, since employers were able to find even younger and more attractive girls who were willing to work at low wages.

Finally, to what extent was children's work tied to family needs? It is possible to agree with the author of a study of Austrian women that working-class parents no longer bore children with the expectation that each additional child would add to family income, as in the period prior to the compulsory-education laws.[80] But one can extend the analysis further by asking if family considerations did not still take precedence over all other considerations. As discussed in chapter 4, large numbers of working-class children worked both before and after school and were expected to contribute all their income to the family. They were also expected to work in the home even if such work kept them from school. Even after beginning to earn an independent income after age 14, children's obligations toward the family continued to be a major one. The two studies of household budgets showed a declining but still meaningful youth contribution to family budgets in the prewar and interwar period. The 1912–14 study revealed that children's earnings provided a portion of the family budget in 32 of the 117 households and that they were more important than those of the wives.[81] The daughter of a delivery man remembered that she gave all her 8-gulden monthly earnings as a servant to her family from age 14 to age 18.[82] Still another recalled that her mother no longer had to take in washing since her brother sent the family $5 a month from his job on a merchant ship.[83]

Youths' family contributions remained important to family budgets in the interwar period because of the massive unemployment
of their parents: the family budget studies of 1925–34 revealed that
children often provided up to 10 percent of family budgets.[84] A
1926 survey of 380 leather-goods apprentices revealed that from
their average earnings of 6–9 schillings a week, 27 gave all, 130
retained only 1–3 schillings, and 104 kept only 3–6 schillings.[85]
Many of those I spoke with remembered the precise amounts they
turned over to the family. One who started work at age 14 in 1924
gave 15 of the 18 weekly schillings that she earned to her family.[86]
The survey of 1,320 women workers revealed that some young girls
were the major wage-earners in their families, and almost all gave
some part of their wages to the family as long as they were part of
the household.[87] A study of German working-class girls found it to
be an "astonishing practice" among the proletariat that girls' earnings were "expropriated" by the parents in the early twentieth
century; two-thirds of the girls questioned gave 65 to 85 percent of
their income to the family.[88]

Tilly and Scott are to a large extent accurate in their assessment
that working-class girls' work was still shaped by family needs in
the early twentieth century.[89] As discussed earlier, many families
found it necessary to put their daughters to work immediately
when they reached the legal school-leaving age so that they might
help support the family financially and permit their brothers to
attend trade school. Little thought was given to girls' occupational
future except to get them into some secure "feminine" occupation
that would provide for them before and especially during marriage. Few broke from this working-class mold even in the interwar
period. Rigler's contention that occupational desires were influenced by a desire for social improvement (*Aufstieg*) is difficult to
accept as an important factor.[90] By far the most important reason
that girls sought to change occupations was to escape poor working conditions or physically taxing labor. The fact that 85 percent
of those in the Leichter study wanted to return to the household
rather than continue to work outside the home raises serious
doubts that a desire for social advancement had any influence on
their decisions. Girls' desires for white-collar jobs were not an attempt to follow a "bourgeois bias," but a desire for less exhausting
work with better work conditions.[91] Although white-collar jobs did
not fulfill girls' expectations completely, they did provide more
security than factory work. The attempt to impose post–World

War II motivations in a primarily nineteenth-century work milieu is misleading.

Throughout the 1890–1938 period, youth's occupational choices were conditioned primarily by the long-term shift to factory production and white-collar jobs, their parents' occupations, and, in the case of girls, family needs and jobs that working-class families considered socially suitable. While males adjusted their occupational desires to meet the economic transformation, female "choices" were limited severely by family needs and the training and occupations open to them. Although the factory might offer better pay than outwork and more free time, parents did not believe that it was socially respectable or that it offered daughters the opportunity to marry well. Although a young girl often could not find full-time work after finishing an apprenticeship in tailoring (dressmaking), parents argued that she could still support herself through piecework at home and after marriage.

The lure of traditional occupations was enhanced by the instability brought on by the war and the economic difficulties of the interwar period. But change was apparent in job choice and attitudes. Males were increasingly choosing jobs because of their intrinsic interest or merely because of better pay, and many females were no longer viewing work as merely an interim stage between school and marriage. As a result of the decline in artisanal work and domestic service coupled with the deskilling of work, occupational choice was much greater in the interwar period. Still, there were sizable differences depending upon the working-class stratum one belonged to. While almost all youth in the upper stratum could expect some form of occupational training, only boys had the possibility of obtaining it in the lower stratum. Job choice was also conditioned by one's social milieu. Those with more schooling tended to choose the better jobs and apprenticeships. Those in the lower stratum were restricted both by their lack of education and by their limited vistas.

6

Youth Culture, Sex, and Marriage

My mother didn't explain sexual matters to us, not at all. We knew absolutely nothing about it.[1]

—*Daughter of a typesetter*

Our youth must be prepared to fight against the sex drive when it challenges the demands of socialist morality.[2]

—*Otto Kanitz, editor of* Die Sozialistische Erziehung

Socialist and bourgeois critics have generally agreed that the typical working-class child suffered physical, social, and psychological damage as a result of the destructive influence of bad city neighborhoods and crowded housing conditions, where youth presumably could not avoid early exposure to the illicit social and sexual activity of their peers, parents, and older siblings. The result was antisocial behavior and a working-class sexual precocity that led to an excessive candidness about sexual matters, sexual promiscuity, illegitimacy, and, in some cases, even prostitution and incest. But recent studies of working-class culture have warned against the imposition of one model of behavior for the entire working class and for all areas. Other studies have suggested that sexual behavior did not abruptly change with urbanization but was tied to rural mentality in many ways, and that the generalization about working-class licentiousness has been much exaggerated. These studies further argue that the working-class adoption of birth-control methods in the late nineteenth century exhibits a restraint that seriously questions previous stereotypes about working-class sexuality. The following examination of youth culture, sexuality, and marriage will reveal even more than the preceding chapters the differences among working-class youth that seriously challenge simple generalizations about working-class behavior.

John Gillis believes that "for virtually all young people, but especially women, the period from 1890–1960 was one of lost status and diminished independence, greater uncertainty and perpetual anxiety, a situation reflected in the growth of distinctive male and female youth subcultures, each with their own distinctive styles and ritual practices."[3] Joseph Kett also views the period after 1890 as a period of institutionalized dependency for youth. As boys were viewed increasingly as "vulnerable, passive and awkward," society moved to segregate youngsters from adults. The result was numerous age-segregated institutions and leisure-time organizations that effectively isolated youth.[4] These institutions and organizations separated males and females so thoroughly, according to Gillis, that homosocial worlds resulted.[5] As the working-class area became settled "urban villages, a feminization for young women and virilization for young men became the norm in Britain. Girls were kept close to home and schooled in feminine tasks with the ultimate objective of making a good marriage. Boys engaged in a rough-and-tumble existence in the streets with limited contact with the female world until age seventeen or after."[6]

When applied in a very general way and with an emphasis on middle-class youth, Gillis's theory has much to recommend it. Certainly middle-class youth and the upper reaches of the working class began to experience a more extensive period of dependence and isolation as they tended to stay in school longer as a result of compulsory education. Also, an increasing number of youth organizations sponsored by religious organizations and political parties separated youth from the adult world. Siegfried Bernfield described this increased dependency in the German-speaking world as stretched puberty (*gestreckten Pubertät*) already in the 1920s.[7] Also, the higher the social stratum, the less youth spent time in the streets among their peers. But this chapter will argue that youth experience after 1890, especially the extent to which youths were becoming dependent or independent, was a complex phenomena that was shaped primarily by class/stratum, gender, area, and age.

There was certainly an extensive effort to isolate youth in Austria into age-specific organizations at the turn of the century. In addition to organizations set up by bourgeois interests to promote youth activities, such as the Boy Scouts (*Pfadfinder*), numerous popular cultural activities such as dance halls, the cinema, and popular sporting events attracted youths' attention. To counter these "bourgeois" influences, the SDAP leadership promoted numerous events (dances, concerts, fests, swimming and bicycle clubs), organizations such as the *Kinderfreunde* (1910), and in the postwar period the Red Falcons (socialist Boy Scouts) in order to obtain youth support. As the discussion of SDAP-organized dances points out below, the party was ineffective in attracting youth away from the bourgeois dance halls. Demographic changes made the small nuclear family, and therefore a youth-centered home, an even greater possibility after the turn of the century, when the one- and two-child family became a reality, first among the bourgeoisie and then among laborers by the interwar period. Since the upper reaches of the working-class could afford to support their children longer, they were increasingly freed from the adult world of work.

In addition to these two cultural milieus, the bourgeois and the SDAP, working-class youth, especially males, were attracted by the even more satisfying street culture. Socialist leaders tried to counter this milieu as resolutely as that of the bourgeoisie. This street culture had existed long before the turn of the century and had attracted much of working-class youth. It threatened to undermine socialist attempts to create "new people" and was therefore constantly under attack by socialist leaders. But much that these youth groups found attractive—smoking, dancing, street dress, fighting—the SDAP was trying to exorcise from youth behavior. For example, the banning of smoking from SDAP-sponsored activities turned many youth away. The SDAP also opposed most of those social and cultural practices that the working class inherited from its peasant and artisanal past. These were viewed as "primitive" by the much more sophisticated SDAP leadership, who were interested in reforming working-class behavior.

There is little doubt that working-class girls, especially after puberty, lost much of their independence. Parents sought to keep daughters at home in order to protect them, to train them for motherhood, and use them for child care. Rada thought respectable [*ordentlich*] behavior and excessive time spent in the streets were incompatible. She lamented the condition of "one of her students who wanted to be a respectable person but was a true street kid."[8] She noted disapprovingly that 38 percent of the working-class children she surveyed spent their Sundays without their parents in the streets or meadows.[9] But street activities for all but girls in the lower stratum stopped abruptly with puberty.[10] Many of the women I interviewed told me that they were not permitted to play in the streets as children.[11] Viethen wrote that "a respectable working-class girl did not go into the streets at night alone. As long as she had no firm friend or fiancé acceptable to her parents, a girl could not leave the house without accompaniment from siblings or parents."[12] The only exceptions were organized functions such as dancing schools, evening courses, and club activities. Although Rada stressed what she considered to be extensive street playing by working-class children, she acknowledged that concerned [*sorgender*] parents forbade it. Rada thought that one need only mention to any working-class mother that her daughter was seen in the streets with boys in order to prevent it. But one mother of a 13-year-old did not find it to be so alarming and responded that "she couldn't run after her grown daughter when she went out with boys."[13] Here we encounter the conflict between Rada's more middle-class attitudes and those of some lower-stratum parents who did not find street activities so damaging. While the more respectable working-class parents would agree with Rada, the remainder would consider such activities normal. The socialist urge to remove temptation from youths' activities led to this blanket condemnation of all street activity. But as Humphries discovered for English working-class youth, "larking about with the lads rarely involved sexual intercourse" due to parental control, lack of privacy, and fear of pregnancy.[14]

Among all working-class strata, parents still severely restricted daughters' leisure pursuits well into the interwar period. "It's terrible that mother won't understand that a girl needs as much freedom and independence as a boy. My brother can do what he wants after work, but I must help my mother with housework even when I come home tired."[15] Girls' attendance at dances was restricted and closely supervised. Leichter estimated that only about 10 percent of the single women in her survey of 1,320 women workers went dancing once a month.[16] Permitting their daughters to attend dances was a major step for parents. Since girls' activities at dances could not be so closely controlled, parents were relinquishing a great deal of the authority they had over them.[17] But parents

tried to maintain their authority by restricting their daughters'
free time. Among the respectable, daughters of working-class parents had to be home by 8 or 9 P.M.[18] The daughter of a silversmith
remarked, "When you had been working awhile, then you could go
out as long as you were home by 8 P.M."[19] One way to enforce hours
was not to give their children a house key, so that they would have
to pay lock-up money [*Sperrgeld'*] if they came home after 10 P.M. In
addition, parents or older brothers often picked up daughters at
social functions and accompanied them home. Usually girls were
not free to go out as they desired until they had moved out of their
parents' home, and this occurred normally only after they married.
A woman recounted how she had to go to dances secretly until she
was married at age 27.[20] As discussed in chapter 5, most working
girls did not make enough money to pay for their own lodging and
remained dependent on their parents until marriage.

The emergence of the cinema before the war brought working-
class youth in closer touch with other social groups, but it was
attended primarily by young men. A prewar survey of more than
100 Viennese school classes found that about 20 percent visited the
cinema regularly and that 76 percent had attended the cinema.[21]
But, typically, younger boys had visited the cinema much more
than even older girls: 35 percent of boys in a Favoriten *Volksschule*
but only 9 percent of girls in a Favoriten *Bürgerschule* reported
regular attendance at the cinema.[22] An interwar survey of male
Ledergalanterie (leather goods) apprentices found that about half of
them attended the cinema regularly.[23] While the trend was toward
greater freedom to attend the cinema during the 1890–1938 period, important gender differences existed.

The picture that emerges from this general description of youth
culture is of a differentiated world dependent upon stratum and
gender. Young men had greater freedom than young women, and
lower-stratum youth had greater freedom than upper-stratum
youth. Also, factory workers had greater freedom than artisanal
apprentices and home-workers. The shorter working hours of the
factory provided more free time, and the greater distance from
parents permitted a more extensive involvement in a youth subculture. Therefore, it is difficult to argue that the general trend during
this period was one of increasing dependency on parents for most
of the working class. It is certainly probable that in the early industrial period in Vienna (the mid-nineteenth century), before the establishment of matrifocal community networks, youth were per-

mitted greater freedom. But any comparison with the peasant and artisanal past would reveal that city dwellers had more freedom. Both peasant and artisanal work required long hours and a close working relationship with parents. City life, especially for those working in factories, meant greater independence. So, if the comparison is with the peasant or artisanal past, Gillis's theory is less apt, and if the comparison is with the early urban factory experience, then his theory has more substance. An examination of working-class youth sexuality may provide greater insights concerning youthful behavior during this period.

The pioneering works of two Viennese socialist women, Hildegard Hetzer and Margarete Rada, provide an important starting point for an assessment of Viennese working-class sexual attitudes.[24] After long periods of observation, both concluded that proletarian girls were too involved in word and deed with sexual matters. Hetzer, from her position as director of a socialist *Hort* for girls, closely observed ten proletarian girls aged 14 to 16 for two years. Based upon these observations, she contended that "they talked about sexual matters with perhaps too much openness at home" and that about half spoke often and openly about such topics as pregnancy, contraception, and other sexual matters, although the other half discussed such things "seldom and quietly." According to Hetzer, those who had sexual relations early became obsessed with sexual matters and, as a result, never discussed more important matters, such as science, art, politics, and nature.[25]

Rada, an elementary teacher in a Viennese working-class district, thought that knowledge of sexual matters was a matter of course among proletarian girls. She recounted how one of her female students explained to her classmates that a couple was having an intimate relationship which she found embarrassing to describe.[26] She was further surprised when she overheard 11-year-old students discussing extramarital relationships. In comparison with middle-class girls, she found that proletarian girls were not as surprised when they began to menstruate.[27] She inferred that working-class girls lost their innocence early when she wrote that the daughter of an administrative official in her class was laughed at by the other girls in her class because of her innocence.[28] This view agrees with a widely held stereotype that middle-class girls were uninformed about sexual matters, while working-class girls knew about sexual acts both through experience and candid discussion of sex. Also, the assumption that candidness about sex comes only from actual sexual experience is questionable. As Hoggart observed in Britain, "sexual matters do seem nearer the surface" in the working class, but this does not necessarily mean that they are "sexually more licentious than others."[29]

Socialist leaders were divided on the sexual question. A minority, including Ernst Fischer and Wilhelm Reich, believed that youth and their parents should be fully informed about sexual matters and that youth should not be constrained by inhibiting bourgeois attitudes about sex. They thought that the typical proletarian youth were sexually disturbed due to a conflict between their advanced knowledge of sexual matters and their lack of sexual activity resulting from their parents petit-bourgeois attitudes, the crowded housing conditions, and young women's fear of pregnancy.[30] Fischer and Reich advised beginning sexual intercourse as soon as youth had attained psychological maturity since it would free youth from their guilt associated with masturbation.[31] But most Austrian socialist leaders, including Julius Tandler, Otto F. Kanitz, Hildegard Hetzer, Charlotte Bühler, and Therese Schlesinger, thought working-class youth were suffering from premature and excessive sexual activity as a result of their exposure to sexual matters. Julius Tandler, in charge of Vienna's Public Welfare Office and a socialist member of the city council, assumed that inferior housing had led to excessive sexual activity and social debilitation among the working class.[32]

Some socialists were particularly concerned about masturbation among the young. Kanitz, editor of *Die sozialistische Erziehung*, responding to a study that claimed 90 percent of young boys masturbated, wrote, "Masturbation? The danger of the lack of restraint is great. What can be done? Abstinence and early marriage."[33] He maintained that those who wished to realize the socialist ideal "must be sexually pure."[34] Kanitz viewed sexual control as part of a necessary self-control demanded by the socialist ideal. Therese Schlesinger advised working-class youth to abstain from sexual intercourse until "they were mature enough to choose the right partner and to take up the obligations of an adult," since "the unbridled satisfaction of the sex drive thwarts the development and deepening of eroticism" and "separates sexual intercourse from reproduction."[35] Both Schlesinger and Hetzer feared that uninhibited sexual activity would lead to large working-class families and crowded housing and thereby not remove those conditions that had led, in their opinion, to the impoverishment and debilitation of the lower working-class stratum.[36] But, Reich, from his experiences as a sex counselor in the Sexual Advice Centers for Workers and Employees, advised that those who had not switched from masturbation to sexual intercourse before the age of twenty could find it difficult making the transition.[37]

Despite Reich's and Fischer's pleas, most socialist leaders were convinced that there was too much sexual activity among working-class youth, and they sought to postpone the onset of sexual inter-course through a propaganda campaign in the socialist press. Un-derlying this perception was the Freudian theory that achievement was made possible through the sublimation of the sex drive. As Schlesinger wrote, "Cultural advance is not possible without the spiritualization and sublimation of a portion of the sex drive."[38] In order to overcome this allegedly excessive sex drive, the socialist party sought to divert the attention of youth from sex through participation in sports and the many SDAP youth organizations. A socialist functionary argued that "we must tie youth between 14 and 17 to the organizations through sports."[39] One of the command-ments of the Red Falcons, the organization for 12- to 14-year-olds, was to be "constantly pure in thought, word and deed."[40] Modern dancing, especially dances such as the Charleston, were forbidden at youth functions in order not to arouse youthful passions.[41] SDAP opposition to the cinema resulted from their fears that it provided too much temptation and diverted youth's attention from cultur-ally edifying events. In order to show the debilitating influence of the cinema, a 1912 survey compared the youths' visits to the cin-ema unfavorably to their visits to St. Stephen's Cathedral.[42] To what extent were socialist fears concerning working-class youths' sexuality real? How much did working-class youth know about sexual matters, to what extent did they actually engage in premari-tal sexual activity, and how were things sexual perceived among the various working-class strata?

At the very bottom of working-class society, among some of the unskilled and seasonal workers, the so-called *Proleten*, socialists' darkest fears were no doubt realized. Housed in the smallest dwell-ings, these larger than normal families also had to take in subten-ants and bed-renters in order to make ends meet. Although the subtenants and bed-renters were not always a negative influence on the families, some no doubt were. Almost all studies of working-class housing in the early twentieth century have noted Adelheid Popp's description of a subtenant's attempt to assault her. As she wrote, "I was not yet fast asleep and I suddenly awoke with a cry of terror. I had detected a hot breath over me, but in the darkness I could not see what it was. My cry awakened my mother, who turned on the light. Our bed-renter—the foot of his bed lay next to the head of our [mother and daughter] bed—had raised himself and was bending over me."[43] Tandler's report that 34 percent of the cases of venereal disease in the Hospital for Children with Venereal Disease came from parents and siblings is also a startling statistic.[44] However, the bulk of the evidence from workers' autobiographies, oral interviews, and crime statistics indicates that such misery was restricted primarily to the lowest stratum of the working class. The vast majority of working-class families, even those with limited economic means, were not sexually promiscuous. In fact, as the rest of this chapter will argue, the majority of working-class families led sexually abstemious lives.

As one quote at the beginning of the chapter indicates, not all working-class children were well informed about sexual matters. Although most of those I spoke with did not discuss sexual matters, those that did informed me that discussion of sex was forbidden (two used the word *tabu*) in their homes.[45] Viethen found that her interviewees were, as youth, not enlightened concerning sexual matters.[46] Reich determined that working-class parents opposed socialist party youth leaders' attempts to instruct youth on sexual matters.[47] Of course, most working-class parents would not have objected had they understood that the youth leaders intended to curb youth's presumed excessive sexual passions. Meacham also discovered that English working-class parents "believed that children were best off knowing and hearing less."[48] This attitude led in some cases to an extreme ignorance about sexual matters. In thinking back on her childhood experiences, the daughter of a silversmith said, "I got my first kiss in Schönbrunn Park . . . then I cried in the night. And my sister said, 'What's the matter?' I told her 'I'm going to have a baby.' She said 'Jesus . . . where were you with him?' I said that he gave me a kiss and I thought I would have a baby."[49]

Despite the stereotype that working-class children were exposed constantly to sexual matters because of their cramped living quarters, it is not clear that they could have known much about sex through observation. As the daughter of a transport worker remembered, "How they [her parents] carried out their love life, I don't know. There was no room. And during the day they worked and the children were there. I think they threw a blanket on the floor at night in order to have sexual intercourse."[50] The son of an artisan recalled, "I was sent to bed early . . . my parents stayed up and worked or talked. And I noticed that my father was near my mother, let's say, sort of on top of my mother, seemingly sleeping. . . . I always heard only my mother's groaning, and I thought that my father was doing something to my mother, and as a boy I was close to my mother, and I was more or less angry with him. I didn't yet understand what it was all about. That they were groans of passion I didn't comprehend. He was doing something to her, but I went back to sleep."[51] What knowledge youth had of sex they gained from their peers. As the son of a stucco worker remembered, "These things went around in similar age groups."[52]

Despite the crowding, most working-class children seldom saw a naked body because most of their parents slept with their clothes on and changed clothing in a corner when others were not looking. As one who was brought up in such an environment recalled, "We never saw our parents naked, although we slept with them as children, never, really never saw it."[53] Viethen found similarly that "living in cramped quarters in no way produced openness and spontaneity in the proletarian family."[54] Parents apparently feared that candidness about sexuality would lead to greater freedom in actual practice. So, instead of explaining things sexual, parents sought to supervise their daughters closely to prevent any possible sexual activity. Elizabeth Roberts found this practice to be common among the English working class as well.[55] Knowledge of childbirth was prevented by sending children to relatives or neighbors when their mothers gave birth. When these observations are added to Hetzer's findings that only about half of the girls she observed spoke incessantly about sexual matters while the others acted as if it were a subject that should not be discussed openly points to the conclusion that knowledge about sex was not as widespread in working-class homes as the stereotype would have it. Rada's contradictory conclusion that "sex played a small role in general" further brings into question the stereotype that all working-class children were obsessed with sex. She noted that "only in four of the sixty cases did involvement with sex push all other interests into the background."[56]

Much of Rada's concern about street activities appears to be a middle-class and SDAP anxiety about working-class sexual precocity. It was a common middle-class perception that working-class youth engaged in early sex, with excessive illegitimacy often the result. A reference in a recent article to the "freer sexual relations of the working class" indicates that present investigations continue to accept a common sexual precocity among all working-class youth.[57] While the age at which youth first had sexual intercourse cannot be firmly established for the early twentieth century due to the secrecy surrounding such experiences, it is possible to make some approximations and thereby arrive at a fuller understanding of working-class sexuality. One interwar study set the average age for first sexual encounters at 18–19 for both sexes.[58] Such an average would certainly not support any argument of sexual promiscuity among the working class. Hetzer acknowledged this when she argued that by 18 or 19 girls had obtained sufficient physical and emotional maturity to not be harmed by sexual intercourse.[59] But there is strong evidence that youth were somewhat more sexually precocious. Reich, from his position as sexual counselor in the Sex Advice Clinics for Workers and Employees, calculated that proletarian youth normally began sexual intercourse at the age of 15 and peasant youth at 13.[60]

Hetzer herself argues that some girls suffered much more than others from premature sexual activity. Obviously such activity would have had to occur before the age of 18. But Hetzer provides convincing proof of early sexual activity for only one of the ten girls she studied.[61] One study of the influence of alcohol on the family did point to much earlier sexual activity. Although this study argued that there was no direct tie between excessive drinking and early sexual activity, it did claim that early sexual activity came to many working-class girls as a result of crowded living conditions. From a total of 738 girls aged 6–14, 287 suffered from the effects of "sexual compulsiveness" [sexueller Triebhaftigkeit] and 85 were "accustomed" to sexual intercourse.[62] The fact that 81 percent of these girls came from the smallest-size apartments (one-half to one and one-half rooms) and one or more of their parents drank excessively indicates that they represented the lowest stratum, the so-called Proleten in Vienna, of the working class.[63] Furthermore, since all 1,143 families in Tandler's study had been under city care for years, a condition that the majority of working-class families would have avoided, is another indication that most must have represented the lowest reaches of the working class.[64] The groups of Hetzer and Tandler/Reich may then represent both ends of a much differentiated working class. In the absence of any more

definitive evidence, the incidence of illegitimacy may provide additional insights into working-class sexuality.

Edward Shorter's view that the first sexual "revolution" occurred as a result of new city dwellers leaving behind traditional
rural values must be questioned for Austria as it has been for England and France.[65] Mitterauer's study of single mothers in Austria
argues convincingly that as the number of factory workers increased strongly toward the end of the nineteenth century, the so-
called sexual revolution had passed.[66] In the case of Vienna, recent
migrants appear to have continued rural sexual practices at first,
followed by a gradual reduction of illegitimate births in the new
city environment. The percentage of illegitimate births in Vienna
declined steadily, from an 1880 level of 45 percent of all births to
42 percent in 1890, 32 percent in 1900, and 29 percent in 1910.[67]
The occupations of most of the mothers bearing illegitimate children were those of the most recent immigrants to the city. Of 3,246
legitimized children in 1904, 1,471 of the mothers were unskilled
factory workers, 268 were temporary workers in the clothing industry, 468 were domestic servants, and a group of 833 gave no occupational information.[68] Domestic servants, the primary occupation of
recent female immigrants, had the highest rate of illegitimacy. In
Vienna in 1910, 4,257 of a total of 4,579 births to domestic servants
were illegitimate.[69]

Men working in the clothing and textile industries had far higher
illegitimacy rates than those in the more modern machine industry; the ratios for 1910 were 35 percent in the clothing industry, 25
percent in textiles, and only one percent in the machine industry.[70]
Higher pay in the machine industry permitted workers to marry
and set up a household earlier and thus avoid illegitimacy. As
Vienna's population became more settled and as the rural influx
subsided, the percentage of illegitimate births declined. The still-
high illegitimacy rate of the prewar period reflects the still-large
influx of workers in the decades immediately before the war. Since
most of these new city dwellers were poor and unable to marry
early and set up a household, they tended to produce more illegitimate children than the more settled inhabitants.[71]

Even with the higher illegitimacy among recent inhabitants of
working-class districts, existing evidence indicates that the working class was not primarily responsible for an illegitimacy rate of
23.4 percent of all Austrian births prior to World War I.[72] In 1910,
illegitimate births comprised a lower percentage of total reported

births in working-class Favoriten than they did in the socially mixed third district and the predominantly middle-class nineteenth district (893 of 5,017 in Favoriten compared to 475 of 2,513 in the third district and 306 of 1,348 in the nineteenth).[73] Of course, the illegitimacy among maids constituted a large portion of the births in the predominantly middle-class areas where they worked. But the evidence from Tandler's study, indicating that the illegitimacy rate among the lower reaches of the working class was not any higher than that for all Vienna, is a clearer indicator of illegitimacy among the poor. From a total of 3,772 children, 734, or 20 percent, were illegitimate compared to an average of 22 percent for all of Vienna between 1927 and 1929.[74]

Also instructive is the fact that the illegitimacy rate for Vienna as a whole was lower than in some parts of the Austrian hinterlands. In 1925, Vienna's 19.75 percent illegitimacy rate was not even half that of Graz's 42.1 percent or Carinthia's 39 percent.[75] After 1917, Vienna's illegitimacy rate dropped below the average for the other Austrian territories and stayed there throughout the interwar period.[76] Many peasants followed the practice of *Verlobungsprobe*, which involved testing a prospective bride's fertility during the period of engagement in order to prevent marrying a woman incapable of bearing children, or in peasant language, not "buy a cat in a sack."[77] Reich estimated that peasant youth began sexual intercourse at about 13, or about two years earlier than working-class youth.[78] Some of the discrepancy between city and country illegitimacy rates could be explained by the greater number of abortions in Vienna. Several medical examiners estimated them to be between 20 and 40 percent of all pregnancies.[79] Undoubtedly, the recourse to abortion was much less frequent among the more devout peasantry of the hinterland. In addition, knowledge of abortion techniques and persons capable of performing abortions were more available in the cities. Knowledge and use of contraceptives could have been more widespread in Vienna, although this is unclear, since many working-class males refused to use condoms because they were relatively expensive—they cost 40 to 50 groschen each—and were thought to reduce sexual satisfaction.[80] According to Reich, the main form of prevention among working-class youth was coitus interruptus.[81] Since this is a rather ineffective form of birth control, it appears that the contraceptives issue cannot explain the lower illegitimacy rate among the working class.

It is also clear that premarital sex and illegitimacy were not looked upon as dishonorable by a large segment of the peasantry and working class. Many argue that illegitimacy was "quasi-honorable" in that it was often tied to marriage. Almost all the German and Austrian workers' autobiographies of the late nineteenth and early twentieth centuries, upon which these commentators rely for their evidence, mention that they had premarital sex with their wives before marriage.[82] Some married after the birth of their first child, but others might wait until the birth of the second or even the third child.[83] As the daughter of an agricultural worker and casual laborer who later moved to Favoriten related, "Well, it was really rather normal when you didn't have any money . . . that you didn't marry. I was born in 1906 and my parents got married in 1909. I was three then. Before me there were two siblings, therefore you could say six years before they got married."[84] A painter's daughter recalling her marriage said, "Yes, yes, I was three months pregnant. . . . My grandmother was also . . . and the same thing happened to her daughter and then we three [sisters] were all three so far. My God, we didn't even know the word sex, that was life."[85]

The large number of legitimized children in Vienna indicates that the practice of marrying the pregnant woman continued in the city environment and that the absence of village social sanctions had little impact on this practice: approximately one-quarter were legitimized through marriage each year, and an untold number continued to be supported in illegal free unions.[86] A large part of the city illegitimacy resulted from couples' disregard for church marriage rather than from an uncontrolled sex drive brought about by the city environment. The percentage of marriage partners listing the same prenuptial address often reached 70 to 80 percent in the early twentieth century.[87] In fact, there was an understood code of honor among the working class that permitted sex between couples who had set up a household but denied it to those without such a commitment.[88] Ultimately, illegitimacy did not result in abandonment, as some have argued, but in the establishment of a household. Another important consideration in evaluating working-class sexuality is the late marriage age, considered below.

As the debate within the SDAP on the sexual question indicates, adult attempts to control and guide youth could produce an even more independent youth. Socialist publications discussed repeatedly the SDAP's failure to lure youth into socialist organizations due to the glamour of "bourgeois" entertainment. An article in *Die*

Praxis in 1930 claimed that "worker youth wanted to dance and they do dance but not with us."[89] The author attributed this to the attractiveness of things associated with popular dance halls— fashionable dress, smoking, and drinking—and despaired that so- cialist dance activities could ever win over those who were already involved in popular dance-hall life, since "our influence over these people is very limited."[90] The SDAP was also losing the sons of party members to radical right-wing political groups during the twenties. The *Arbeiter Zeitung* warned members repeatedly to pre- vent their sons from joining such organizations.[91] This genera- tional revolt was also played out within the socialist milieu in 1934, when an autonomous youth movement, the *Jungfront*, re- jected the pacifist, compromising style of the SDAP leadership in the face of rightist opposition. The younger generation's resort to militancy has been explained as frustration with the leadership's anemic response to the rightist Fatherland Front's attacks and as a generational revolt growing out of the street culture of working- class youth.[92]

   The first theory contends correctly that the party leadership wanted to educate youngsters in SDAP youth organizations, such as the Red Falcons or the Union of Socialist Working Youth (SAJ), but sought to limit youth to purely educational concerns lest they develop a political activism inconsistent with party leadership.[93] There was already historical precedent for such opposition, since youth had opposed the party's support for the government during World War I.[94] During the twenties, the prudish SDAP attitude concerning drinking and sexual activity further alienated many youths. Conflict developed between leaders and youth over frank SAJ discussions of sexual issues. When the SAJ called for action against fascism in 1931, the SDAP leadership removed some of the SAJ leaders. The SDAP tried to incorporate the youth movement by setting up the Young Socialist Front—the *Jungfront*—in 1932 for youths aged 21 to 25. The *Jungfront* developed its own momentum and resisted party attempts to control it. So while the *Jungfront* continued its agitation for action against the right, the party leader- ship stuck to a long view that socialism would ultimately win through the SDAP's strategy of education and working within the system. The activist opposition that emerged in the party in 1933 and provided the spark for the armed opposition to the right in 1934 was initiated by *Jungfront* members.[95]

   Another theory has attempted to get at the underlying motiva-

tion for youth opposition both to party leadership and to the rightist onslaught against the left by tying it to youth street culture.[96] In
defending their neighborhood or district against "invaders" when
they were growing up, youth had developed an intense identification with their districts. In the 1930s, as members of the *Jungfront*
or the paramilitary socialist *Schutzbund*, they defended their neighborhoods against rightist paramilitary invasions. During the heavy
unemployment after 1929, young men had spent most of their time
in the streets and nearby fields, where they often sought food. The
rightist invasion violated their social realm and threatened to
block one of their main sources of nourishment.[97] Much of the overt
opposition to the right during the military suppression of the left in
February 1934 developed spontaneously among youth-dominated
groups of the *Schutzbund*, which had waited in vain for the socialist leadership to issue a call to arms. They were shocked and dis-
mayed that much of the older generation had not joined in a massive strike against the right that might have crippled the government and made a successful military revolt more likely.

If youth, defined to a large extent as the period of dependency on
the family, was not brought to a close with separation from parents
by employment, it was with marriage. The increasing age of marriage due to the shortage and costs of housing and the necessity to
contribute to the parents' household as long as possible stretched
the period from the end of school to marriage to a decade or more
by the interwar period. For females, this period was one of court-
ship and full-time work but little independence. Unless employed
as domestic servants, girls rarely lived away from their parents,
even when they became apprentices. They were expected to contribute financially to their parents' household, share in some of the
household work, and master those tasks they would need to know
in order to run their own household. In fact, since much of
dressmaking and other textile work was still done in the home,
daughters often worked with their mothers until marriage. Most
males became independent long before marriage, although they
still might provide financial aid to the family until they married.

The marriage age dropped steadily throughout the nineteenth
century and then stabilized between 1890 and 1938. One study
calculates that 50 percent of lower-class males were marrying between the ages of 24 and 30 in the 1890s compared with only 30
percent at mid-century.[98] The *Austrian Statistical Handbook* establishes that the average Viennese marriage age stayed within this

range during the entire period 1890–1938; average marriageable age for men in 1913 and 1931 was 28.8 and 28.6, respectively, with the corresponding averages for women of 26.4 and 25.5.[99] But the age at which Viennese most often married was somewhat lower— 26 for men and 23 for women in 1930–31.[100] British averages were similar. The average Edwardian male married at 27, while his interwar counterpart married at 29; for females the averages were 25 for the prewar period and 26 for the interwar period.[101] Very few Viennese men married before age 25. Figures for the 1910–34 period indicate a slight tendency toward more marriages in the 20– 24 year-old age cohort but a still-small incidence of marriage in these years: In 1910, only 4,084 of 104,184 men and 22,097 of 112,438 women were or had been married during these years; and for 1934, 5,052 of 71,183 men and 17,000 of 85,881 women were or had been married.[102] For the age cohort 25–29, about half of the women were still single in 1910 (52,899 of 105,249), while a slightly lower 48 percent were single in 1934 (47,720 of 96,182).[103]

For the working class, the marriage age was slightly higher. The 1931 study of 1,300 female industrial workers indicates that only a minority were marrying before age 25; from a total of 164 aged 21– 25, about 30 percent (50) were or had been married.[104] Although there was a shortage of males in Vienna as a result of World War I, it would have influenced marriage among the age cohort 16–25 very little, since their possible mates would not have fought in the war unless they married someone six years their senior. The evidence from other surveys and my own calculations indicates that such an age gap between mates was rare. The average marriage age for men and women in St. Johann parish was 28.34 and 25.97, respectively, in 1910, and 28.59 and 26.53 in 1936.[106] A still-sizable proportion of the age cohort 26–30 in Leichter's study was single (108 of 266). This group would of course be more influenced by the war-related shortage of males. Since this was the age cohort that normally had the highest incidence of marriage, many of the unmarried in this survey would remain single.

From this rather lengthy discussion of marriage age, it is apparent that females remained single for about a decade after school. Although much documentary evidence indicates a small incidence of common-law relationships, my evidence indicates that a large number began living together before marriage and thus cut their ties with their parents' household. It appears that couples refused to acknowledge common-law relationships unless it was absolutely necessary. For example, the 1934 census revealed that only 1,811 of 51,601 Favoriten households (3.5 percent) contained common-law mates.[107] Leichter's sample of 1,300 industrial workers listed only nine-tenths of a percent as involved in any common-law relation-ship.[108] But both of these surveys are contradicted by other, official evidence and by my parish studies, which indicate that the number who began to live together before marriage was much higher. For 1912, 62.46 percent of the married couples in Ottakring and 69.12 percent of those in Brigittenau came from the same building.[109] It is possible that a few came from different apartments in the building, but most were probably already living together. Evidence from the parish archives shows a similarly high percentage living at the same address at the time of marriage. Of the 212 marriages in 1910 in St. Johann parish, 157 couples listed the same address. Since separate addresses were listed in the other cases, the address was not just their future marriage address.[110] Normally, the prospective groom moved in with the bride-to-be's parents. This practice was common in Austria among the peasantry as well as the working class.

Marriage or the possibility of marriage was the dominant influ-ence in working-class girls' lives. Work was still viewed by many as only a temporary stage in women's lives prior to marriage or as a necessary duty to supplement family income. As discussed in chap-ter 5, Leichter found that 95.3 percent of married female workers would have given up their work if their husbands had earned enough to support the family.[111] But more significant in terms of the continuation of traditional attitudes was the response of 68.1 per-cent of the single working girls that they would quit work if their fathers or future husbands earned enough to support them.[112] Such attitudes were often the determining factor in job choices. As a sur-vey of 500 women concluded, those taking up occupations in the interwar years were heavily influenced by their parents' attitudes about what occupations would enhance or reduce their daughters' chances for marriage.[113] As a result, working-class girls were often restricted to those occupations that would prepare them for house-hold tasks after marriage: dressmaking, domestic service, washing, ironing, etc. Even such occupations as sales clerk, nurse, hair-dresser, and office worker were suspect, since they necessitated con-siderable mingling with men.[114] Factory work in general, particu-larly in the metal industry, was thought to be damaging to a girl's marriage prospects. Laws were passed in 1919 prohibiting women and youth under 18 from working at night, thus reducing the competition of women and youth for jobs under the guise of protecting women's virtue.[115] This is not to say that some working-class girls did not begin to look at work in a different way. As noted in chapter 4, job choices began to change away from occupations identified with the home. But such choices might have changed more rapidly had opposition not existed toward "unfeminine" occupations.

For many working-class girls, the traditional role of housewife and mother was fulfilling enough. Marriage brought purpose to their lives. Many I interviewed spoke with pride about their ability to manage a household on their husbands' meager incomes. As one proudly exclaimed, "Studied? No. But I knew everything a housewife should know."[116] Meacham contends that the wife's central position within the household was one of the reasons she decided to marry, despite the hardships it might bring. In fact, marriage often provided an escape from the hardships at home. Although conditions might not be any better, the new wife would at least have more control over her life and perhaps an improved standard of living. A woman from a family of nine children remarked that she married "so that I could get out of my house and he so that he could get away from his family . . . at last to get away and have your own home, right, for that you had to get married."[117] It was also expected that a woman would marry. Marriage provided proof of a woman's adulthood and femininity.[118] Gillis also argues that the working class "measured maturity in marriage."[119]

The choice of mate included "instrumental" as well as emotional considerations. Shorter's contention that individual emotional considerations completely overcame instrumental (economic) attitudes by the nineteenth century inadequately explains mate selection in Vienna.[120] Since working-class youths tended increasingly to court away from home and chose their mates with less interference from their parents, emotional considerations began to play a greater role in their choice. But many of those I interviewed spoke about marriage partners being chosen because they might provide greater material support. Male white-collar workers were often preferred, since they could not lose their jobs as easily as manual laborers.[121] Such a consideration got added emphasis in the interwar period, when massive unemployment among manual laborers increased the attractiveness of white-collar workers. Those who worked for the city transportation system were especially attractive catches because they had a steady income with less chance of losing their jobs. A woman recalled that "a tramway worker who received

a monthly salary was a rich man then."[122] One of Viethen's interviewees remarked that "one didn't hear about love. In most cases
one married where one had a better prospect."[123] Her respondents
also noted the advantages of marrying salaried employees because
of their greater job security and pensions.[124] World War I had destroyed many working-class girls' illusions about marrying rich.
With so few available men and tough economic times, most women
settled for any available man.[125]

Contrary to the argument that geographic endogamy had ended
by the twentieth century, the vast majority of Viennese males
chose their brides from the same district, although the census figures are compromised due to the number of couples who were
already living together before marriage and gave the same address.[126] Since laborers seldom ventured out of their own district,
their mates were overwhelmingly from the same district. In 1905, a
little over 84 percent of Favoriten grooms (1,220 of 1,445) married
women from their own district.[127] Since 66 percent of the 1,220
came from the same building and were probably living together
before marriage, it is impossible to determine how many lived in
the same district before they began living together. However, only
225 of the 1,445 came from outside Favoriten and 415 came from
other parts of Favoriten.[128] Comparable figures for a predominantly middle-class district such as the fourth shows that only 48
percent of grooms—with 30 percent listing the same building—
married women from their own district.[129] For 1910, the percentage increased slightly for Favoriten to 87 percent—with 71 percent
from the same building—and to 63 percent for the fourth district.[130]

Socially, traditional marriage patterns endured. Working-class
couples continued to marry almost exclusively within their own
occupational stratum in the twentieth century. The fact that most
occupants of Favoriten chose their mates within Favoriten and
from a similar occupational category is rather formidable proof of
a continuing class endogamy. Of the 212 males marrying in Favoriten's St. Anton's Church in 1938, only fifteen married someone
who was from a higher occupational category.[131] In most of the
fifteen exceptions, marriages occurred between unskilled workers
and lower-level white-collar workers who were ill-paid and often
only one generation removed from unskilled labor themselves. The
vast majority of marriages were between unskilled workers or between unskilled workers and women who did not work outside

their parents' home.[132] The Viennese evidence supports Tilly and Scott's speculation that class endogamy existed far into the twentieth century.[133]

Both sexual practices and marriage patterns indicate that working-class attitudes and behavior were heavily influenced by traditional rural and urban values. The city environment tended to reduce rather than increase sexual promiscuity. Although conditions among the lowest stratum of the working class were damaging, especially from a middle-class perspective, their attitudes and practices represent only one segment of a socially and economically complex working class. The gradual decrease in illegitimacy beginning in the mid-nineteenth century, combined with the extended period between puberty and marriage age in the early twentieth century (which should have produced increased illegitimacy if the theory about working-class licentiousness were true), indicates sexual restraint rather than license.[134] The Viennese experience suggests that the working class is not a monolithic group, and the imposition of a cultural-depravity theory on the whole working class will conceal the real diversity and richness of working-class culture.

7

Conclusion

I will suggest in conclusion that we can doubt whether a simple modernization model fits even twentieth-century working-class culture, for the legacy of traditionalism from the nineteenth century retains considerable hold.[1]
—Peter Stearns, "The Effort at Continuity in Working-Class Culture"

The youth from worker families became so multiform during the twenties . . . that the concept Arbeiter *and* proletariat *became at this point sociologically meaningless.[2]*
—Heinz Kluth, "Arbeiterjugend—Begriff und Wirklichkeit"

Early twentieth-century Europe was caught up in a battle between the forces of modernization and traditionalism. While the factory system, major demographic changes, and popular forms of entertainment made inroads into the attitudes and behavior of lower-class youth, traditional (peasant and artisanal) attitudes and practices continued to influence the entire laboring population. Traditionalism postponed a full adolescent experience for most lower-stratum youth and perpetuated the authoritarian family, the need to sacrifice independence for the good of the family, the inequality of the sexes, the concrete and the practical, the miminizing of schooling, and a continuing religious observance despite attacks on religion among anticlerical working-class groups.

Although adolescence came to the upper classes in the late nineteenth century, traditionalism slowed its full penetration into the working class. If adolescence is defined as a preparatory phase in the life-cycle when youth are separated from the adult world of work and responsibility, then only a few males from the upper stratum of manual laborers experienced it in the period before World War I. Adolescence for most working-class girls was spent under the close supervision of mothers. Since most girls began work immediately after leaving the upper primary school and had taken on adult roles even earlier in their families, only a few girls in skilled working-class homes had some possibility of extending that freedom from adult concerns normally associated with the adolescent stage.[3] Only the massive demographic/economic changes of the war and inter-war period, combined with bourgeois attempts to isolate youth in age-specific institutions, gave the forces of modernization the upper hand. In the interwar period working-class youth were spending much more time under the tutelage of adults in the schools and youth organizations. Those primarily male youths who rejected the adolescent model of extended dependency and submissiveness adopted by bourgeois and socialist leaders formed an antagonistic subculture tied to the street culture of their childhood.

Family size and function changed dramatically between 1890 and 1938. The decline in the average number of children from more than five to about one and the sharp reduction in subletting brought an end to the half-open family and a different relationship between parents and children. By the interwar period, almost all children were staying in school until age 14 and few were working before or after school, as was common in the prewar period. With only one or two children to care for, parents did not have to force youth out of the home at about age 14, as was still common in the prewar period. While it cannot be established definitively, closer, more emotional relationships between children and parents became a reality with the smaller families. Although few of those I interviewed spoke harshly of their parents, some recalled the lack of parental attention they experienced while growing up between 1900 and 1920. The stereotype of an unfeeling, authoritarian, hard-drinking father ruling with an iron fist might have still occurred among a few lower-stratum families, but it was not the rule among the majority of working-class families.

While there was a general trend between 1890 and 1938 to extend more equal treatment to young women, they continued to play a secondary role to young men. It was not unusual even in the interwar period to hear remarks similar to those reported in *Die Sozialistische Erziehung:* when asked about his sister's death, a young boy responded, "Oh, it doesn't matter. Girls are good-for-nothing."[4] While parents were not so insensitive as this young boy, their traditional attitudes constrained the working-class girl much more than her male counterpart. Too much independence on the part of girls was met with opposition from parents who considered them to be "getting above themselves" (*über den Kopf gewachsen sind*).[5] The attitude toward girls was similar to that in England, where, as Dyhouse found, "The growing girl tended to be seen as a problem when and where she showed signs of cherishing anything resembling autonomy."[6] Berlanstein argued that Parisian mothers "used their emotional ascendency over children to socialize them to dependence and submissiveness."[7] There were differences, depending upon the family's rough or respectable attitudes. Although girls from "respectable" working-class homes might have better job and training opportunities, they were normally much more restricted during their leisure time than girls from "rough" homes.

While girls tended increasingly to perform tasks in industry and service similar to those of boys, although at lower pay, traditional attitudes continued to limit their occupational training primarily to female-dominated occupations such as textiles. As discussed in chapters 4 and 5, parents sent their sons to trade school or found them an apprenticeship, while they sent their daughters out to work in factory or service jobs or kept them at home to aid with family artisanal tasks. If asked to defend this action, most would have responded that there were insufficient funds to support all the children in trade school or apprenticeship and it was absolutely essential for males to have a trade. Girls, on the other hand, could be supported by their husbands or the sewing skills that almost all females learned. The view that working-class girls could be supported by their husbands proved to be a particularly destructive attitude, since many women did not marry in the interwar period due to the shortage of males after World War I.

Traditionally inclined parents would have defended their position by responding that girls needed to have some practical occupation that would give them security in case they did not marry or their husbands were incapacitated or unemployed. Such parents must have felt vindicated when during the depression in the interwar period a few families were supported solely by the wife's income from sewing. Again and again, fathers forced their daughters to learn a traditional skill such as sewing or dressmaking so they would have something to fall back on in case they failed. Parents' traditional attitudes limited their daughters' opportunities at the same time that their occupational possibilities were expanding in the industrial and service areas.

Most working-class girls would have agreed with their parents. As a young girl responded to Rada, "Needlework . . . that is a peaceful and sensible work for girls."[8] In responding to my question concerning occupational goals, a bricklayer's daughter described this world of reduced possibilities when she responded, "Yes, we all really knew what we wanted to do. . . . Everyone learned a skill, a practical skill."[9] Of the girls studied by Leichter in the late twenties, 44 percent selected their occupations because they provided a good preparation for marriage.[10] Many of the women I interviewed who were born between 1890 and 1914 had accepted the traditional peasant and artisanal practice that girls should subordinate their occupational goals to those of their brothers. Those girls who insisted on occupational goals in conflict with family wishes were considered to be "aggressive, unfeminine women."[11] Only in the twenties, with the smaller working-class families, did girls have an enhanced chance to gain occupational training through trade schools and apprenticeships. But the apprentices were by this time often used merely as casual laborers and were not taught the skills of a trade, and the few trade school openings were still being filled by males.

This world of the concrete and the practical with its limited possibilities shaped many of the working-class attitudes toward society and its institutions. Schooling, for example, played a much different role in working-class culture than it did in bourgeois culture. As discussed in chapter 4, some working-class youth tended to view the schools almost as alien institutions. They seemed to working-class youth and parents to have little practical value for the real world of work. This attitude partially explains parental hostility to their daughters' "excessive" reading, which would, in their opinion, not prepare them for an occupation. Much more important was occupational training or early work that would relieve family finances. As a result, before World War I, working-class children stayed in school only as long as required by law. Schooling for all except the children in the upper reaches of the working class meant the *Volksschule* (elementary school) and the *Bürgerschule* (upper-elementary school).[12] As late as 1928, a writer in the socialist magazine *Die sozialistische Erziehung* argued that proletarian children were not inferior to bourgeois children and were even superior in practical matters and in knowledge of every-day affairs and that schools should stress these latter aspects of education rather than strictly academic subjects.[13]

The curriculum changes that the Vienna city government pushed through in the 1920s did include some training in skills for all students. Since children of unskilled and casual laborers did not see the value of schooling, and some experienced the schools primarily as disciplinary institutions, they were often involved in a vicious cycle of disobedience to school authorities, with the resultant punishment. A survey of punishment in schools carried out in 1922 showed that proletarian boys were spanked more frequently than bourgeois boys. It was in effect a clash between the dominant culture—including some Social Democratic leaders who had accepted its cultural attitudes—which wished to remake working-class children in its own image, and a portion of the laboring population, which refused to accept its rules and cultural values. But contrary to Humphries's view that most working-class boys were involved in such opposition, many working-class children meekly accepted penalties handed down by their superiors. The survey revealed that a higher percentage of working-class boys than bourgeois children agreed that school spankings were necessary.[14] Such a response resulted from the deferential attitude learned by youth in many working-class homes.[15]

By the interwar period, socialist control over Vienna's educational system and a changing working-class attitude toward the schools reduced the conflict between the schools and working-class children. With fewer children, a greater acceptance of the importance of education, and city pressure on parents to keep their children in school because of the shortage of jobs, more working-class children stayed in school longer. But few working-class children attended the academic secondary schools even in the interwar period, since an advanced academic environment was still alien to the vast majority of the working class, few secondary schools existed in the working-class districts, and family priorities were directed more toward short-term objectives, such as immediate financial contributions to the family, rather than long-term objectives or a petit-bourgeois striving for status. Most working-class parents could simply not afford to put their children through eight years of secondary school.

The proletarian rejection of the secondary schools is also tied to a fear of rapid change and too much youth independence from the family. Change meant venturing into unknown and possibly dangerous areas and pursuits. Since most parents did not find the bourgeois obsession with getting ahead so compelling, they did not think it necessary to push their children into advanced schooling. Most working-class parents thought such schooling would only alienate their children from them, as well as bring other undesirable changes into their lives. The son of a brickworker told me that his parents most feared change, "the ultramodern things or political things."[16] With their lives already full with long hours of work and everyday duties, few working-class families had time for political or other involvements that would complicate their lives. As a small-scale milliner told me, "Everyday affairs ate us up."[17] The constant socialist lament that workers did not become politically involved was often a result of this lack of free time.

Another traditional practice among women workers and youth that had a declining but still-important influence was religion. The stereotype of a nonpracticing, unbelieving, anticlerical proletariat is an obfuscation. Even workers involved in the Social Democratic party were normally anticlerical but not necessarily antireligious. Their wives and children might still attend religious services because it was traditional practice in their neighborhood or because religion provided an outlet for their troubles. However, it is difficult to find definitive evidence concerning religious views. Oral interviews are most unreliable when asking questions concerning beliefs in the past, since the respondents cannot recall precisely what they believed at that time, and they tend to read back into that period the beliefs that they held later. For example, those who became functionaries in the Social Democratic party almost always contend that they rejected religion very early.

A typical response to my questions concerning religious beliefs as a child came from the son of a blacksmith, who said, "I'll tell you something. I got a "5" [lowest score] in religion in the first *Volksschule* class. My mother was very upset about it, but my father said, 'that doesn't make any difference, the main thing is that he is doing well in the other subjects.' "[18] Yet, the worker autobiographies from the turn of the century indicate that most working-class women continued to practice religion or at least require that their children attend services and even religious instruction.[19] A socialist teacher and Free Thinker (*Freidenker*) complained that thousands of white-clad girls in the "most proletarian of all proletarian districts, Favoriten," marched in the Corpus Christi processions in 1926.[20] Wilhelm Reich wrote, "There are thousands of proletarian families that are religious and the more we penetrate the petit-bourgeois proletariat the deeper resides religion."[21] A 1924 survey by Otto Kanitz concerning the religious beliefs of 39 children of workers politically active in the Social Democratic party revealed that about one-half (19) believed in God.[22] Many of those I interviewed explained that they had attended church services as a child. As one woman told me, "We were not very religious, but we kids had to go to church and our parents told us it would not harm us and it didn't."[23] Most of the working-class homes continued to have religious pictures decorating their walls. Normally a picture of Mary hung over the bed of their parents. With the exception of those who adopted a strong animosity to religion and left the church at their parents' urging during their youth, most of the remainder continued to attend church services because of their continuing belief in God, their parents' belief that religious teachings "wouldn't hurt" their children, or merely out of habit but without any strong religious convictions.

While traditionalism brought a similarity to working-class attitudes and practices, Gillis's commentary that "we should not be surprised to find a variety of youth cultures within a particular locality or even within a particular class" has been echoed by those studying Austrian working-class and youth culture.[24] The diversity has led me as well as others to reject the lumping of all proletarian children into one homogenous mass. As one such study found, "What proletarian childhood at the turn of the century meant is so different that one must reject painting a similar black (*grau in grau*) undifferentiated picture of the situation."[25] Another rejects Otto Rühle's blanket condemnation of the proletarian family as *grau in grau* and an unfavorable agency of socialization.[26] Kluth argued that the youth experience became so varied in the twenties that even the terms "worker" and "proletariat" became meaningless.[27] So, despite the strong uniformities, working-class youths' lives and attitudes could differ depending upon family attitudes, social stratum, gender, and nearness to the Social Democratic party.

Those in the upper stratum who were involved in the Social Democratic subculture and concerned about respectable behavior were a type of labor aristocracy. The higher income and smaller families in this stratum gave youth many advantages: a bed of their own, better clothing and food, greater opportunities to study or obtain occupational training, and more leisure. This upper group was separated from most workers in terms of expectations. Artisans tended to send their children to secondary school no matter how great the sacrifice, while the skilled workers in this upper stratum were, with a few exceptions, satisfied with occupational training. In other words, skilled workers were interested in finding stable jobs for their children but not in obtaining some exalted social status for them. But youth were much more closely supervised in their leisure activities than those in the lowest stratum. Youth in the lowest stratum were constrained by their family's low income, large numbers, crowded housing, and traditional views on education and training. Girls in this stratum had few opportunities because of the sacrifices they had to make for the family. Their brothers might be able to obtain an apprenticeship, but they normally began work early as day laborers. One of the few advantages enjoyed by youth in the lowest stratum was more freedom in their leisure time. Their parents' absence from the home gave them greater freedom to play in the streets and gain some release from adult domination at home and in school.

While those in the middle stratum encountered many of the problems of those in the lowest stratum, their steadier employment and greater inclination to adopt respectable behavior patterns brought about greater stability for their children. Although this stratum was often exposed to instability due to unemployment or illness, the families normally had support from their neighborhood and relatives to get them through the hard times. Because of these families' respectable behavior, only the boys had a great deal of freedom to play in the streets. By the interwar period, boys from the middle stratum could gain occupational training or enter a trade school, but at most, girls could expect training in the textile industry or an ill-paying job as a service worker. While there could be sizable differences among youth in these three strata, the death of the father or long-term unemployment could bring severe instability to even the families of skilled workers. But families in the upper two strata had greater chances to survive because of their more fixed domicile and therefore more extensive support groups.

The experience of youth, then, could be quite different depending on the group to which one belonged. Yet there were similarities that bound all working-class groups together. Basic to all attitudes and activities were traditionalism and one's class/strata position. The further down the social ladder one was located, the more difficult it was to obtain life's necessities or to change one's economic or social situation. At the very top of working-class society, it was possible by the interwar period to gain sufficient training or education to change one's status, but the poor economic and social conditions of the interwar period and the working-class tendency to sacrifice for the good of the entire family led few to take the necessary steps. As late as the interwar period, only a few children from the upper reaches of the working class attended a secondary school or sought work or a spouse outside the area of their birth. Most working-class youth were locked into certain occupations because of their parents' traditional attitudes and their own lack of training and resources. If they sought a change in their situation, it was normally only a limited one that would permit them to escape some of the hardships experienced by their parents.

Despite these limited vistas and opportunities, most working-class youth did not lead a life of despair and want. The smaller families, more settled existence, and improving economic conditions that characterized the two upper strata of the Viennese working class by the last decade before World War I permitted families to direct more attention to each child. While working-class families may not have achieved that familialization model of most bourgeois families, they were not as destructive of youth as they have often been depicted. The ability of working-class families to cope with scarcity is still one of the least-known aspects of working-class life. If this work has contributed something to our understanding of the day-to-day existence of working-class families and youth and to the continuity of working-class existence, it will have achieved its purpose.

Appendix: Labor Strata

Gender	Interview	Father's Occupation	Number of Siblings	Education	Occupation	Number of Children
				UPPER		
M	6	Shoemaker	1	Volks/Bürgerschule, Apprentice	Shoemaker	4
F	7	Tailor	9	Volks/Bürgerschule	Maid	4
M	8	Upholsterer	8	Volks/Bürgerschule, Vocational School	Salesman	1
F	9	Locksmith	0	Volks/Bürgerschule	Unskilled	1
M	10	Tram Conductor	1	Volks/Bürgerschule, Vocational School	Salaried Employee	2
F	12	Tram Employee	1	Volks/Bürgerschule, Vocational School	Housewife	3
M	15	Baker	3	Volks/Bürgerschule, Vocational School	Clerk	0
F	16	Bakery Worker	2	Volks/Bürgerschule, Vocational School	Dressmaker	2
M	17	Galvanizer	5	Volks/Bürgerschule, Vocational School	Sign Painter	0
F	20	Postman	5	Volks/Bürgerschule	Maid	1
F	23	Shoemaker	4	Volks/Bürgerschule, Vocational School	Unskilled	0
F	28	Transport Employee	2	Volks/Bürgerschule, Vocational School	Hat Maker	3
F	29	Baker	1	Volks/Bürgerschule, Pedagogic Institute	Teacher	0
F	30	Printer	2	Volks/Bürgerschule	Seamstress	0
F	31	Foreman	1	Volks/Bürgerschule, Vocational School	Housewife	0

Appendix (continued)

Gender	Interview	Father's Occupation	Number of Siblings	Education	Occupation	Number of Children
F	32	Shoemaker	3	Volks/Bürgerschule	Dressmaker	1
F	35	Skilled Worker	1	Volks/Bürgerschule, Vocational School	Clerk	0
F	36	Tobacco Shop	2	Volks/Hauptschule	Father's Shop	3
M	39	Carpenter	5	Volks/Realschule	Carpenter	2
M	41	Dyer	4	Volks/Bürgerschule, Vocational School	Dyer	0
F	42	Baker	2	Volks/Bürgerschule	Unskilled	Single
M	46	Tram Foreman	1	Volks/Bürgerschule, Vocational School	Fireman	0
F	50	Shoemaker	6	Volks/Bürgerschule	Hotel Director	0
M	51	Railroad Inspector	1	Volks/Bürgerschule, Vocational School	Clerk	1
F	52	Galvanizer	1	Volks/Bürgerschule, Vocational School	Clerk	1
M	53	Woodworker	3	Volks/Bürgerschule, Vocational School	Taxi Driver	0
F	55	Transportation Clerk	2	Volks/Bürgerschule, Vocational School	Hat Shop	0
F	57	Warehouse Foreman	3	Volks/Bürgerschule, Vocational School	Bank Clerk	0
F	60	Government Clerk	2	Volks/Bürgerschule	Unskilled	Single
F	66	Tailor	5	Volks/Bürgerschule, Conservatory	Seamstress	1
F	67	Bookkeeper	7	Volks/Bürgerschule	Housewife	1

1	F	Typesetter	2	Volks/Bürgerschule	Clerk	2
4	M	Machine Fitter	5	Volks/Bürgerschule, Vocational School	Machine Fitter	1
11	F	Railroad Worker	1	Volks/Mittelschule	Sales Clerk	2
13	M	Mason	2	Volks/Bürgerschule, Vocational School	Machine Fitter	0
14	M	Blacksmith	1	Volks/Bürgerschule	Fitter	1
19	F	Wood Dealer	8	Volks/Bürgerschule	Housewife	1
21	M	Farmer	9	Volksschule	Butcher	1
22	F	Lathe Operator	2	Volks/Bürgerschule	Dressmaker	0
24	M	Painter	5	Volks/Hauptschule	Painter	4
26	F	Blacksmith	4	Volks/Bürgerschule	Seamstress	0
33	M	Tailor	2	Volks/Bürgerschule, Vocational School	Engraver	0
40	M	Mason	4	Volks/Bürgerschule	Clerk	0
44	M	Unskilled	2	Volks/Bürgerschule	Engraver	0
45	F	Locksmith	1	Volks/Bürgerschule	Seamstress	0
47	F	Lithographer	6	Volks/Bürgerschule, Vocational School	Shop Foreman	0
48	F	Shoemaker	6	Volks/Bürgerschule, Vocational School	Clerk	1
49	F	Typesetter	6	Volksschule	Nurse	1
54	F	Typesetter	4	Volks/Bürgerschule	Seamstress	2
59	M	Unskilled	1	Volks/Bürgerschule, Apprentice	City Administrator	1
65	M	Bag Maker	2	Volks/Bürgerschule, Vocational School	Clerk	0
69	F	Carpenter	1	Volks/Bürgerschule, Vocational School	Clerk	Single

Appendix (*continued*)

Gender	Interview	Father's Occupation	Number of Siblings	Education	Occupation	Number of Children
				LOWER		
F	2	Unskilled	5	Volks/Bürgerschule	Housewife	1
F	3	Farmer	10	Volksschule	Unskilled	1
F	5	Unskilled	5	Volksschule	Unskilled	Single
F	25	Unskilled	2	Volks/Bürgerschule, Vocational School	Typesetter	0
F	27	Cook (Mother)	1	Volks/Bürgerschule	Casual Labor	0
M	34	Unskilled	1	Volks/Bürgerschule, Apprentice	Unemployed	—
F	37	Delivery Man	4	Volks/Bürgerschule	Maid	0
M	38	Mason	6	Volksschule	Unskilled	0
M	43	Unskilled	2	Volks/Bürgerschule, Vocational School	Tailor	0
F	56	Mason	10	Volks/Bürgerschule	Unskilled	0
F	58	Factory Carpenter	10	Volks/Bürgerschule, Vocational School	Seamstress	1
F	61	Carpenter	8	Volks/Bürgerschule	Unskilled	3
F	62	Shoemaker	3	Volks/Bürgerschule	Unskilled	0
F	63	Weaver	3	Volks/Bürgerschule	Unskilled	0
F	64	Carpenter	6	Volks/Bürgerschule	Restaurant Worker	2
M	68	Bakery Helper	2	Volks/Bürgerschule	Unskilled	3
F	70	Mason	6	Volks/Bürgerschule	Unskilled	0

NOTES

INTRODUCTION

1. Otto Rühle, *Das proletarische Kind* (Munich, 1922) and *Die Seele des proletarischen Kindes* (Dresden, 1925). Otto Felix Kanitz, *Das proletarische Kind in der bürgerlichen Gesellschaft* (Jena, 1925). For a recent example of a reductionist study of Vienna in the interwar period, see Alfred Frei, *Rotes Wien: Austromarxismus und Arbeiterkultur* (Berlin, 1984). An exception would be the subtle Marxian analyses of individuals such as Eric Hobsbawm.

2. For an elaboration of this theory, see C. C. Harris, *The Family and Industrial Society* (London, 1983), chapter 4.

3. G. S. Hall, *Adolescence: Its Psychology and Its Relations to Physiology, Anthropology, Sociology, Sex Crime, Religion and Education*, 2 vols. (New York, 1904). Gareth Stedman Jones, *Outcast London* (London, 1970).

4. John Clarke, Chas Critcher, and Richard Johnson, *Working-Class Culture: Studies in History and Theory* (New York, 1979).

5. Stephen Humphries, *Hooligans or Rebels? An Oral History of Working-Class Childhood and Youth 1889–1939* (Oxford, 1981). Elizabeth Roberts, *A Woman's Place: An Oral History of Working-Class Women 1890–1914* (Oxford, 1984).

6. John Gillis, *Youth and History: Tradition and Change in European Age Relations, 1770–Present* (New York, 1981), 218.

7. Philippe Aries, *Centuries of Childhood: A Social History of Family Life* (New York, 1962).

8. Dieter Langewiesche's study of working-class reading habits, while an important addition to our knowledge of the working class, is still primarily history from the perspective of the Social Democratic party. Dieter

Langewiesche, *Zur Freizeit des Arbeiters: Bildungsbestrebungen und Freizeit-gestaltung österreichischer Arbeiter im Kaiserreich und in der Ersten Republik* (Stuttgart, 1979).

9. Gillis, Preface, x–xi.

10. Among Austrian examples, I would include the following: Michael John, *Hausherrenmacht und Mieterelend. Wohnverhältnisse und Wohner-fahrung der Unterschichten in Wien 1890–1923* (Vienna, 1982), and *Wohn-verhältnisse sozialer Unterschichten im Wien Kaiser Franz Josephs* (Vienna, 1984); Hubert Ch. Ehalt, *Geschichte von Unten*, (Vienna, 1984); and the works cited in note 13.

11. Rühle, Kanitz. Hildegard Hetzer, *Kindheit und Armut: Psycholo-gische Methoden in Armuts-Forschung und Armutsbekämfung* (Leipzig, 1929) and *Zur Psychologie des Wohnens: Beiträge zur städtischen Wohn- und Siedelwirtschaft* (Munich, 1930). Ernst Hanisch's perceptive article, "Arbeit-erkindheit in Österreich vor dem Ersten Weltkrieg," in *Internationales Ar-chiv für Sozialgeschichte der deutschen Literatur*, vol. 7 (1982), that the concept of a "bleak childhood" (*schwarzen Kindheit*) had become a cliché among those writing about laboring families, p. 115. Hanisch's article was the first Austrian study that concentrated on the real everday experiences of workers' children.

12. Hetzer; Margarete Rada, *Das reifende Proletariermädchen* (Vienna, 1931); Charlotte Bühler, *Kindheit und Jugend: Genese des Bewusstseins* (Leipzig, 1928) and *Das Seelenleben des Judgenlichen* (Jena, 1927).

13. Michael Mitterauer, *Geschichte der Jugend* (Frankfurt am Main: 1986).

14. Wolfgang Neugebauer, *Bauvolk der kommenden Welt: Geschichte der sozialistischen Jugendbewegung in Österreich* (Vienna, 1975).

15. Although Hanisch's article, cited in note 11, cannot qualify as a full-scale study, it did provide me with many insights and is an important early attempt to get at the life of working-class children.

16. My interviews are in both tape and transcribed form and will be lodged in the University of Notre Dame Archives, 607 Hesburgh Library.

17. For fuller discussions of oral-history evidence, see Reinhard Sieder, "Geschichten erzählen und Wissenschaft treiben," in Gerhard Botz and Josef Weidenholzer, *Mündliche Geschichte und Arbeiterbewegung* (Vienna-Cologne: Böhlau, 1984). Gerhard Botz, "Oral History—Wert, Probleme, Möglichkeiten der Mündliche Geschichte," in Gerhard Botz and Josef Weidenholzer, eds., *Mündliche Geschichte und Arbeiterbewegung* (Vienna-Cologne, 1984), 32.

18. Ehmer, "The artisan family . . . ," passim.

19. For excellent insights on housing see Feldbauer's *Stadtwachstum und Wohnungsnot: Determinanten unzureichender Wohnungsversorgung in Wien, 1848 bis 1914* (Vienna, 1977).

20. Monika Glettler, *Die Wiener Tschechen um 1900* (Vienna, 1972), 76. Karl Brousek, *Wien und seine Tschechen* (Vienna, 1980), 20. Brousek argues that one-quarter of Vienna's population in 1914 had its origins in the Czech lands, but only one-tenth of the population was recognized as Czech or Slovak in the census returns, 25.

21. Lutz Roth, *Die Erfindung des Jugendlichen* (Munich, 1983), 12.

22. Anson Rabinbach, "Politics and Pedagogy: The Austrian Social Democratic Youth Movement 1931–32," in *Journal of Contemporary History* 13 (1978).

CHAPTER 1

1. Interview 25. Taped and transcribed interviews are on file in the University of Notre Dame Archives, 607 Hesburgh Library.
2. Interview 70.
3. Josef Ehmer, *Familienstruktur und Arbeitsorganisation im frühindustriellen Wien* (Munich, 1980).
4. David F. Good, *The Economic Rise of the Habsburg Empire, 1750–1914* (Berkeley, Calif., 1984), 239.
5. Gerhard Meissl, "Im Spannungsfeld von Kundenhandwerk, Verlagswesen und Fabrik," in Renate Banik-Schweitzer and Gerhard Meissl, *Industriestadt Wien: Die Durchsetzung der industriellen Marktproduktion in der Habsburgerresidenz* (Vienna, 1983), 186.
6. Peter Feldbauer, *Stadtwachstum und Wohnungsnot* (Vienna, 1976), 35.
7. Meissl, 182–84.
8. Ibid., 180.
9. Feldbauer, 35.
10. Banik-Schweitzer, 33.
11. Meissl, 180, table 13.
12. Josef Ehmer, "Wiener Arbeitswelten um 1900," in Hubert Ch. Ehalt, Gernot Heiss, and Hannes Stekl, eds., *Glücklich ist, Wer Vergisst . . . ?: Das andere Wein um 1900* (Vienna, 1986), 195.
13. Renate Schweitzer, "Die Entwicklung Favoritens zum Arbeiterbezirk," in *Wiener Geschichtsblätter* 29, 4 (1974), 262.
14. *Statistisches Jahrbuch der Stadt Wien für das Jahr 1901*, Vienna, 1903, 67. Hereafter cited as *SJSW*.
15. Ehmer, *Familienstruktur*, 61, 81–82.
16. *SJSW*, 1910, 45.
17. Ibid.
18. Feldbauer, 39.
19. Interviews 4–8, 10, 16, and 20 in Appendix.
20. *SJSW*, 1901, 44.
21. Monika Glettler, *Die Wiener Tschechen um 1900* (Vienna, 1972), 32. Few now accept the Austrian Census figures from 1910 that show only 98,000 Slavic-speaking inhabitants. Estimates of the Slavic-speaking population range from 400,000 to 600,000. Glettler, 29.
22. Glettler, 61.
23. Parish records in the personal possession of the author. The two major Roman Catholic parishes in Favoriten before World War I were St. Johann and St. Anton. I surveyed all 212 grooms who were residents of Favoriten and married in St. Johann parish in 1938 and an equal number for 1910.
24. *Volkszählung*, 1934, 14–15.

25. Feldbauer, 40.

26. Ibid., table 41.

27. *Die Frau*, March 1932; *Die Wohnung*, March 1938, 2.

28. *SJSW*, 1910, 45, 58–59.

29. See Appendix.

30. Käthe Leichter, *So Leben Wir* (Vienna, 1931), 91.

31. Hofstetter, 3.

32. Ehmer, 55.

33. Philippovich.

34. *SJSW*, 1910, 59, 108–9.

35. Felix Kanitz, "Mieterschutz und Erziehung," in *Die sozialistische Erziehung*, September 1928.

36. *Die Wirksamkeit des Stadtschulrates fuer Wien, 1925–26*, 52.

37. Benedikt Kautsky, *Die Wirtschaftlichen und sozialen Folgen des Wohnungsrechtes in Österreich in Schriften des Vereins für Sozial Politik*, 177, part 3 (Vienna, 1930).

38. *Die Wohnung*, July 1930, 31.

39. Rainer Bauböck, *Die Wohnungsverhältnisse im Sozialdemokratischen Wien, 1919–1934* (Salzburg, 1979), 20.

40. Wilhelm Kosian, "Das Realeinkommen verschiedener Berufsgruppen des Arbeiterstandes u. das der öffentliche Beamten in Österreich in der Epoche 1910–1949" (Dissertation: University of Vienna, 1978), 32–39.

41. For a thorough treatment of the Christian Social movement, see John Boyer, *Political Radicalism in Late Imperial Vienna: Origins of the Christian Social Movement, 1848–1897* (Chicago, 1981).

42. Richard Evans, ed., *The German Working Class 1888–1933: The Politics of Everyday Life* (London, 1982), 30. Vernon L. Lidtke, *The Alternative Culture: Socialist Labor in Imperial Germany* (New York, 1985), 20.

43. Dieter Langewiesche, "Arbeiterkultur in Österreich: Aspekte, Tendenzen und Thesen," in Gerhard Ritter, ed., *Arbeiterkultur* (Königstein, 1979), 53.

44. Lidtke, 19.

45. Dieter Langewiesche, *Zur Freiheit des Arbeiters: Bildungsbestrebungen und Freiheitgestaltung österreichischer Arbeiter im Kaiserreich und in der Ersten Republik* (Stuttgart, 1979), 43.

46. Interview 70. Alexander Plato found that children of Communist Party members in the Ruhr during the Weimar period stayed in the church and took religious instruction. Alexander Plato, " 'Ich bin mit allen gut ausgekommen' oder war die Ruhrarbeiterschaft vor 1933 in politische Lager zerspalten?" in Lutz Niethammer, ed., *Faschismus Erfahrungen im Ruhrgebeit: Lebensgeschichte und Sozialkultur im Ruhrgebiet 1930 bis 1960*, vol. 1 (Berlin-Bonn, 1983), 52.

47. E. P. Thompson, *The Making of the English Working Class* (New York, 1966), 9.

48. *Arbeiterzeitung*, 15 November 1913, 9. Although no official designation of Kreta existed, local inhabitants thought of this area as distinct from the rest of Favoriten. Newspapers, such as the socialist *Arbeiterzeitung*, also referred to this area as the Kreta. Today a Gasthaus named the

KretaStüberl operates in the heart of this area. Some I questioned thought the name came from the Kreta's relative isolation, like the island Crete, on the edge of the district. But it may be that the name refers to the Cherethites (Krethi), a tribe from Philistia, the foreign mercenaries of King David who constituted his bodyguard. Today the phrase "Krethi und Plethi" in German refers to riff-raff (*Gesinde*). The meaning apparently derives from the motley nature of David's mercenary followers. I wish to thank Dr. Albert Wimmer of the Department of Modern Languages at the University of Notre Dame for this insight.

49. Interviews 6, 8, and 10 contain the fullest references to the Kreta area.

50. Interview 45.

51. Interview 56.

52. *Arbeiterzeitung*, 14 July 1912, 10.

53. Monika Glettler, *Die Wiener Tschechen um 1900* (Vienna, 1972), 52.

54. Glettler, 227.

55. Interview 43.

56. *Das Kleine Blatt*, 8 May 1927, 6.

57. Glettler, 43.

58. Ibid., 57.

59. Interview 10.

60. Standish Meacham, *A Life Apart: The English Working Class, 1890–1914* (Cambridge, Mass., 1977), 27.

61. Interview 8.

62. Interview 4.

63. Interview 2.

64. Interview 61.

65. Interview 1.

66. Interview 53.

67. Interview 4.

68. Of course, the Austrian designation for floor level is different, since the ground floor in Austria would be called the *parterre* and the second floor would be designated as the first floor.

69. Michael John, *Wohnverhältnisse sozialer Unterschichten im Wien Kaiser Franz Josephs* (Vienna, 1984), 91. Margarete Rada did not consider the children of skilled workers to be a part of this upper level in a working-class district. She did not believe that the children of skilled workers differed in behavior from those of unskilled workers. She provided very little proof for this assertion, however. Margarete Rada, *Das reifende Proletariermädchen* (Vienna and Leipzig, 1931), 18. Albert Kaufmann places lower-level service workers and officials with skilled and unskilled workers in a lower stratum (*Unterschicht*). Albert Kaufmann, "Soziale Schichtung und Berufsstatistik," in *Soziologie Forschung in Österreich*, Leopold Rosenmayr and Sigurd Höllinger, eds. (Vienna, 1969), 324.

70. Interview 62.

71. Josef Ehmer, "Schuster zwischen Handwerk und Fabrik," in Helmut Konrad and Wolfgang Maderthaner, eds., *Neuere Studien zur Arbeitergeschichte*, vol. 1 (Vienna, 1984). Josef Ehmer, "The Artisan Family in

Nineteenth-Century Austria: Embourgeoisement of the Petite Bourgeoisie?" in Geoffrey Crossick and Heinz-Gerhard Haupt, eds., *Shopkeepers and
Master Artisans in Nineteenth-Century Europe* (London, 1984).

72. John, *Wohnverhältnisse*, 88.

73. Ibid., 33.

74. Reinhard Sieder, "Vata, derf i aufstehn?" Kindheitserfahrungen in
Wiener Arbeiterfamilien um 1900," in Hubert Ch. Ehalt, Gernot Heiss, and
Hannes Stekl, eds., *Glücklich ist, Wer Vergisst . . . ?* 45. Josef Ehmer's essay
on the artisan family cited in note 71 is a good introduction to artisanal
attitudes.

75. Ehmer, *Wiener Arbeitswelten*, 200.

76. Ibid.

77. John, *Wohnverhältnisse*, 82.

78. Sieder, "*Vata*," illustration following p. 48.

79. Ibid., 46.

80. Ibid.

81. See Appendix.

82. Eva Viethen, "Wiener Arbeiterinnen Leben zwischen Familie, Lohnarbeit und politischen Engagement," (Dissertation, University of Vienna,
1984), 178.

83. See Appendix.

84. Reinhard Sieder, "Housing Policy, Social Welfare, and Family Life
in 'Red Vienna,' 1919–1934," unpublished manuscript, 17.

85. Interview 49.

86. Interview 68.

87. Ibid.

88. Interview 45.

89. Interview 31, p. 15 of the interviews carried out by the Institute for
Economic and Social History at the University of Vienna. Primary inter-
viewers were Reinhard Sieder, Gottfried Pirhofer, and Michael John. Hereafter referred to as Institute Interviews.

90. Institute Interview 22, 31.

91. Interview 60.

92. Josef Ehmer, "Familie und Klasse: Zur Entstehung der Arbeiterfamilie in Wien," in Michael Mitterauer and Reinhard Sieder, eds., *Historische Familienforschung* (Frankfurt am Main, 1982).

93. Sieder, "*Vata*."

CHAPTER 2

1. Interview 31.

2. Interview 39.

3. Hildegard Hetzer, *Zur Psychologie des Wohnens: Beiträge zur städtischen Wohn- und Siedelwirtschaft* (Munich, 1930), 5.

4. Margarete Rada, *Das reifende Proletariermädchen* (Vienna, 1931), 9.

5. Dieter Langewiesche, "Politische Orientierung und soziales Verhalten: Familien und Wohnverhältnisse von Arbeitern in 'roten' Wien der
Ersten Republik," in Lutz Niethammer, ed., *Wohnen im Wandel* (Wupper-

tal, 1979). Peter Marcuse, "The Housing Policy of Social Democracy: Determinants and Consequences," in Anson Rabinbach, ed., *The Austrian Socialist Experiment: Social Democracy and Austromarxism, 1918–1934* (Boulder, 1985).

6. Renate Schweitzer, "Die Entwicklung Favoritens zum Arbeiterbezirk," in *Wiener Geschichtsblätter*, 29, 4 (1974), 259.

7. Peter Feldbauer, *Stadtswachstum und Wohnungsnot* (Vienna, 1976), 203. In 1917 about half of the apartments in the working-class districts of Favoriten, Ottakring, and Floridsdorf contained only one room and a kitchen: Favoriten, 21,898 of 43,673; Ottakring, 24,828 of 49,482; Floridsdorf, 11,407 of 22,834. Another one-sixth of the apartments in Favoriten and Ottakring and one-fifth of those in Floridsdorf were listed as one-room kitchen/cabinet dwellings: Favoriten, 7,224 of 43,673; Ottakring, 7,931 of 49,482; Floridsdorf, 4,647 of 22,834. The next most common category of apartments in Favoriten and Ottakring was the smallest size possible, a cabinet. The cabinet dwellings comprised 4,617 of the living units in Favoriten and 5,205 of those in Ottakring. In a more middle-class district, such as the third, about one-quarter of the apartments were one room and kitchen (10,787 of 42,232) and only 1,452 were cabinet apartments. *Die Ergebnisse der Wohnungszählung in Wien vom Jahre 1917* (Vienna, 1918), table 1.

8. Institute Interview 31, 37.

9. Feldbauer, 315–16.

10. Ibid., 205. Rainer Bauböck, "Zur sozialdemokratischen Wohnungspolitik 1919–1934: Mieterschutz, Wohnungsanforderung und kommunaler Wohnbau unter besonderer Berücksichtigung Wiens" (Dissertation: University of Vienna, 1976), 5.

11. Michael John, *Wohnverhältnisse sozialer Unterschichten im Wien Kaiser Franz Josephs* (Vienna, 1984), 241–42.

12. See Appendix. The father's occupation was the major criteria used in sorting out the interviews. Parents in the upper stratum were either small masters or lower-level city/government employees. Parents in the lowest stratum were casual laborers with large families, except in cases where the father had died or abandoned the family.

13. Feldbauer, 117.

14. *Wirtschaftsrechnungen und Lebensverhältnisse von Wiener Arbeiterfamilien in den Jahren 1912 bis 1914: Erhebung des K. K. Arbeitsstatistischen Amtes im Handelsministerium* (Vienna, 1916), 62.

15. Charles Gulich, *Von Habsburg zu Hitler*, vol. 2 (California, 1948), 78.

16. Langewiesche, 173.

17. Anton Schubert, *Ziffern zur Frage des niederösterreichischen Tscheneinschlages* (Vienna, 1909), 17.

18. Interview 65.

19. Josef Mooser, *Arbeiterleben in Deutschland 1900–1970* (Frankfurt am Main, 1984), 143.

20. Feldbauer, 205.

21. Interview 58.

22. Interview 49.

23. Interview 61.

24. Feldbauer, appendix, 323.
25. Interview 54.
26. Interview 59.
27. Interview 40.
28. Interview 49.
29. Eva Viethen, "Wiener Arbeiterinnen Leben zwischen Familie, Lohnarbeit und politischen Engagement" (Dissertation: University of Vienna, 1984), 187.
30. John, 62.
31. Viethen, 178–91.
32. Schweitzer, 263.
33. Michael John, *Hausherrenmacht und Mieterelend, Wohnverhältnisse und Wohnerfahrung der Unterschichten in Wien, 1890–1923* (Vienna, 1982), 3.
34. Bauböck, 109.
35. John, *Wohnverhältnisse*, 26.
36. For a fuller discussion, see the articles by Langewiesche and Marcuse cited in note 5.
37. Marcuse, 215. Bauböck, 109. Bauböck estimates the change from 13.7 percent in 1912 to 2.65 percent in 1925.
38. *Ergebnisse der Wohnungs- und Geschäftsaufnahme*, 1934, 18.
39. *Die Unzufriedene*, 15 December 1928.
40. *SJSW*, New Series 3, 1930–35, 7.
41. See Appendix.
42. *Volkszählung*, 1934, 159.
43. Reinhard Sieder, *Housing Policy, Social Welfare, and Family Life in 'Red Vienna', 1919–1934,"* unpublished manuscript, 18.
44. See Wegs and Viethen interviews. The Viethen interviews can be found at the Institute for Folklore in Vienna.
45. Josef Ehmer, *Familienstruktur und Arbeitsorganization im frühindustriellen Wien* (Munich, 1980), 457.
46. James H. Jackson, "Overcrowding and Family Life: Working-Class Crisis in Late Nineteenth-Century Duisburg," in Richard J. Evans and W. R. Lee, eds., *The German Family* (Totowa, N.J., 1981), 217.
47. Standish Meacham, *A Life Apart*, 37.
48. Langewiesche, 172.
49. Roman Sandgruber, "Gesindestuben, Kleinhäuser und Arbeiterkasernen," in Lutz Niethammer, *Wohnen im Wandel* (Wuppertal, 1979), 107.
50. Interview 69.
51. Interview 36.
52. Interview 38.
53. Interview 17.
54. Interview 4.
55. Interview 67.
56. Interview 28.
57. Interview 38.
58. Interview 53.
59. Interview 36.
60. Michael John, *Wohnverhältnisse*, 199.

61. Interview 31.

62. Interview 48.

63. Hildegard Hetzer, *Kindheit und Armut* (Leipzig, 1929), 41.

64. Claude S. Fischer et al., *Networks and Places: Social Relations in the Urban Setting* (New York, 1977), 201.

65. Interview 26.

66. Interview 58.

67. Interview 15.

68. Interview 17.

69. John, *Hausherrenmacht*, 118.

70. Interview 4.

71. Institute Interview 25, second conversation, 22.

72. Interview 45.

73. Interviews 43, 47, and 49.

74. John, *Wohnverhältnisse*, 199.

75. Interview 35.

76. John Gillis, *For Better, For Worse: British Marriages, 1600 to the Present* (New York, 1985), 352.

77. Viethen, 63.

78. Robert Wegs, "Working-Class Respectability: The Viennese Experience," *Journal of Social History* 15 (Summer 1982).

79. See interviews in Notre Dame Archives.

80. Louise Tilly and Joan Scott, 193.

81. Interview 26.

82. Interview 36.

83. Ibid.

84. Interview 47.

85. Carl Ziak, *Von der Schmelz auf den Gallitzinberg* (Vienna, 1969), 15.

86. Ibid.

87. Rada, 11.

88. Richard Johnson, "Three Problematics: Elements of a Theory of Working-Class Culture," in John Clarke, Chas Critcher, and Richard Johnson, eds., *Working-Class Culture: Studies in History and Theory* (New York, 1979), 237.

89. Wegs, "Working-Class Respectability," 624.

90. Richard Hoggart, *The Uses of Literacy: Changing Patterns in English Mass Culture* (New Jersey, 1957), 76.

91. *Arbeiterzeitung*, 12 June 1932, 18.

92. *Die Frau*, 1 August 1929.

93. *Arbeiterzeitung*, 18 October 1931, 20.

94. Institute Interview, 10, 18.

95. Institute Interview, 24, 10.

CHAPTER 3

1. *Bildungsarbeit*, 9 October 1922, 74.

2. Interview 17.

3. John Clarke, Chas Critcher, and Richard Johnson, eds., *Working-Class Culture: Studies in History and Theory* (New York, 1979).

4. Philip Greven, *The Protestant Temperament: Patterns of Child-Rearing, Religious Experience, and the Self in Early America* (New York, 1977). Peter Stearns, "Emotionology: Clarifying the History of Emotions and Emotional Standards," *American Historical Review* 90, 4 (October 1985).

5. Josef Ehmer, "Frauenarbeit und Arbeiterfamilie in Wien: Vom Vormärz bis 1934," in *Geschichte und Gesellschaft*, 7, 3/4, 457.

6. Margarete Rada, *Das reifende Proletariermädchen* (Vienna-Leipzig, 1931). Hildegard Hetzer, *Kindheit und Armut* (Leipzig, 1929).

7. Josef Ehmer, 461. Ehmer cites Rada's dissertation, "Das reifende Proletariermädchen in seiner Beziehung zur Umwelt" (University of Vienna, 1931). This quote was not retained in her book, published by the Verlag für Jugend und Volk in 1931.

8. Hetzer, 38.

9. Interview 3, 20.

10. Interview 3.

11. Interview 20.

12. Eva Viethen, "Wiener Arbeiterinnen Leben zwischen Familie, Lohnarbeit und politischen Engagement" (Dissertation: University of Vienna, 1984), 49.

13. Viethen, 51.

14. Interview 48.

15. Interview 12.

16. Viethen, 274.

17. Robert Hofstätter, *Die arbeitende Frau: Ihre wirtschaftliche Lage, Gesundheit, Ehe und Mutterschaft* (Vienna, 1929), 288.

18. John Gillis, *Youth and History: Tradition and Change in European Age Relations, 1770–Present*, expanded student edition (New York, 1981), 187.

19. Interview 38.

20. Interview 31.

21. Hofstätter, 225. Hofstätter lists the number of abortion arrests in 1921, 1922, and 1923 as 288, 376, and 460, respectively.

22. Interview 11.

23. Hofstätter, 288.

24. Käthe Leichter, *So Leben Wir: 1320 Industriearbeiterinnen berichten über ihr Leben* (Vienna, 1931), 55.

25. Reinhard Sieder argues that men took no part in discussions concerning pregnancy, birth, and abortion. This position is inconsistent with Sieder's thesis that males dominated the working-class family. It also disregards the heterogeneity of the Viennese working class, which Sieder accepts. See Reinhard Sieder, "Vata derf i aufstehn?" Kindheitserfahrungen in Wiener Arbeiterfamilien um 1900," in Hubert Ch. Ehalt, Gernot Heiss, and Hannes Stekl, eds., *Glücklich ist, Wer Vergisst . . . ?: Das andere Wien um 1900* (Vienna, 1986), 71.

26. See Appendix.

27. Birgit Bolognese-Leuchtenmuller, "Unterversorgung und mangelnde Betreuung der Kleinkinder in den Unterschichtenfamilien als

soziales Problem des 19. Jahrhunderts," in Herbert Knittler, *Wirtschafts-und Sozialhistorische Beiträge* (Vienna, 1979), 414.

28. Gottfried Pirhofer, "Linien einer kulturpolitischen Auseinandersetzung in der Geschichte des Wiener Arbeiterwohnbaues," in *Wiener Geschichtsblätter*, 33, 1 (1978), 21.

29. J. Robert Wegs, "Working-Class Respectability: The Viennese Experience," in *Journal of Social History* 15 (Summer 1982).

30. Otto Felix Kanitz, "Erziehung, Schule u. Klassenkampf," in *Die sozialistische Erziehung*, February 1923. Otto Rühle, *Das proletarische Kind* (Munich, 1922).

31. Ibid., 52.

32. Gottfried Pirhofer and Reinhard Sieder, "Zur Konstitution der Arbeiterfamilie im roten Wien: Familienpolitik, Kulturreform, Alltag und Asthetik," in Michael Mitterauer and Reinhard Sieder, eds., *Historische Familienforschung* (Frankfurt am Main, 1982), 339.

33. Ibid., 339–40.

34. Viethen, 62–90.

35. Elizabeth Roberts, *A Woman's Place: An Oral History of Working-Class Women, 1890–1940* (Oxford, 1984), 3.

36. Wegs, 623. Elizabeth Roberts (ibid., 112) makes a similar argument for English working-class mothers.

37. Siegfried Reck, *Arbeiter nach der Arbeit: Sozialhistorische Studie zu den Wandlungen des Arbeiteralltags* (Lahn-Giessen, 1977), 118. Reck makes a similar case for Germany.

38. Rühle, 85.

39. Hetzer, 18.

40. Ibid., 30.

41. *Die sozialistische Erziehung*, July/August 1926. The average number of children in their families was 3.2, and 56 percent of the mothers were employed outside the home.

42. Rada, 21.

43. Ibid., 30.

44. Ibid.

45. Hetzer, 19.

46. Interviews 3, 56, and 58 in Appendix.

47. Interview 49.

48. Interview 65.

49. Interview 4.

50. Interview 48.

51. Interview 31.

52. Interview 54.

53. Interviews 28 and 31.

54. Interview 32.

55. Interview 41.

56. Interview 20.

57. Standish Meacham, *A Life Apart: The English Working Class, 1890–1914* (Cambridge, Mass., 1977).

58. Interview 39.

59. Ibid.

60. Interview 17.
61. Interviews 35 and 44.
62. Interview 15.
63. Interviews 45, 47, and 48.
64. Interview 16.
65. Institute Interview 11.
66. Reinhard Sieder, "Gassenkinder," in *Aufrisse, Zeitschrift für Politische Bildung* (April 1985), 14.
67. Viethen, 255.
68. Institute Interview 23, 5.
69. Interview 9.
70. Institute Interview 23, 16.
71. Hetzer, 19, table 2.
72. Hetzer, 48.
73. Hannes Stekl, " 'Sei es wie es wolle, es war doch so schön,' Bürgerliche Kindheit um 1900 in Autobiographien," in Hubert Ch. Ehalt, Gernot Heiss, and Hannes Stekl, eds., *Glücklich ist, Wer Vergisst . . . ?: Das andere Wien um 1900* (Vienna, 1986), 27.
74. Klemens Dorn, *Favoriten: Der 10 Wiener Gemeindebezirk* (Vienna, 1928), 210.
75. Ibid.
76. Ibid.
77. Ibid., 212.
78. Eva Tesar, *Hände auf die Bank . . . Erinnerungen an den Schulalltag* (Vienna, 1986), 222.
79. A. Tesarek, "Strafen in Schule und Haus," in *Die Sozialistische Erziehung*, 2, December 1922, 272.
80. Rada, 64.
81. Interviews 6, 8, and 17. These interviews were cited as interviews 43 and 41 in an article by Hans Safrian and Reinhard Sieder, "Gassenkinder—Strassenkämpfer: Zur politischen Sozialisation einer Arbeitergeneration in Wien 1900 bis 1938," in Lutz Niethammer and Alexander von Plato, *"Wir kriegen jetzt andere Zeiten": Auf der Suche nach der Erfahrung des Volkes in Nachfaschistischen Ländern* (Berlin-Bonn, 1985), 121, 122. These interviews will no longer appear as interviews 41 and 43 but will carry my numbers 6 and 8 in the future.
82. Interview 8.
83. Interview 11.
84. Interview 8.
85. Ibid.
86. Wilfried Konnert, *Favoriten im Wandel der Zeit* (Vienna, 1974), 94.
87. Anton Langer, "Die Disziplinarklasse als Erziehungsfaktor in Dienste der Jugendfürsorge," in *Zeitschrift für Kinderschutz und Jugendfürsorge* 2, 5 (May 1910), 271. Karl Ziak maintains that the *Plattenbrüder* would sometimes take watches and packages from passersby. Karl Ziak, *Von der Schmelz auf den Gallitzinberg* (Vienna, 1969), 12.
88. Emmerich Tauber, "Die Freizeitbeschäftigung der schulentlassenen männlichen Jugend," in *Zeitschrift für Kinderschutz, Familien- und Berufsfürsorge* 17 (July/August 1925), 133.

89. Langer, 279.

90. Tauber, 134.

91. *Zeitschrift für Kinderschutz, Familien- und Berufsfürsorge* 17 (July/ August 1925), 143. The number of punishable offenses had increased from 6,015 in 1914 to 14,896 by 1918; it dropped to a prewar level of 5,556 in 1923.

92. Rada, 67. Gillis (196) and Humphries make a similar case for British youth. Stephen Humphries, *Hooligans or Rebels? An Oral History of Working-Class Childhood and Youth, 1889–1939* (Oxford, 1981), 24.

93. *Das Kleine Blatt*, 10 May 1927, 2.

94. Interview 17.

95. Interview 41.

96. Interview 40.

97. Mike Brake, *The Sociology of Youth Culture and Youth Subcultures: Sex and Drugs and Rock'n'roll?* (London, 1980), 45. Clarke, 251. Geoff Mungham and Geoff Pearson, *Working-Class Youth Culture* (London, 1976), 154.

98. Reinhard Sieder in his article "Gassenkinder," which utilized some of my interviews, has come to a similar conclusion. Both Alexander Plato and Margarete Flecken have argued that a family's political views or social type played no role in street youth groups and activities. Alexander Plato, " 'Ich bin mit allen gut ausgekommen' oder war die Ruhrarbeiterschaft vor 1933 in politische Lager zerspaltet," in Lutz Niethammer, ed., *"Die Jahre weiss man nicht, wo man die heute hinsetzen soll": Faschismus Erfahrungen im Ruhrgebiet: Lebengeschichte und Sozialkultur im Ruhrgebiet 1930 bis 1960*, vol. 1 (Berlin, 1983), 52. Margarete Flecken, *Arbeiterkinder im 19. Jahrhundert: Eine sozialgeschichtliche Untersuchung ihrer Lebenswelt* (Weinheim, 1981), 153.

99. See Interview 8.

100. Rada, 65.

101. Interview 15.

102. Interview 17.

103. Interview 3.

104. Bettina Hirsch (ed. and comment), *Anton Proksch und seine Zeit* (Vienna, 1977), 12.

105. Interview 43.

106. Interview 8.

107. Ziak, 9.

108. Humphries (206) came to similar conclusions concerning English youths' forays into the countryside.

CHAPTER 4

1. Interview 10.

2. Interview 56.

3. John Gillis, *Youth and History* (New York, 1981), 165. Daniel K. Lapsley, Robert D. Enright, and Ronald C. Serlin, "Toward a Theoretical Perspective on the Legislation of Adolescence," *Journal of Early Adoles-*

cence 5, no. 4 (1985). Detlev J. K. Peukert, *Jugend Zwischen Krieg und Krise, Lebenswelten von Arbeiter Jugend in der Weimarer Republik* (Cologne, 1987), 84.

4. For a discussion of this theme in other countries, see Gillis, 194. Jurgen Reyer, *Wenn die Mütter arbeiten gingen* (Cologne, 1983), 196–203. Standish Meacham, *A Life Apart* (Cambridge, Mass., 1977), 174. Richard Hoggart, *The Uses of Literacy: Changing Patterns in English Mass Culture* (New Jersey, 1957). See Hoggart (21), for an elaboration of this theme.

5. Otto Glöckel, *Drillschule, Lernschule, Arbeitsschule* (Vienna, 1928). Otto Felix Kanitz, "Erziehung, Schule und Klassenkampf," in *Die sozialistische Erziehung* 3, 2 (February 1923).

6. Hildegard Hetzer, *Kindheit und Armut* (Leipzig, 1929), 67. Gillis, 165.

7. Stephen Humphries, *Hooligans or Rebels? An Oral History of Working-Class Childhood and Youth, 1889–1939* (Oxford, 1981), 54. Mike Brake, *The Sociology of Youth Culture and Youth Subcultures: Sex and Drugs and Rock'n'roll?* (London, 1980), 57.

8. Elizabeth Roberts, *A Woman's Place: An Oral History of Working-Class Women, 1890–1940* (Oxford, 1984), 28.

9. Not only did those I interviewed not attend kindergarten, but many did not even believe that kindergartens existed in the early twentieth century.

10. Ludwig Battista, *Die österreichische Volksschule* (Vienna, 1937), 20.

11. Käthe Leichter, *So Leben Wir: 1320 Industriearbeiterinnen berichten über ihr Leben* (Vienna, 1931), 94–96. A typical day in a *Hort* would include a mid-day lunch after school followed by the completion of school assignments and supervised play until parents came at about 6 P.M. Since a typical *Hort* included some handwork instruction for older children, especially needlework, more girls attended. *Die sozialistische Erziehung*, February 1924, 55, and May 1924, 195.

12. Ibid.

13. Leichter, 95. Dieter Langewiesche, *Zur Freizeit des Arbeiters: Bildungsbestrebungen und Freizeitgestaltung österreichischer Arbeiter im Kaiserreich und in der Ersten Republik* (Stuttgart, 1979), 339.

14. Gerda Kautsky, "Familie oder Kindergarten," *Die Unzufriedene* 9, 4 (April 1929), 77–78.

15. Institute Interview 12, 35.

16. Kautsky, 77–78.

17. The number of city kindergartens increased from 11 in 1897 to 29 in 1922 and 111 in 1931. The number of students rose from 1,533 in 1897 to 5,871 in 1922 and 9,356 in 1931. Felix Czeike, *Wirtschafts- und Sozialpolitik der Gemeinde Wien in der ersten Republik (1919–1934)* (Vienna, 1959), 2, 177. Birgit Bolognese-Leuchtenmüller, "Unterversorgung und mangelnde Betreuung der Kleinkinder in den Unterschichtenfamilien als soziales Problem des 19. Jahrhunderts," in Herbert Knittler, ed., *Festschrift für Alfred Hoffman zum 75 Geburtstag: Wirtschafts- und sozialhistorische Beiträge* (Vienna, 1979), 429. Another 49 kindergartens were operated by societies (*Vereinen*) and private individuals in 1897. *Zeitschrift für Kinderschutz und Jugendfürsorge* 2, 5 (May 1910), 138. Hereafter cited as *ZKJ*. In 1926

Favoriten had eight city and eight private kindergartens with a total of 1,267 pupils. Klemens Dorn, *Favoriten* (Vienna, 1928), 85–86.

18. Most of the city-run kindergartens were people's kindergartens (*Volkskindergärten*) that began at 7 A.M. and were open until 5 or 6 P.M. Pupils received breakfast free and lunch at a minimal price. *Blätter für das Wohlfahrtswesen der Stadt Wien*, 22 (November/December 1923), 81.

19. Interview 11, second conversation.

20. Interview 71.

21. Edith Rigler, *Frauenleitbild und Frauenarbeit in Österreich vom ausgehenden 19 Jahrhundert bis zum Zweiten Weltkrieg* (Vienna, 1976), 103.

22. Josef Meixner, "Knabenhorte, Jugendbündnisse und Jugendwehren als Stätten der Volkserziehung," in *ZKJ* 3, 7 (July 1911), 210.

23. *ZKJ* 2 (January/February 1910), 41.

24. *ZKJ* 3, 7 (July 1911), 207–9.

25. Fritz Kolb, "Klares Wollen," in *Die Sozialistische Erziehung* 1, 1924.

26. Hans Safrian and Reinhard Sieder, "Gassenkinder—Strassenkämpfer," in Lutz Niethammer and Alexander von Plato, eds., *"Wir Kriegen jetzt andere Zeiten": Auf der Suche nach der Erfahrung des Volkes in Nachfaschistischen Ländern* (Berlin-Bonn, 1985), 126.

27. Interviews 10, 29, and 39.

28. Interview 11, second conversation.

29. Gillis (193) poses a similar argument for British youth.

30. *Arbeiterzeitung*, 27 August 1912.

31. Ibid.

32. Ibid.

33. Interview 49.

34. Interview 26.

35. *Der Schul- u. Kinderfreund* 5 (November 1924), 82.

36. "Berufsberatungsamt der Stadt Wien und der Arbeiterkammer," *Zeitschrift für Kinderschutz, Familien- und Berufsfürsorge* 15, 5 (1923), 94. Hereafter cited as *ZKFB*.

37. *Arbeiterzeitung*, 14 February 1923, 8.

38. *Das Kleine Blatt*, 14 July 1927, 8.

39. Hans Pamperl, "Warnung vor Schulauftritt während des Schuljahres," *Die Unzufriedene* 8, 6 (February 1928), 3.

40. Leichter, 19.

41. Margarete Rada, *Das reifende Proletariermädchen* (Vienna, 1931), 85.

42. Louise Tilly and Joan Scott, *Women, Work and the Family* (New York, 1978), 181.

43. Hans Fischl, *Wesen und Werden der Schulreform in Österreich* (Vienna, 1929), 105.

44. *Bildungsarbeit* 14, 10 (October 1927), 181–82.

45. August Wesely, "Schulreform, Volk und Bildung," in *Die sozialistische Erziehung*, October 1923, 227.

46. *Arbeiterzeitung*, 9 September 1923.

47. Karl Ziak, *Von der Schmeltz auf den Gallitzinberg* (Vienna, 1969), 45.

48. Student records are kept in the individual schools. Unfortunately the records of the one *Gymnasium* in Favoriten were destroyed during World War II. But the records of a *Realschule* (stressing technical subjects

and modern languages) on the Schuhmeierplatz in Ottakring are intact. Children from working-class homes were much more likely to attend a *Realschule* than a *Gymnasium*, since the latter stresses classical languages and preparation for the university. I examined the entering and graduating classes for the school years 1909/10, 1928/29, 1929/30, and 1935/36.

49. Ibid.

50. Michael John, *Wohnverhältnisse sozialer Unterschichten im Wien Kaiser Franz Josephs* (Vienna, 1984), 83. Hartmut Kaelble calculates that only 2.8 percent of the 10- to 19-year-old age group attended secondary school in Austria compared with Germany's 3.2 percent, France's 2.6 percent, and England's 2.4 percent. Kaelble, *Soziale Mobilität und Chancengleichheit* (Göttingen, 1983), 177.

51. Glöckel, 23.

52. Ernst Papanek, *The Austrian School Reform* (New York, 1962), 106.

53. Wegs and Viethen interviews.

54. Peukert, 84.

55. Oskar Achs and Eva Tesar, *Schule damals-Schule heute: Otto Glöckel und die Schulreform* (Munich, 1985), 13.

56. Wenzel Holek, *Lebensgang eines deutsch-tschechischen Handarbeiters* (Jena, 1909), 33.

57. Adelheid Popp, *Die Jugendgeschichte einer Arbeiterin* (Munich, 1927), 4.

58. Humphries, 54.

59. Institute Interview 40.

60. Roberts, 24.

61. *Arbeiterzeitung*, 3 September 1913.

62. Julius Deutsch, "Gegen die Kinderarbeit," in *Der Kampf* 1, 10 (1 July 1908), 460.

63. Reginald Bray, *Boy Labour and Apprenticeship* (London, 1911), 62.

64. Gertrude Langer-Ostrawsky, "Wiener Schulwesen um 1900," in Hubert Ch. Ehalt, Gernot Heiss, and Hannes Stekl, eds., *Glücklich ist, Wer Vergisst . . . ?: Das andere Wien um 1900* (Vienna, 1986), 102.

65. Rada, 78.

66. Interview 49.

67. Rada, 29.

68. Gillis, 194. Reyer, 198–203. Hoggart, chapters 7–10.

69. Reyer, 198.

70. Interview 10.

71. Interview 35.

72. Anna Maier, "Wie ich reif wurde," in *Gedenbuch: 20 Jahre österreichische Arbeiterinnenbewegung*, 108.

73. Rada, 62. German working-class parents held similar attitudes. Margarete Flecken argues that German parents considered reading an "unnecessary waste of time." Flecken, *Arbeiterkinder im 19. Jahrhundert* (Weinheim, 1981), 169.

74. Ibid.

75. Michael Mitterauer, *Sozialgeschichte der Jugend* (Frankfurt am Main, 1986), 38.

76. *Arbeiterzeitung*, 27 August 1912.

77. Glöckel, 19.

78. Rada, 14.

79. Interview 45.

80. Rada, 66. Ellen Ross claims that English youth were also very effective at "discouraging 'superior' airs." Ross, " 'Not the Sort that Would Sit on the Doorstep': Respectability in Pre-World War I London Neighborhoods," *International Labor and Working Class History*, no. 27 (Spring 1985), 44.

81. Institute Interview 25, second conversation, 21.

82. Rada, 47.

83. Charles Gulich, *Austria from Habsburg to Hitler*, vol. 1 (Berkeley, 1948), 561.

84. Rada, 37.

85. Interview 36.

86. Rada, 14.

87. Rada, 7.

88. Interview 44.

89. *Die Unzufriedene*, 25 February 1928.

90. Rigler, 38.

91. Most followed a traditional working-class occupational pattern as described in chapter 5.

92. Interview 61.

93. Institute Interview 41, 3.

94. Langer-Ostrawsky, 102.

95. Rada, 78.

96. Institute Interview 10, second conversation, 19.

97. Viethen, 208. Interview with Maria Malina.

98. Viethen, 202–16.

99. *Erhebung über die Kinderarbeit in Österreich im Jahre 1908*, part 2, 235.

100. Langer-Ostrawsky, 107.

101. Herbert Steiner, ed., *Käthe Leichter, Leben und Werk* (Vienna, 1973), 305.

102. Carol Dyhouse, *Girls Growing Up in Late Victorian and Edwardian England* (London, 1981), 103.

103. Tilly and Scott, 177.

104. See Appendix.

105. Interview 8.

106. Interview 54.

107. Interview 10.

108. *Statistisches Jahrbuch der Stadt Wien*, 1929, 257.

109. Ibid.

110. *Realschule* records in Ottakring.

111. *Arbeiterzeitung*, 14 February 1923.

112. *Die Frau*, 1 August 1932, 509–10.

113. Humphries, 89. Brake, 57.

114. Brake, 57.

115. Mary Jo Maynes, *Schooling in Western Europe: A Social History* (Albany, 1984), 151.

116. Marsha Rozenblit, *The Jews of Vienna, 1867–1914: Assimilation and Identity* (Albany, 1984), 109.

117. A. Tesarek, "Strafen in Schule und Haus," *Die Sozialistische Erziehung,* 2 (December 1922), 270.

118. Kaelble, 199. Kaelble shows that while university attendance increased 2.8 percent yearly before 1914, it sank to only about one-half that during the interwar years. Kaelble calculates that in 1911 only 2 percent of the university students in Austria and 3 percent in Germany came from working-class homes. In the 1930s the Austrian percentage climbed to 4 percent but dropped to 2 percent for Germany. Kaelble, 204, 206, 214.

119. *Wirtschaftsrechnungen und Lebensverhältnisse von Wiener Arbeiterfamilien in den Jahren 1912 bis 1914* (Vienna, 1916). Benedikt Kautsky, ed., "Die Haushaltstatistik der Wiener Arbeiterkammer 1925–1934," in *International Review for Social History* (Leiden, 1937).

CHAPTER 5

1. Interview 37.
2. Interview 49.
3. Interview 45.
4. See chapter 1, page 14.
5. Edith Rigler, *Frauenleitbild und Frauenarbeit in Österreich: Vom ausgehenden 19 Jahrhundert bis zum Zweiten Weltkrieg* (Vienna, 1976), 123.
6. *Handbuch der Frauenarbeit in Österreich* (Vienna, 1930), 30.
7. Gerhard Meissl, "Industriearbeit in Wien 1830–1913," in *Jahrbuch des Vereins für Geschichte der Stadt Wien,* vol. 36, 1980, Table 20.
8. *Arbeit und Wirtschaft,* 1 February 1930, 130.
9. Rigler, 57, 63.
10. Camilla Theimer, *Frauenarbeit in Österreich* (Vienna, 1909), 41, 42, 62. Rigler, 57, 63.
11. *Arbeit und Wirtschaft,* 1 March 1933.
12. *Die Frau,* 1 July 1929, 19.
13. *Arbeit und Wirtschaft,* 1 June 1929, 457.
14. *Die Frau,* 1 June 1929.
15. Leichter, *So Leben Wir,* 8.
16. Elise Di Pauli, "Die Arbeiterin in der Schuhindustrie," in *Handbuch,* 111.
17. Josef Ehmer, "Schuster zwischen Handwerk und Fabrik," in Helmut Konrad and Wolfgang Maderthaner, eds., *Neuere Studien zur Arbeitergeschichte* (Vienna, 1984), 5.
18. Rigler, 148. Olegnik, 82.
19. Ibid.
20. Paul Lazarsfeld, *Jugend und Beruf* (Jena, 1931), 9.
21. Ibid., 19.
22. John Gillis, *Youth and History* (New York, 1981), 182.
23. Ibid.

24. *Erhebung über die Kinderarbeit in Österreich im 1908*, part 2 (Vienna, 1911), 15.

25. Sigismund Peller, "Wirtschaftsrechnungen und Lebensverhältnisse von Wiener Arbeiterfamilien in den Jahren 1912 bis 1914," in *Sonderheft der Sozialen Rundschau*, 58.

26. Ehmer, 202.

27. Trauungsbuch, Pfarre St. Johann Evangelist, 1938. Trauungsbuch, Pfarre St. Anton, 1938. [Parish marriage records for St. Anton Parish in Favoriten in 1938.] Information was obtained through a comparison of marriage and birth records in St. Anton and St. Johann churches.

28. Trauungsbuch, Pfarre St. Johann Evangelist, 1910.

29. Robyn Dasey, "Women's Work and the Family," in Richard Evans, ed., *The German Family* (London, 1981), 243.

30. Interview 67.

31. Trauungsbuch, Pfarre St. Johann Evangelist, 1910.

32. See Interviews 12, 16, 28, 31, 45, 48, and 55 in Appendix.

33. Eva Viethen, "Wiener Arbeiterinnen Leben zwischen Familie, Lohnarbeit und politischen Engagement"(Dissertation: University of Vienna, 1981), 220–54.

34. Manfred Seiser, "Die wirtschaftliche und soziale Lage der Wiener Arbeiterjugend zwischen 1918 und 1934" (Dissertation: University of Vienna, 1981), 12.

35. Ibid.

36. Karl Reininger, "Berufswünsche und Berufseinstellung von 12–14 jährigen Volksschülern," in Paul Lazersfeld, *Jugend und Beruf*, 104.

37. *Arbeiterzeitung*, 14 February 1923.

38. Ibid., 109.

39. Ibid., 117.

40. Standish Meacham, *A Life Apart: The Englis'. Working Class, 1890–1914* (Cambridge, Mass., 1977), 178.

41. *Schul- u. Kinderfreund*, 5, (6 June 1924), 43.

42. Emmerich Maros, "Zur Frage der Berufsberatung," in *Die sozialistische Erziehung*, June 1926, 145–47.

43. Interview 58.

44. Liesl Zerner, "Die jugendliche Arbeiterin," in *Handbuch*, 144.

45. Peller, 54.

46. See female respondents in Appendix.

47. *Zeitschrift für Kinderschutz, Familie und Berufsfürsorge*, vol. 15, 1923, 93.

48. Interview 45.

49. Interview 16.

50. Interview 37.

51. Rada, 10.

52. *Die Frau*, 1 August 1932, 509–10.

53. Ibid.

54. Reininger, 107.

55. Ibid., 117.

56. Zerner, 142.

57. Rigler, 111–12.

58. Institute Interview 18, 34.

59. Adelheid Popp, *Die Jugendgeschichte einer Arbeiterin* (Vienna, 1922), 3.

60. Leichter, *So Leben Wir . . . 1320 Industriearbeiterinnen berichten über ihr Leben* (Vienna, 1931), 54.

61. *Arbeit und Wirtschaft*, 1 June 1929, 457.

62. Seiser, 11.

63. Ibid., 12.

64. Gerhard Meissl, "Für mich wäre es Freiheit, wenn ich in die Fabrik gienge," Zum Wandel der Arbeitsorganisation und Arbeitserfahrung in Wien zwischen 1890 und 1914, in *Archiv 1985 Jahrbuch des Vereins für Geschichte der Arbeiterbewegung*, vol. 1, 1985, 29.

65. Leichter, 54.

66. Zerner, 142. Michael Mitterauer and Reinhard Sieder, *The European Family* (Chicago, 1982), 107. Manfred Seiser (10–11) contends that the small shops (*Kleinbetriebe*) saved themselves by using apprentice labor, essentially youth, working long hours and at low pay.

67. Amalie Pölzer, "Erinnerungen," in *Gedenkbuch* (Vienna, 1930), 103.

68. Dasey, 238.

69. Meacham, 180.

70. Rigler, 124.

71. Leichter, 18.

72. Interview 33. Dasey found that a similar misuse of apprentices was widespread in Germany; Dasey, 238.

73. Leichter, 14.

74. Paul Lazersfeld, "Zur Berufseinstellung des jungendlichen Arbeiters," in Paul Lazersfeld, *Jugend und Beruf*, 169.

75. Seiser, 35.

76. Leichter, 18.

77. *Arbeit und Wirtschaft*, 1 January 1932, 41–42.

78. Ibid., 47.

79. *Arbeiterzeitung*, 5 November 1932. Holcombe found that an English shop girl was considered to be used up at age 21. Lee Holcombe, *Victorian Ladies at Work* (Hamden, Conn.: 1973), 114.

80. Rigler, 38.

81. Peller, 59.

82. Interview 37.

83. Interview 58.

84. Kautsky, *Die Haushaltsstatistik der Wiener Arbeiterkammer 1925–1934* (Leiden, 1937), 15.

85. Seiser, 123.

86. Interview 61.

87. Leichter, 129.

88. Elizabeth Franzen-Hellersberg, *Die jugendliche Arbeiterin: Ihre Arbeitsweise und Lebensform* (Tübingen, 1932), 47.

89. Tilly and Scott, 185.

90. Rigler, 149.

91. Ibid., 139.

CHAPTER 6

1. Interview 20.
2. Otto F. Kanitz, *Die sozialistische Erziehung*, April 1922, 87.
3. John Gillis, *For Better, For Worse: British Marriages, 1600 to the Present* (New York, 1985), 262.
4. Joseph F. Kett, *Rites of Passage: Adolescence in America, 1790 to the Present* (New York, 1977), 6.
5. Gillis, 260.
6. Ibid., 268.
7. Klaus R. Allerbeck and Leopold Rosenmayr, *Einführung in die Jugendsociologie: Methoden, Theorien, und empirische Materialien* (Heidelberg, 1976), 25.
8. Rada, 67.
9. Ibid., 66.
10. Viethen, 218.
11. Interviews 25, 28.
12. Viethen, 255.
13. Rada, 71.
14. Humphries, 139.
15. Aline Furtmuller, "Frauenarbeit und Frauenbewusstsein," in Käthe Leichter, *Handbuch der Frauenarbeit in Österreich* (Vienna, 1930), 465.
16. Käthe Leichter, *So Leben Wir* (Vienna, 1931), 82, 109, 115.
17. Michael Mitterauer, *Sozialgeschichte der Jugend* (Frankfurt am Main, 1986), 26.
18. Sofie Lazarsfeld, *Sexuelle Erziehung* (Vienna, 1931), 21.
19. Institute Interview 12, 22.
20. Institute Interview 24.
21. Robert Lang, "Das Kinematographentheater und seine Gefahren für die Jugend," in *Zeitschrift für Kinderschutz u. Jugendfürsorge* 4, no. 3 (March 1912), 73.
22. Lang, 74.
23. Manfred Seiser, "Die wirtschaftliche und soziale Lage der Wiener Arbeiterjugend zwischen 1918 und 1934" (Dissertation: University of Vienna, 1981), 128.
24. Hildegard Hetzer, "Sexualleben und Interessenkreis pubertierender Mädchen," in *Zeitschrift für Pädagogische Psychologie*, vol. 30, 1929. Rada, *Das reifende Proletariermädchen*. Hetzer, *Kindheit und Armut* (Leipzig, 1929).
25. Hetzer, 449–53.
26. Rada, 72.
27. Ibid., 69.
28. Ibid., 71.
29. Richard Hoggart, *The Uses of Literacy: Changing Patterns in English Mass Culture* (New Jersey, 1957), 67.
30. Ernst Fischer, *Krise der Jugend* (Vienna, 1931), 43, 56.
31. Wilhelm Reich, *Sexualerregung und Sexualbefriedigung* (Vienna, 1929), 56.
32. Julius Tandler, *Die Sozialbilanz der Alkoholikerfamilie* (Vienna, 1936).

33. Kanitz, 89.

34. Ibid., 91.

35. Therese Schlesinger and Paul Stein, "Leitsätze für die sexuelle Aufklärung der Jugend," in *Bildungsarbeit* 19, 12 (December 1932), 236.

36. Hetzer.

37. Wilhelm Reich, *Geschlechtsreife, Enthaltsamkeit, Ehemoral: Eine Kritik der bürgerlichen Sexualreform* (Vienna, 1930), 80–85.

38. Reich, *Sexualerregung*, 236.

39. *Die Praxis*, 9, 3 (March 1930).

40. Anton Tesarek, *Das Buch der Roten Falken* (Vienna, 1926).

41. Institute Interview 37.

42. *Zeitschrift für Kinderschutz u. Jugendfürsorge* 4 (March 1912), 74.

43. Adelheid Popp, *Die Jugendgeschichte einer Arbeiterin* (Munich, 1927), 19.

44. Paul Stein, *Arbeiterzeitung*, 8 November 1932, 14. Stein argued further that the Viennese situation was not as desperate as that in Berlin due to Vienna's less crowded apartments.

45. Interviews 10 and 15.

46. Eva Viethen, "Wiener Arbeiterinnen Leben zwischen Familie, Lohnarbeit und politischen Engagement" (Dissertation: University of Vienna, 1984), 350.

47. Reich, *Geschlechtsreife*, 89.

48. Standish Meacham, *A Life Apart: The English Working Class, 1890–1914* (Cambridge, Mass.: 1977), 159.

49. Institute Interview 12, 13.

50. Interview 49.

51. Institute Interview 31, 38.

52. Institute Interview 20, 33.

53. Gottfried Pirhofer and Reinhard Sieder, "Zur Konstitution der Arbeiter Familie im Roten Wien: Familien Politik, Kulturreform, Alltag und Asthetik," in *Historische Familienforschung*, Michael Mitterauer and Reinhard Sieder, eds. (Frankfurt am Main, 1982), 243.

54. Viethen, 350.

55. Elizabeth Roberts, *A Woman's Place: An Oral History of Working-Class Women 1890–1940* (Oxford, 1984), 15.

56. Rada, 76.

57. Ernst Hanisch, "Arbeiterkindheit in Österreich vor dem Ersten Weltkrieg," in *Internationales Archiv für Sozialgeschichte der deutschen Literatur*, vol. 7, 1982, 122.

58. Hetzer, *Kindheit und Armut*, 55.

59. Ibid.

60. Reich, *Geschlechtsreife*, 88.

61. Hetzer, *Kindheit und Armut*, 51.

62. Tandler, 39.

63. Ibid., 40.

64. Ibid., 17.

65. Edward Shorter, *The Making of the Modern Family*. See similar arguments in Weeks, *Sex, Politics and Society*, for England (61) and in Cissie

Fairchild, "Female Sexual Attitudes and the Rise of Illegitimacy: A Case Study," *Journal of Interdisciplinary History* 8, no. 4 (Spring 1978).

66. Mitterauer, *Ledige Mütter*, 103.

67. Maximilian Angerer, "Studien zur Sozialgeschichte der Wiener Bezirke I, VII und X in der Zeit zwischen 1869 und 1910" (Dissertation: University of Vienna, 1957), 70.

68. *Statistischen Jahrbuch der Stadt Wien für das Jahr 1904*, 64–65. Hereafter cited as *SJSW*.

69. *SJSW*, 1910, 68.

70. Ibid. Only 21 of 4,001 births to couples in the machine industry were illegitimate, compared with 93 of 405 in the textile industry and 1,239 of 3,593 in the clothing industry. Schomerus's study of illegitimacy in Esslingen produced similar results. He found that about 35.7 percent of mothers in the textile industry gave births to illegitimate children, compared with 31.6 percent in the machine industry. Heilwig Schomerus, "The Family Life-Cycle: A Study of Factory Workers in Nineteenth-Century Wurttemberg," in Richard J. Evans and W. R. Lee, *The German Family* (London, 1981), 185.

71. Mitterauer, *Ledige Mütter*, 106.

72. *Österreichische Statistischen Handbuch für 1932*, 17. Hereafter *ÖSH*.

73. *SJSW*, 1910, 1912, 55–60.

74. Tandler, 28. *ÖSH*, 1932, 17.

75. *Arbeiterzeitung*, 8 April 1913, 10.

76. *ÖSH*, 1932, 17.

77. Siegfried Reck, *Arbeiter nach der Arbeit: Sozial-historische Studie zu den Wandlungen des Arbeiteralltags* (Lahn-Giessen, 1977), 114. Jeffrey Weeks, *Sex, Politics and Society*, 60. R. P. Neuman reached similar conclusions for German workers in his essay "Industrialization and Sexual Behavior: Some Aspects of Working-Class Life in Imperial Germany," in Robert J. Bezucha, ed., *Modern European Social History* (Lexington, Mass., 1972), 285–86. Donata Elschenbroich described premarital pregnancy among the peasantry as a "conditio sine qua non." Elschenbroich, *Kinder werden nicht geboren: Studien zur Entstehung der Kindheit* (Frankfurt am Main, 1980), 121.

78. Reich, *Geschlechsreife*, 88.

79. W. Latzko, *Wiener Medizinische Wochenschrift*, no. 26, 1924, 1387.

80. Reich, *Sexualerregung*, 20.

81. Ibid., 17.

82. Reck, 113. Stefan Bajohr, "Illegitimacy and the Working Class: Illegitimate Mothers in Brunswick, 1900–1933," in Richard J. Evans, ed., *The German Working Class, 1888–1933* (London, 1982), 148. Michael Mitterauer and Reinhard Sieder, *Vom Patriarchat zur Partnerschaft* (Munich, 1977), 145. Michael Mitterauer, *Ledige Mütter*, 55.

83. Wenzel Holek, *Lebensgang eines deutsch-tschechischen Handarbeiters* (Jena, 1909), 234.

84. Institute Interview 40, 10.

85. Institute Interview 10, 23.

86. *SJSW*, 1904, 64–65. *SJSW*, 1901, 128. *SJSW*, 1904, 64. *SJSW*, 1905,

68. From 3,000 to 4,000 children were legitimized each year from 1900 to 1904, while the yearly illegitimate totals reached between 16,000 and 17,000.

87. *SJSW*, 1912, 54. *SJSW*, 1901, 124. In 1912, figures for district 20 were 69.12 and for district 16, 62.46. Percentages in 1901 were 81.69 for Favoriten, 72.99 for district 20, and 70.48 for district 16. For the upper-class district 1, the percentage was only 19.11.

88. Mitterauer, 106. Mike Brake, *The Sociology of Youth Culture and Youth Subcultures: Sex and Drugs and Rock'n'roll* (London, 1980), 141.

89. *Die Praxis*, 9 (March 1930), 68.

90. Ibid.

91. *Arbeiterzeitung*, 1 April 1923, 17.

92. Anson Rabinbach, "Politics and Pedagogy: The Austrian Social Democratic Youth Movement 1931–32," *Journal of Contemporary History* 13 (1978), 337–56. Hans Safrian and Reinhard Sieder, "Gassenkinder— Strassenkämpfer: Zur politischen Sozialisation einer Arbeitergeneration in Wien 1900–1938," in Lutz Niethammer and Alexander von Plato, eds., *"Wir Kriegen jetzt andere Zeiten": Auf der Suche nach der Erfahrung des Volkes in Nachfaschistischen Ländern* (Berlin-Bonn, 1985).

93. Rabinbach, 341.

94. Charles Gulich, *Austria from Habsburg to Hitler*, vol. 2 (Berkeley, 1948), 587–88.

95. Rabinbach, 352.

96. Safrian and Sieder.

97. Ibid., 147.

98. Josef Ehmer, *Familienstruktur und Arbeitsorganization im frühindustriellen Wien* (Munich, 1980), 184.

99. *ÖSH*, 1932, 11.

100. Ibid., 14.

101. Weeks, 25, 201.

102. Albert Kaufmann, *Demographische Struktur und Haushaltsstatistik*, index 1.1, 1.2.

103. Ibid.

104. Käthe Leichter, *So Leben Wir*, 9. While this percentage is about 10 percent higher than that for all Viennese, the one-year difference in the age cohorts would reduce the disparity somewhat. The sample has some drawbacks. The group has a lower percentage of the 16–30-year cohort than the female workers as a whole. Still this does not alter these findings, since this group was examined independent of any other age cohort. Moreover, it is advantageous for our purposes in that it includes primarily those women working in larger factories—62 percent worked in factories with more than 100 employees—and therefore is composed of industrial rather than the more traditional artisanal and small-shop workers. It represents workers who were most influenced by the factory modernizations and rationalizations of the postwar period.

105. Trauungsbuch, Pfarre St. Johann Evangelist, 1910, 1938.

106. Leichter, *So Leben Wir*, 9.

107. *Die Ergebnisse der österreichischen Volkszählung vom 22 März 1934* (Vienna, 1935), 159.

108. Leichter, *So Leben Wir*, 9.

109. *SJSW*, 1912, 54.

110. Trauungsbuch, Pfarre St. Johann Evangelist, 1910.

111. Leichter, *So Leben Wir*, 55.

112. Ibid.

113. Ursula Lehr, *Die Frau im Beruf*, 69.

114. Ibid., 167. Pirhofer and Sieder (345) argue that even a position as a domestic was considered preferable to that of a factory position.

115. Edith Rigler, *Frauenleitbild und Frauenarbeit in Österreich vom ausgehenden 19 Jahrhundert bis zum Zweiten Weltkrieg* (Vienna: 1976), 104.

116. Interview 67.

117. Institute Interviews 19, 17, and 29.

118. Viethen, 307.

119. Gillis, 288.

120. Shorter, passim.

121. This view was mentioned by almost all I interviewed.

122. Pirhofer and Sieder, 347.

123. Viethen, 305.

124. Ibid.

125. Viethen, 300, 315.

126. Louise Tilly and Joan Scott, *Women, Work and Family* (New York: Holt, Rinehart and Winston, 1978), 191.

127. *SJSW*, 1905, 1907. 45.

128. Ibid.

129. Ibid.

130. *SJSW*, 1912, 1914, 54.

131. Results from the parish record study in the personal possession of the author.

132. Ibid.

133. Tilly and Scott, 192.

134. Elizabeth Roberts (73) contends, based upon similar evidence for English women, that one might more easily argue that the illegitimacy rate represents sexual restraint rather than license.

CHAPTER 7

1. Peter Stearns, "The Effort at Continuity in Working-Class Culture," *Journal of Modern History* 52 (December 1980). Ernst Hanisch argued similarly in "Arbeiterkindheit in Österreich vor dem Ersten Weltkrieg," in *Internationales Archiv für Sozialgeschichte der deutschen Literatur*, vol. 7, 1982, 109–47.

2. Heinz Kluth, "Arbeiterjugend—Begriff und Wirklichkeit," in Helmut Schelsky, *Arbeiterjugend Gestern und Heute* (Heidelberg, 1955), 74.

3. Carol Dyhouse makes a similar argument for English working-class girls. Dyhouse, *Girls Growing Up in Late Victorian and Edwardian England* (London, 1981), chapter 4.

4. Trude Wiechert, "Mädchenerziehung von heute—nicht von gestern,"

in *Die Hausliche Erziehung/Die Sozialistische Erziehung,* 10 (November 1930), 255.

5. Wiechert, 254.

6. Dyhouse, 138.

7. Lenard R. Berlanstein, *The Working People of Paris, 1871–1914* (Baltimore, 1984), 144.

8. Margarete Rada, *Das reifende Proletariermädchen* (Vienna-Leipzig, 1931), 32.

9. Interview 70.

10. Käthe Leichter, *So Leben Wir* (Vienna, 1932), 70.

11. Edith Rigler, *Frauenleitbild und Frauenarbeit in Österreich vom ausgehenden 19 Jahrhundert bis zum Zweiten Weltkrieg* (Vienna, 1976), 162.

12. Ernst Hanisch contends that the *Volksschule* was the proletarian school in the period before World War I since almost all working-class children finished the *Volksschule,* but not all finished the upper-elementary school, the *Bürgerschule.* But many working-class children were attending the *Bürgerschule* prior to World War I. "Arbeiterkindheit in Österreich vor dem Ersten Weltkrieg," in *Internationales Archiv für Sozialgeschichte der deutschen Literatur,* vol. 7, 1982, 140.

13. G. Bäumer, "Sind Proletarierkinder 'minderbegabt,' " in *Die Häusliche Erziehung/Die Sozialistische Erziehung,* 8 (March 1928), 81.

14. A. Tesarek, "Strafen in Schule und Haus," in *Die Sozialistische Erziehung,* 2 (December 1922), 270.

15. Berlanstein, 144. Marsha Rosenblit, *The Jews of Vienna, 1867–1914: Assimilation and Identity* (Albany, 1984), 109.

16. Interview 43.

17. Interview 55. [Alltag hat uns aufgefressen].

18. Interview 14.

19. Hanisch, 124.

20. Wolfgang Maderthaner, "Kirche und Sozialdemokratie: Aspekte des Verhältnisse von politischem Klerikalismus und sozialistischer Arbeiterschaft bis zum Jahre 1938," in Helmut Konrad and Wolfgang Maderthaner, eds., *Neuere Studien zur Arbeitergeschichte,* vol. 3 (Vienna, 1984), 539.

21. Wilhelm Reich, *Der Sexuelle Kampf der Jugend* (Vienna, 1932), 126.

22. Otto F. Kanitz, *Die sozialistische Erziehung,* January 1924, 7.

23. Interview 31.

24. John Gillis, *Youth and History: Tradition and Change in European Age Relations, 1770–Present* (New York, 1981), 218.

25. Eva Viethen, "Wiener Arbeiterinnen Leben zwischen Familie, Lohnarbeit und politischen Engagement" (Dissertation: University of Vienna, 1984), 46.

26. Hanisch, 120.

27. Heinz Kluth, "Arbeiterjugend—Begriff und Wirklichkeit," in Helmut Schelsky, ed., *Arbeiterjugend—gestern und heute* (Heidelberg, 1955).

Bibliography

PRIMARY SOURCES

ARCHIVES

Allgemeines Verwaltungsarchiv, Vienna (AVA)
Bundesministerium des Inneren
SD Archiv
Archiv der Bundespolizeidirektion
Strafprozessakten
Bezirksmuseum Favoriten (10 Bezirk)
Bezirksmuseum Liesing (23 Bezirk)
Dokumentationsarchiv des österreichischen Widerstandes (Vienna)
Trauungsbücher, Pfarre St. Anton, 1900–1920, 1938
Trauungsbücher, Pfarre St. Johann Evangelist, 1900–1920, 1938
Verein für Geschichte der Arbeiterbewegung

GOVERNMENT PUBLICATIONS

Amtsblatt der Stadt Wien, 1892–1911, 1920–30, 1933–36.
Die Arbeitszeit in den Fabriksbetrieben Österreichs. Vienna, 1908.
Die Arbeits- und Lebensverhältnisse der Wiener Lohnarbeiterinnen: Ergebnisse und Stenographisches Protokoll der Enquete über Frauenarbeit abgehalten in Wien vom 1 März bis April 1896. Vienna, 1897.
Bericht der Gewerbe-Inspektoren, 1913, 1914, 1926–28 (Name changed to Amtstätigkeit der Gewerbe-Inspektorate in 1928).
Bericht über die Industrie, den Handel und die Verkehrsverhältnisse in Wien und Niederösterreich. Vienna, 1907.

Berufsstatistik nach den Ergebnissen der Volkszählung vom 31 Dezember 1910 in Österreich, Vienna, 1916.

Die Bewegung der Bevölkerung in den Jahren 1914 bis 1921. Vienna, 1923.

Die Ergebnisse der Ausserordentlichen Volkszählung vom 31 Jänner 1920. Vienna, 1921.

Die Ergebnisse der Erhebung der Wohnungsverhältnisse in Wien am 22 März, 1934. Vienna, 1935.

Die Ergebnisse der österreichischen Volkszählung vom 22 März 1934. Vienna, 1935.

Die Ergebnisse der Volkszählung vom 31 Dezember 1910 in der K. K. Reichshaupt- und Residenzstadt Wien. Vienna, 1911.

Die Ergebnisse der Wohnungszählung in Wien vom Jahre 1917. Vienna, 1918.

Erhebung über die Kinderarbeit in Österreich im Jahre 1908. Vienna, 1911.

Krankheits- und Sterblichkeitsverhältnisse bei den nach den Gesetze vom 30 März 1888 (R. G. Bl. nr. 33), betreffend die Krankenversicherung der Arbeiter, eingerichteten Krankenkassen in den Jahren 1896–1910. Vienna, 1913.

Löhne und Lebenshaltung der Wiener Arbeiterschaft im Jahre 1925. Vienna, 1928.

Das neue Wien: Städtewerk, vols. 1–4, 1926–28.

Das öffentliche Armenwesen in Wien. Eine Skizze seiner *geschichtlichen Entwicklung*. Vienna, 1946.

Olegnik, Felix. *Historische Statistische Übersichten von Wien*. 3 vols. Vienna, 1956–57.

Rationalisierung, Arbeitswissenschaft und Arbeiterschutz. 2d expanded edition, Vienna, 1928.

Sedlaczek, Stefan. *Die definitiven ergebnisse der Volkszählung vom 31 Dezember 1890 in der K. K. Reichshaupt- und Residenzstadt Wien*. Vienna, 1891.

Statistische Monatschrift. Vienna, 1890–1911.

Statistische Mitteilungen der Stadt Wien. Vienna, 1925–26.

Statistisches Handbuch für die Republik Österreich, 1920–1935. Vienna.

Statistisches Jahrbuch der Stadt Wien, 1901–1912, new issue 1–2, 1929–1934. Vienna.

Statistisches Taschenbuch der Stadt Wien, 1926–1934. Vienna.

Vergleich der berufsstatistischen Ergebnisse der Volkszählungen 1934–1951–1961. Vienna, 1968.

Vorläufige Ergebnisse der Volkszählung vom 31 Dezember 1900 in den im Reichsrathe vertretenen Königreichen und Ländern. Vienna, 1901.

Wirtschaftsrechnungen und Lebensverhältnisse von Wiener Arbeiterfamilien in den Jahren 1912 bis 1914. Erhebung des K. K. Arbeitsstatistischen Amtes im Handelsministerium. Vienna, 1916.

Wirtschaftsstatistisches Jahrbuch. Kammer für Arbeiter und Angestellte in Wien, 1924–29, 1932–33. Vienna, 1925–34.

Das Wohlfahrtsamt der Stadt Wien und seine einrichtungen, 1921–1931. Vienna, 1931.

INTERVIEWS

Seventy-one interviews of elderly former inhabitants of working-class districts in Vienna in 1978–79. Transcribed interviews available in the University of Notre Dame Archives, 607 Hesburgh Library.

Interviews carried out by the Institute for Economic and Social History [Institut für Wirtschaft und Sozialgeschichte] at the University of Vienna from 1980 to 1982. Primary interviewer, Reinhard Sieder.

Interviews carried out by Eva Viethen. Transcribed interviews available in the Institute for Folklore [Institut für Volkskunde], Vienna.

SECONDARY SOURCES

BOOKS

Achs, Oskar, and A. Krassnigg. *Drillschule- Lernschule- Arbeitsschule: Otto Glöckel und die österreichische Schulreform in der Ersten Republik.* Vienna: Jugend und Volk, 1974.

Adler, Alfred, and Carl Furtmüller. *Heilen und Bilden: Arztlichpädagogische Arbeiten des Vereins für Individualpsychologie.* Munich: Ernst Reinhardt, 1914.

Aichorn, August. *Verwahrloste Jugend.* New York: Viking, 1935.

Allerbeck, Klaus, and Leopold Rosenmayr. *Einfünrung in die Jugendsoziologie: Theorien, Methoden und empirische Materialien.* Heidelberg: Quelle & Mayer, 1976.

Altfahrt, Margit, ed al. *Die Zukunft liegt in der Vergangenheit: Studien zum Siedlungswesen der Zwischenkriegszeit.* Vienna: Franz Deuticke, 1983.

Andics, Hellmut. *Der Staat, der keiner wollte, Österreich 1918–1938.* Vienna: Herder, 1962.

Appelt, Erna. *Von Ladenmädchen, Schreibfräulein und Gouvernanten: Die weiblichen Angestellten Wien zwischen 1900 und 1934.* Vienna: Verlag für Gesellschaftskritik, 1985.

Aries, Philippe. *Centuries of Childhood: A Social History of Family Life.* New York: Vintage Books, 1962.

Arlt, Ilse. *Die Grundlagen der Fürsorge von Wien.* Vienna: Schulbücher, 1921.

Ausch, Karl. *Als die Banken fielen: Zur Soziologie der politischen Korruption.* Frankfurt: Europa, 1968.

Backe, Bruno. *Die sozialräumliche Differenzierung in Florisdorf.* Vienna: Notring, 1968.

Banik-Schweitzer, Renate. "Zur Bestimmung der Rolle Wiens als Industriestadt für die wirtschaftliche Entwicklung der Habsburgermonarchie." *Industriestadt Wien: Die Durchsetzung der industriellen Marktproduktion in der Habsburgerresidenz.* Vienna: Franz Deuticke, 1983.

Banik-Schweitzer, Renate, and Gerhard Meissl, eds. *Historischer Atlas von Wien,* vol. 1. Vienna: Jugend und Volk, 1981.

Barker, Elizabeth. *Austria, 1918–1972.* London: Macmillan, 1973.

Battista, Ludwig. *Die Körperliche und geistige Entwicklung des Schulkindes und ihre Beziehungen zur Schühlerbeobachtung und zu den Bildungsaufgaben der Schule.* Vienna, Leipzig, and New York: Deutscher Verlag für Jugend und Volk, 1924.

Battista, Ludwig. *Die österreichische Volksschule: Ihr Werden, ihre äusseren Arbeitsbedingungen und ihre Erziehungs und Bildungsarbeit.* Vienna: Österreichischer Bundesverlag, 1937.

Bauböck, Rainer. *Wohnungsverhältnisse in Sozialdemokratische Wien, 1919–1934.* Salzburg: Neugebauer, 1979.

Berlanstein, Lenard R. *The Working People of Paris, 1871–1914.* Baltimore: The Johns Hopkins University Press, 1984.

Bernfeld, Siegfried. *Die Neue Jugend und die Frauen.* Vienna: Kamonen, 1914.

Bernfeld, Siegfried. *Von Gemeinschaftsleben der Jugend, Quellenschriften zur seelischen Entwicklung.* Vienna: 1922.

Berninger, Wilhelm, and Albrecht Pubker. *Zur Berufswahl für Mädchen und junge Frauen.* Vienna: Österreichischer Schulbücher, 1924.

Bodner, John. *Workers' World: Kinship, Community, and Protest in an Industrial Society, 1900–1940.* Baltimore: The Johns Hopkins University Press, 1982.

Bodzenta, Erich. *Die österreichische Gesellschaft.* Vienna: 1972.

Bolognese-Leuchtenmüller, Birgit. *Bevolkerungsentwicklung und Berufsstruktur.* Vienna: Europa, 1978.

Borscheid, Peter, and Hans J. Teuteberg, eds., *Ehe, Liebe, Tod: Zum Wandel der Familie, der Geschlechts- und Generations- beziehungen in der Neuzeit.* Münster: F. Coppenrath, 1983.

Botz, Gerhard, Hans Hautmann, and Helmut Konrad. *Geschichte und Gesellschaft.* Festschrift für Karl R. Stadler zum 60. Geburtstag. Vienna: Europa, 1974.

Botz, Gerhard, Hans Hautmann, Helmut Konrad, and J. Weidenholzer, eds. *Bewegung und Klasse. Studien zur österreichischen Arbeitergeschichte.* Vienna: Europa, 1978.

Botz, Gerhard, and J. Weidenholzer. *Mundliche Geschichte und Arbeiterbewegung.* Vienna and Cologne: Böhlau, 1984.

Boyer, John W. *Political Radicalism in Late Imperial Vienna: Origins of the Christian Social Movement, 1848–1897.* Chicago: University of Chicago Press, 1981.

Brake, Mike. *The Sociology of Youth Culture and Youth Subcultures: Sex and Drugs and Rock'n'roll.* London: Routledge and Kegan Paul, 1980.

Branca, Patricia. *Women in Europe since 1750.* London: Croom Helm, 1978.

Braun, Stephanie, and Carla Zaglitz. *Frauenbewegung, Frauenbildung und Frauenarbeit in Österreich.* Vienna: 1930.

Bray, Reginald. *Boy Labour and Apprenticeship.* London: Constable, 1911.

Breich, Otto, and Gerhard Fritsch. *Finale und Auftakt: Wien, 1898–1914.* Salzburg: Otto Müller, 1964.

Broch, Herman. *Hofmannsthal und seine Zeit.* Munich: R. Piper, 1964.

Brousek, Karl. *Wien und seine Tschechen.* Vienna: Geschichte und Politik, 1980.

Bruckner, Adele. *Vom Alltag*. Vienna: Verlag der Socialpadogogischen Gesellschaft, 1925.

Bühler, Charlotte, and Hildegard Hetzer. *Testing Children's Development from Birth to School Age*. New York: Farrar and Rhinehart, 1935.

Bühler, Charlotte. *Kindheit und Jugend: Genese des Bewusstseins*. Leipzig: S. Hezel, 1928.

Bühler, Charlotte. *Das Seelenleben des Jugendlichen*. Jena: Gustav Fischer, 1927.

Bühler, Charlotte. *Quellen und Studien zur Jugendkunde*. Jena: Gustav Fischer, 1926.

Bühler, Karl. *Die geistige Entwicklung des Kindes*. 5th edition. Jena: Gustav Fischer, 1929.

Buttinger, Joseph. *In the Twilight of Socialism*. New York: Praeger, 1953.

Buttinger, Joseph. *Ortswechsel: Die Geschichte meiner Jugend*. Frankfurt am Main: Neue Kritik, 1979.

Clarke, John, Chas Critcher, and Richard Johnson. *Working-Class Culture: Studies in History and Theory*. New York: St. Martin's Press, 1979.

Comfort, Alex. *Sex in Society*. London: Penguin, 1966.

Conze, W. *Sozialgeschichte der Familie in der Neuzeit Europas*. Stuttgart: Ernst Klett, 1976.

Crankshaw, Edward. *Vienna: The Image of a Culture in Decline*. London: Macmillan, 1938.

Crossick, Jeffrey, and Heinz-Gerhard Haupt, eds. *Shopkeepers and Master Artisans in Nineteenth-Century Europe*. New York: Methuen, 1984.

Czeike, Felix, and Helga Schmidt. *Franz Schuhmeier*. Vienna: Europa, 1964.

Czeike, Felix. *Wirtschafts und Sozialpolitik der Gemeinde Wein: In der ersten Republik (1919–1934)*. Vienna: Jugend und Volk, 1958–59.

Czeike, Felix. *Liberale, Christlichsoziale und Sozialdemokratische Kommunalpolitik (1861–1934)*. Vienna: Geschichte und Politik, 1962.

Czeike, Felix, and Walter Lugasch. *Studien zur sozialgeschichte von Ottakring und Hernals, Weiner Schriften II*. Vienna: Jugend und Volk, 1955.

Danneberg, Robert. *Der finanzielle Marsch auf Wien*. Vienna: Sozialdemokratischen Partei.

Danneberg, Robert. *Hochverrater der Wirtschaft und der Republik*. Vienna: Sozialdemokratischen Partei, 1931.

Danneberg, Robert. *Vienna under Socialist Rule*. London: The Labour Party, 1928.

Danneberg, Robert. *The New Vienna*. London: The Labour Party, 1931.

Demos, John. *Past, Present, and Personal: The Family and the Life Course in American History*. New York: Oxford, 1987.

de Mause, Lloyd. *The History of Childhood*. New York: Psychohistory Press, 1974.

Dermutz, Suzanne. *Der österreichische Weg: Schulreform und bildungspolitik in der Zweiten Republik*. Innsbruck: University of Innsbruck, Gesellschafts Politik, 1983.

Deutsch, Hugo. *Eine Umfrage über die Ausgaben für alkoholische Getränke bei 2302 Krankenkassemitgliedern*. Vienna: Sonderdruck, 1909.

Deutsch, Julius. *Der Burgerkrieg in österreich Eine Darstellung Von Mit- kampfern und Augenzeugen.* Karlsbad: Graphia, 1934.

Deutsch, Julius. *Ein weiter Weg: Lebenserinnerungen.* Vienna: Amalthea, 1960.

Deutsch, Julius. *Geschichte der österreichischen Gewerkschaftsbewegung.* Vi- enna: Wiener Volksbuchhandlung, 1929–32.

Deutsch, Julius. *Sport und Politik.* Berlin: J. H. W. Dietz, 1928.

Deutsch, Julius. *Unter roten Fahnen! Von Rekord-zum Massenport.* Vienna: Organisation Wien der Sozialdemokratischen Partei, 1931.

Dorn, Klemens. *Favoriten: Ein Heimatbuch des 10 Wiener Gemeindebezirkes.* Vienna: Jugend und Volk, 1928.

Dottrens, Robert. *The New Education in Austria.* New York: The John Day Company, 1930.

Duczynska, Ilona. *Workers in Arms: The Austrian Schutzbund and the Civil War of 1934.* New York: Monthly Review Press, 1978.

Dyhouse, Carol. *Girls Growing Up in Late Victorian and Edwardian En- gland.* London: Routledge and Kegan Paul, 1981.

Ehalt, Hubert Ch., ed., *Geschichte von Unten.* Vienna: Böhlau 1984.

Ehalt, Hubert Ch., ed. *"Glüchlich ist, Wer Vergisst . . . ?" Das andere Wien um 1900.* Vienna: Böhlau, 1986.

Ehmer, Josef. *Familienstruktur und Arbeitsorganization im frühindustriellen Wien.* Munich: R. Oldenbourg, 1980.

Elschenbroich, Donata. *Kinder werden nicht geboren: Studien zur Ent- stehung der Kindheit.* Frankfurt am Main: Pädagogische Extra Buch- handlung, 1980.

Evans, Richard. *The Feminist Movement in Germany, 1894–1933.* New York: Sage Studies, 1976.

Evans, Richard. *The German Working Class, 1888–1933: The Politics of Everyday Life.* London: Croom Helm, 1981.

Evans, Richard, and W. R. Lee. *The German Family: Essays on the Social History of the Family in Nineteenth- and Twentieth-Century Germany.* London: Croom Helm, 1981.

Feldbauer, Peter. *Kinderelend in Wien Von der Armenflege zur Jugend fürsorge 17–19 Jahrhundert.* Vienna: Verlag für Gesellschaftskritik, 1980.

Feldbauer, Peter. *Stadtwachstum und Wohnungsnot: Determinanten unzu- reichender Wohnungsversorgung in Wien, 1848 bis 1914.* Vienna: Geschichte und Politik, 1977.

Field, Frank. *The Last Days of Mankind: Karl Kraus and His Vienna.* New York: St. Martin's, 1967.

Fischer, Claude S. *Networks and Places: Social Relations in the Urban Set- ting.* New York: The Free Press, 1977.

Fischer, Claude S. *To Dwell Among Friends: Personal Networks in Town and City.* Chicago: University of Chicago Press, 1982.

Fischer, Ernst. *An Opposing Man.* London: Allen Lane, 1974.

Fischer, Ernst. *Krise der Jugend.* Vienna: Hess, 1931.

Fischl, Hans. *Wesen und Werden der Schulreform in Österreich.* Vienna: Jugend und Volk, 1929.

Flecken, Margarete. *Arbeiterkinder im 19. Jahrhundert: Eine sozialgeschicht-liche Untersuchung ihrer Lebenswelt.* Weinheim: Beltz, 1981.

Fout, John, ed. *German Women in the Nineteenth Century: A Social History.* New York: Holmes & Meier, 1984.

Franzen-Hellersberg, Lisbeth. *Die jugendliche Arbeiterin Ihre Arbeitsweise und Lebensform: Ein Versuch sozialpsychologischer Forschung zum Zweck der Umwertung proletarischer Tatbestände.* Tübingen: J. C. B. Mohr, 1932.

Frei, Alfred. *Rotes Wien: Austromarxismus und Arbeiterkultur.* Berlin: DVK, 1984.

Frei, Bruno. *Das Elend Wiens.* Vienna: Wiener Graphischen Werkstätte, 1921.

Frei, Bruno. *Judisches Elend.* Vienna: R. Löwit, 1920.

Freundlich, Emmy. *Die Genossenschaftsbewegung im Lande u. der Gemeinde Wien.* Vienna: Sozialdemokratischen Partei, 1930.

Frischauer, Willi. *Twilight in Vienna.* London: Collins, 1938.

Gainham, Sarah. *Night Falls on the City.* London: Collins, 1967.

Gedenkbuch: 20 Jahre österreichische Arbeiterinnenbewegung. Vienna: Volks-buchhandlung, 1912.

Gestrich, Andreas. *Traditionelle Jugendkultur und Industrialisierung.* Göt-tingen: Vandenboeck & Ruprecht, 1986.

Gillis, John. *For Better, For Worse: British Marriages, 1600 to the Present.* New York: Oxford, 1985.

Gillis, John R. *Youth and History: Tradition and Change in European Age Relations, 1770–Present,* expanded student edition. New York: Aca-demic Press, 1981.

Glettler, Monika. *Die Wiener Tschechen um 1900.* Vienna: R. Oldenbourg, 1972.

Glöckel, Otto. *Drillschule, Lernschule, Arbeitsschule.* Vienna: Sozialdemo-kratischen Partei, 1928.

Golias, Edward. *Am Tore des Lebens: Über sexuelle Aufklärung und Sittlich-keit.* Leipzig: Neuer Akademie Verlag, 1919.

Good, David F. *The Economic Rise of the Habsburg Empire 1750–1914.* Berkeley: University of California Press, 1984.

Goody, Jack. *The Development of the Family and Marriage in Europe.* Cam-bridge: Cambridge, 1983.

Gruber, Ignaz. *Die Haushaltung der arbeitenden Klassen.* Jena: Gustav Fischer, 1887.

Gulich, Charles. *Austria from Habsburg to Hitler,* 2 vols. Berkeley: Univer-sity of California Press, 1948.

Hahn, Georg, Angelica and Friedrich Götz, and Brigitte Marcher, eds., *Kinder, Küche, Kleider: Historische Texte zur Mädchenerziehung.* Vi-enna: Europa, 1982.

Handbuch der Frauenarbeit in Österreich. Vienna: Kammer für Arbeiter und Angestellte, 1930.

Hanhart, Dieter. *Arbeiter in der Freizeit: Eine sozialpsychologische Unter-suchung.* Bern: Hans Huber, 1964.

Hannak, Jacques. *Im Sturm eines Jahrhunderts, eine volkstümliche*

Geschichte der sozialistische Partei Österreichs. Vienna: Wiener Volksbuchhandlung, 1952.

Hannak, Jacques. *Karl Renner und Seine Zeit: Versuch einer Biographie.* Vienna: Europa, 1965.

Hardy, Charles O. *The Housing Program of the City of Vienna.* Washington, D.C.: Brookings Institution, 1934.

Haraven, Tamara K. *Amoskeag: Life and Work in an American Factory-Town.* New York: Pantheon Books, 1978.

Haraven, Tamara K. *Family Time and Industrial Time: The Relationship Between the Family and Work in a New England Industrial Community.* Cambridge: Cambridge University Press, 1982.

Haraven, Tamara K., ed. *Transitions: The Family and the Life Course in Historical Perspective.* New York: Academic Press, 1978.

Harris, C. C. *The Family and Industrial Society.* London: George Allen & Unwin, 1983.

Hautmann, Hans, and Rudolf Kropf. *Die österreichische Arbeiterbewegung von Vormärz bis 1945: Sozialökonomische Ursprünge ihrer Ideologie und Politik.* Vienna: Europa, 1976.

Heinz, Karl. *Kampf und Aufstieg: Die Geschichte der sozialistischen Arbeiterjugendbewegung Österreichs.* Vienna: 1932.

Hetzer, Hildegard. *Kindheit und Armut: Psychologische Methoden in Armutsforschung und Armutsbekämpfung.* Leipzig: S. Hirzel, 1929.

Hetzer, Hildegard. *Mutterlichkeit: Psychologische Untersuchung der grundformen mutterlicher Haltung.* Leipzig: S. Hirzel, 1937.

Hetzer, Hildegard. *Testing Children's Development from Birth to School Age.* New York: Farrar & Rinehart, 1935.

Hetzer, Hildegard. *Zur Psychologie des Wohnens: Beiträge zur städtischen Wohn- und Siedelwirtschaft.* Munich: Duncker & Humblot, 1930.

Hiner, N. Ray, and Joseph M. Hawes. *Growing Up in America: Children in Historical Perspective.* Urbana: University of Illinois Press, 1985.

Hirsch, Bettina, ed. *Anton Proksch und seine Zeit.* Vienna: Europa, 1977.

Hoffmann, E. *Vorschulerziehung in Deutschland: Historische Entwicklung im Abriss.* Witten, 1971.

Hofstätter, Robert. *Die arbeitende Frau: Ihre wirtschaftliche Lage, Gesundheit, Ehe und Mutterschaft.* Vienna: Moritz Perles, 1929.

Hoggart, Richard. *The Uses of Literacy: Changing Patterns in English Mass Culture.* New Jersey: Essential Books, 1957.

Holcombe, Lee. *Victorian Ladies at Work.* Hamden, Conn.: Archon Books, 1973.

Holek, Heinrich. *Unterwegs: Eine Selbstbiographie.* Vienna: Bugra, 1927.

Holek, Wenzel. *Lebensgang eines deutsch-tschechischen Handarbeiters.* Jena: E. Diederichs, 1909.

Hörnle, Edwin. *Die Arbeiterklasse und ihre Kinder.* Berlin: G. Sieber, 1921.

Huck, Gerhard, ed. *Sozialgeschichte der Freizeit: Untersuchungen zum Wandel der Alltagskultur in Deutschland.* Wuppertal: Peter Hammer, 1980.

Humphries, Stephen. *Hooligans or Rebels? An Oral History of Working-Class Childhood and Youth, 1889–1939.* Oxford: Blackwell, 1981.

Hurt, J. S. *Elementary Schooling and the Working Classes, 1860–1918.* London: Routledge and Kegan Paul, 1979.

Institüt für Höhere Studien/Wien. *Strukturen der sozialen Ungleichheit in Österreich: Analysen zur Klassenstruktur und sozialen Schichtung in Österreich*, 3 vols. Vienna, 1978.

Jedlicka, Ludwig, and Rudolf Neck. *Österreich 1927 bis 1938*. Vienna: Geschichte und Politik, 1973.

Joeres, Ruth-Ellen B., and Annete Kuhn, eds. *Frauen in der Geschichte*, vol. 6. Düsseldorf: Schwann, 1985.

Johansen, Erna M. *Betrogene Kinder: Eine Sozialgeschichte der Kindheit*. Frankfurt am Main: Fischer, 1978.

John, Michael. *Hausherrenmacht und Mieterelend. Wohnverhältnisse und Wohnerfahrung der Unterschichten in Wien 1890–1923*. Vienna: Gesellschaftskritik, 1982.

John, Michael. *Wohnverhältnisse sozialer Unterschichten im Wien Kaiser Franz Josephs*. Vienna: Europa, 1984.

Jolles, Hiddo M. *Wien, Stadt ohne Nachwuchs; sozialwissenschaftliche Betrachtungen ueber den Geburtenrueckgang in der alten Donaustadt*. Assen: Van Gorcum, 1957.

Jugendnot und Jugendberatung: Vier Vorträge gehalten in der Gründversammlung des Vereins für Jugendberatung in Wien. Vienna: Wien II, 1929.

Kaelble, Hartmut. *Soziale Mobilität und Chancengleichheit*. Göttingen: Vandenhoeck & Ruprecht, 1983.

Kanitz, Otto F. *Das proletarische Kind in der bürgerlichen Gesellschaft*. Jena: Urania, 1925.

Kautsky, Benedikt. *Die Haushaltsstatistik der Wiener Arbeiterkammer 1925–1934*. Leiden: E. J. Brill, 1937.

Kautsky, Carl. *Der Kampf gegen den Geburten Rückgang*. Vienna: Wiener Volksbuchhandlung, 1924.

Kautsky, Carl. *Soziale Hygiene der Frau: Eine sozialmedizinische Darstellung des weiblichen Geschlechtslebens*. Prague: Graphia Karlsbad, 1931.

Kett, Joseph F. *Rites of Passage: Adolescence in America, 1790 to the Present*. New York: Basic Books, 1977.

Kimml, Anton. *Jugendparlament der Ersten Republik: Der Jugendbeirat der Arbeiterkammer, Wien, 1924–1938*. Vienna: Europa, 1965.

Klezl, Felix. *Beruf und Betrieb: Ihre begriffliche Abgrenzung und ihre Bedeutung für das Standeproblem*. Vienna: Österreichischer Wirtschaftsverlag, 1934.

Knapp, Vincent J. *Austrian Social Democracy, 1889–1914*. Washington, D.C.: University Press of America, 1980.

Knittler, Herbert, ed. *Festschrift für Alfred Hoffman zum 75 Geburtstag: Wirtschafts- und sozialhistorische Beiträge*. Vienna: Geschichte und Politik, 1979.

Knodel, John. *The Decline of Fertility in Germany, 1871–1939*. Princeton: Princeton University Press, 1974.

Komlos, John, ed. *Economic Development in the Habsburg Monarchy in the Nineteenth Century: Essays*. Boulder: Columbia University Press, East European Monographs, 1983.

Konnert, Wilfried. *Favoriten im Wandel der Zeit*. Vienna: Kurt Mohl, 1974.

Konrad, Helmut, and Wolfgang Maderthaner, eds. *Neuere Studien zur Arbeitergeschichte*. 3 vols. Vienna: Europa, 1984.

Kreissler, Felix. *Von der Revolution zur Annexion, 1918–38.* Vienna: Europa, 1970.

Kreymeyer, Norbert, Bernhard Scherzinger, Gerd Koch, and Volkhard Brandes, eds. *Heute schon gelebt? Alltag und Utopie.* Offenbach: Verlag 2000, 1981.

Langewiesche, Dieter. *Zur Freizeit des Arbeiters: Bildungsbestrebungen und Freizeitgestaltung österreichischer Arbeiter im Kaiserreich und in der Ersten Republik.* Stuttgart: Klettcola, 1979.

Lazarsfeld, Paul. *Jugend und Beruf.* Jena: Gustav Fischer, 1931.

Lazarsfeld, Sofie. *Technik der Erziehung.* Leipzig: S. Hirzel, 1929.

Lazarsfeld, Sofie. *Sexuelle Erziehung.* Vienna: Moritz Perles, 1931.

Lazarsfeld, Sofie. *Wie die Frau den Mann erlebt.* Vienna: Verlag für Sexualwissenschaft, 1932.

Lazarsfeld, Sofie. *Vom häuslichen Frieden.* Vienna: Moritz Perles, 1926.

Lefebvre, Henri. *Das Alltagsleben in der modernen Welt.* Frankfurt am Main: Suhrkamp, 1972.

Lehr, Ursula. *Die Frau im Beruf: Eine psychologische Analyse der weiblichen Berufstätigkeit.* Frankfurt am Main: Athenäum, 1969.

Leichter, Käthe. *So Leben Wir . . . 1320 Industriearbeiterinnen berichten über ihr Leben.* Vienna: Arbeit und Wirtschaft, 1931.

Leichter, Käthe. *Wie Leben die Wiener Heimarbeiter?* Vienna: Arbeit und Wirtschaft, 1923.

Leichter, Otto. *Glanz und Elend der Ersten Republik: Wie es zum österreichischen Bürgerkrieg kam.* Vienna: Europa, 1964.

Leser, Norbert. *Zwischern Reformismus und Bolschewismus: Der Austromarxismus als Theorie und Praxis.* Vienna: Europa, 1968.

Levenstein, Adolf. *Die Arbeiterfrage: Mit besonderer Berucksichtigung der sozialpsychologischen Seite des modernen Grossbetriebes und psychophysischen Einwirkungen auf die Arbeiter.* Munich: Ernst Reinhardt, 1912.

Lichtenberger, Elizabeth, and Hans Bobek. *Wien: Bauliche Gestalt und Entwicklung seit der mitte des 19 Jahrhunderts.* Cologne and Graz: Böhlau, 1966.

Lidtke, Vernon. *The Alternative Culture: Socialist Labor in Imperial Germany.* New York: Oxford, 1984.

Mayer, Amalie, et al. *Geschichte der österreichischen Mädchenmittelschule.* Vienna: Österreichischer Bundesverlag, 1952.

Maynes, Mary Jo. *Schooling in Western Europe: A Social History.* Albany: SUNY Press, 1984.

Mayreder, Rosa. *Das Haus in der Landskrongasse.* Vienna: E. Mensa, 1948.

Meacham, Standish. *A Life Apart: The English Working Class 1890–1914.* Cambridge: Harvard University, 1977.

Medick, Hans, and David Warren Sabean. *Interest and Emotion: Essays on the Study of Family and Kinship.* Cambridge: Cambridge University, 1984.

Mitterauer, Michael. *Ledige Mütter: Zur Geschichte illegitimer Geburten in Europa.* Munich: C. H. Beck, 1983.

Mitterauer, Michael, and Reinhard Sieder. *The European Family: Patriar-*

chy to Partnership from the Middle Ages to the Present. Chicago: University of Chicago Press, 1982.

Mitterauer, Michael, and Reinhard Sieder. *Vom Patriarchat zur Partnerschaft: Zum Strukturwandel der Familie.* Munich: C. H. Beck, 1977.

Mitterauer, Michael, and Reinhard Sieder, eds. *Historische Familienforschung.* Frankfurt an Main: Suhrkamp, 1982.

Mitterauer, Michael. *Sozialgeschichte der Jugend.* Frankfurt am Main: Suhrkamp, 1986.

Möller, Heinrich. *Geschichte der Schumacher Österreichs, 1871–1931.* Vienna, 1931.

Montane, H. *Die Prostitution in Wien: Ihre Geschichte und Entwicklung von den Anfängen bis zur Gegenwart.* Vienna: Paula Rasch, 1925.

Moore, Barrington. *Injustice: The Social Bases of Obedience and Revolt.* White Plains, N.Y.: M. E. Sharpe, 1978.

Mooser, Josef. *Arbeiterleben in Deutschland, 1900–1970.* Frankfurt am Main: Suhrkamp, 1984.

Mosser, Peter, and Theodor Reitterer. *Die Mittelschulen in Österreich,* vol. 1. Vienna, 1929.

Mössler, Adolf. *Österreichische Volksschulzustände: Ein Wort an das Volk und seine Lehrer.* Vienna: Brand, 1897.

Muchow, Hans H. *Jugend und Zeitgeist: Morphologie der Kulturpubertät.* Reinbek bei Hamburg: Rohwolt, 1962.

Mungham G., and G. Pearson, eds. *Working Class Youth Culture.* London: Routledge and Kegan Paul, 1976.

Musgrove, F. *Youth and the Social Order.* Bloomington: Indiana University Press, 1964.

Muuss, Rolf E. *Theories of Adolescence.* New York: Random House, 1968.

Neugebauer, Wolfgang. *Bauvolk der kommenden Welt: Geschichte der sozialistischen Jugendbewegung in Österreich.* Vienna: Europa, 1975.

Niedhardt, Friedhelm. *Die Familie in Deutschland.* Opladen: Leske, 1966.

Neidhardt, Friedhelm. *Die junge Generation.* Opladen: Leske, 1970.

Niethammer, Lutz, ed. *Faschismus Erfahrungen im Ruhrgebiet: Lebensgeschichte und Sozialkultur im Ruhrgebiet 1930 bis 1960,* vol. 1. Berlin: Dietz, 1983.

Niethammer, Lutz. *Lebenserfahrung und kollektives Gedächtnis: Die Praxis der "Oral History."* Frankfurt am Main: Suhrkamp, 1985.

Neithammer, Lutz, ed. *Wohnen im Wandel.* Wuppertal: Peter Hammer, 1979.

Niethammer, Lutz, and Alexander von Plata, eds. *"Wir Kriegen jetzt andere Zeiten": Auf der Suche nach der Erfahrung des Volkes in Nachfaschistischen Ländern.* Berlin and Bonn: Dietz, 1985.

Otruba, Gustav. *Österreichs Wirtschaft im 20. Jahrhundert.* Vienna: Österreichischer Bundesverlag, 1968.

Papanek, Ernst. *The Austrian School Reform: Its Bases, Principles and Development—The Twenty Years Between the Two World Wars.* New York: Frederick Fell, 1962.

Pelinka, Anton. *Stand Oder Klasse? Die christliche Arbeiterbewegung Österreichs 1933 bis 1938.* Vienna: Europa, 1972.

Petzold, Alfons. *Das Leben des Arbeiters*. Vienna: Jungbrunnen, 1930.
Petzold, Alfons. *Das Rauhe Leben*. Vienna: Österreichischer Bundesverlag, 1964.
Pfoser, Alfred. *Literatur und Austromarxismus*. Vienna: Löcker, 1980.
Pollitzer, Johann. *Die Lage der Lehringe im Kleingewerbe in Wien*. Tübingen, 1900.
Pollock. Linda A. *Forgotten Children: Parent-Child Relations from 1500 to 1900*. Cambridge: Cambridge University, 1983.
Popp, Adelheid. *Die Jugendgeschichte einer Arbeiterin*. 3d edition enlarged. Munich: Ernst Reinhardt, 1927.
Rabb, Theodore K., and Robert I. Rotberg. *The Family in History: Interdisciplinary Essays*. New York: Harper & Row, 1971.
Rabinbach, Anson. *The Crisis of Austrian Socialism: From Red Vienna to Civil War, 1927–1934*. Chicago: University of Chicago Press, 1983.
Rada, Margarete. *Das reifende Proletariermädchen*. Vienna: Jugend und Volk, 1931.
Reck, Siegfried. *Arbeiter nach der Arbeit: Sozialhistorische Studie zu den Wandlungen der Arbeiteralltags*. Lahn-Giessen: Focus, 1977.
Reich, Wilhelm. *Der Sexuelle Kampf der Jugend*. Vienna: Sexpol, 1932.
Reich, Wilhelm. *Geschlechtsreife, Enthaltsamkeit, Ehemoral: Eine Kritik der bürgerlichen Sexualreform*. Vienna: Münster, 1930.
Reich, Wilhelm. *Sexualerregung und Sexualbefriedigung*. Vienna: Münster, 1930.
Reininger, Karl. *Über soziale Verhaltungswesen in der Vorpubertät*. Vienna: Jugend und Volk, 1924.
Reulecke, Jürgen, and Wolfhard Weber. *Fabrik, Familie, Feierabend: Beiträge zur Sozialgeschichte des Alltags im Industriezeitalter*. Wuppertal: Peter Hammer, 1978.
Reyer, Jürgen. *Wenn die Mutter arbeiten gingen . . . Eine sozialhistorische Studie zur Entstehung der öffentlichen Kleinkindererziehung im 19. Jahrhundert in Deutschland*. Cologne: Pahl-Rugenstein, 1983.
Rigler, Edith. *Frauenleitbild und Frauenarbeit in Österreich vom ausgehenden 19 Jahrhundert bis zum Zweiten Weltkrieg*. Vienna: Geschichte und Politik, 1976.
Ringer, Fritz. *Education and Society in Modern Europe*. Bloomington: Indiana University Press, 1979.
Ritter, Gerhard A. *Arbeiterkultur*. Königstein: Athenäum, 1979.
Roberts, Elizabeth. *A Woman's Place: An Oral History of Working-Class Women, 1890–1940*. Oxford: Basil Blackwell, 1984.
Robins, David, and Philip Cohen. *Knuckle Sandwich: Growing up in the Working-class City*. Harmondsworth: Penguin, 1978.
Rozenblit, Marsha L. *The Jews of Vienna, 1867–1914: Assimilation and Identity*. Albany: SUNY Press, 1984.
Rübelt, Lothar. *Österreich zwischen den Kriegen*. Vienna: Molden, 1979.
Rühle, Otto. *Das proletarische Kind*. Munich: Albert Langen, 1922.
Rühle, Otto. *Die Seele des proletarischen Kindes*. Dresden: Am anderen Ufer, 1925.
Rühle, Otto. *Illustrierte Kultur- und Sittengeschichte des Proletariats*. Berlin: Neuer Deutscher, 1930.

Sauer, Walter, ed. *Der dressierte Arbeiter.* Munich: Beck, 1984.

Schelsky, Helmut, ed. *Arbeiterjugend Gestern und Heute.* Heidelberg: Quelle & Meyer, 1955.

Scheu, Andreas. *Eine Biographie.* Vienna: Europa, 1968.

Scheu, Andreas. *Umsturzkeime, Erlebnisse eines Kämpfers.* Vienna: Wiener Volksbuchhandlung, 1923.

Schlesinger, Therese. *Wie Will und wie soll das Proletariat seine Kinder erziehen?* Vienna: Frauen-Reichskomitees, 1921.

Schofield, Michael. *The Sexual Behavior of Young People.* London: Penguin, 1968.

Schreiber, Adele. *Mutterschaft.* Vienna: Albert Langen, 1913.

Schubert, Anton. *Ziffern zur Frage des niederösterreichischen Tschecheneinschlages.* Vienna: Bundes des Deutschen in Niederösterreich, 1909.

Shell, Kurt. *The Transformation of Austrian Socialism.* New York: SUNY, 1962.

Shorter, Edward. *The Making of the Modern Family.* New York: Basic Books, 1975.

Siegl, May Hollis. *Reform of Elementary Education in Austria.* New York, n.p., 1933.

Siemering, Hertha. *Arbeiterbildungswesen in Wien und Berlin.* Karlsruhe: G. Braunsche, 1911.

Siemering, Hertha, and Eduard Spranger. *Weibliche Jugend in unserer Zeit.* Leipzig: Quelle & Meyer, 1932.

Sommerville, C. John. *The Rise and Fall of Childhood.* Beverly Hills: Sage Library of Social Research, 1982.

Stein, Leopold. *Die Sprache des Kindes und ihre Fehler.* Vienna: Moritz Perles, 1926.

Steiner, Herbert, ed. *Käthe Leichter: Leben und Werk.* Vienna: Europa, 1973.

Steiner, Herbert. *Die kommunistische Partei Österreichs von 1918–1933.* Vienna: Europa, 1968.

Suppan, Arnold. *Die österreichischen Volksgruppen: Tendenzen ihrer gesellschaftlichen Entwicklung im 20. Jahrhundert.* Munich: R. Oldenbourg, 1983.

Tandler, Julius. *Die Sozialbilanz der Alkoholikerfamilie. Ein sozial- med. u. sozialpsychol. Untersuchung.* Vienna: Gerold, 1936.

Teuteberg, Hans J., and Gunter Wiegelmann. *Der Wandel der Nahrungsgewohnheiten unter dem Einfluss der Industrialisierung.* Göttingen: Vandenhoeck & Ruprecht, 1972.

Theimer, Camilla. *Frauenarbeit in Österreich.* Vienna: A. Opitz. Opiss, 1909.

Thompson, Paul. *The Edwardians.* London: 1975.

Thompson, Paul. *The Voice of the Past: Oral History.* Oxford: Oxford University Press, 1978.

Tichy, Marina. *Alltag und Traum: Leben und Lexture der Wiener Dienstmädchen um die Jahrhundertwende.* Vienna: Böhlau, 1984.

Tilly, Charles, ed. *An Urban World.* Boston: Little, Brown, 1974.

Tilly, Louise A., and Joan W. Scott. *Women, Work, and Family.* New York: Holt, Rinehart and Winston, 1978.

Traxler, Gabrielle. *Zwischen Tradition und Emanzipation: Probleme der Frauenarbeit in Österreich.* Vienna: W. Braumüller, 1973.

Ueberhorst, Horst. *Frisch, Frei, Stark und Treu: Die Arbeitersportbewegung in Deutschland, 1893–1933.* Düsseldorf: Peter Hammer, 1973.

Vecerka, L. *Das soziale Verhalten von Mädchen während der Reifezeit.* Jena: Gustav Fischer, 1926.

Vicinus, Martha, ed. *Suffer and Be Still: Women in the Victorian Age.* Bloomington: Indiana University Press, 1972.

Wagner, Richard. *Geschichte der Kleiderarbeiter in Österreich im 19 Jahrhundert und im ersten Viertel des 20 Jahrhunderts.* Vienna: Gewerkschaft der Kleiderarbeiter Österreichs, 1930.

Weber, Therese, ed. *Häuslerkindheit: Autobiographische Erzählungen.* Vienna: Böhlau, 1984.

Weeks, Jeffrey. *Sex, Politics and Society.* London: Longman, 1981.

Weidenholzer, Josef. *Auf dem Weg zum "Neuen Menschen": Bildungs- und Kulturarbeit der österreichischen Sozialdemokratie in der Ersten Republik.* Vienna: Europa, 1981.

Wheaton, Robert, and Tamara K. Hareven. *Family and Sexuality in French History.* Philadelphia: University of Pennsylvania Press, 1980.

Wiegelmann, Gunter, ed. *Kultureller Wandel in 19 Jahrhundert.* Göttingen: Vandenhoeck & Ruprecht, 1973.

Winter, Max. *Das goldene Wiener Herz.* Berlin: Herman Seeman, 1905.

Winter, Max. *Im unterirdischen Wien.* Berlin: Herman Seeman, 1905.

Ziak, Karl. *Von der Schmelz auf den Gallitzinberg.* Munich: Jugend und Volk, 1969.

Zwahr, Hartmut. *Zur Konstituierung des Proletariats als Klasse: Strukturuntersuchung über das Leipziger Proletariat während der industriellen Revolution.* Berlin: Akademie Verlag, 1978.

ARTICLES

Allen, Ann Taylor. "Gardens of Children, Gardens of God: Kindergartens and Day-Care Centers in Nineteenth-Century Germany." *Journal of Social History* (Spring 1986), 433–50.

Bach, David. "Warum haben wir keine sozialdemokratische Kunstpolitik." *Der Kampf,* 22, March 1929.

Banik-Schweitzer, Renate. "Entwicklung Favoritens zum Arbeiterbezirk." In *Wiener Geschichtsblätter,* 29, issue 4 (1974).

Bolognese-Leuchtenmüller, Birgit. "Unterversorgung und mangelnde Betreuung der Kleinkinder in den Unterschichtfamilien als soziales Problem des 19. Jahrhunderts." In Herbert Knittler, ed., *Wirtschafts- und sozialhistorische Beiträge: Festschrift für Alfred Hoffman zum 75 Geburtstag.* Vienna: Geschichte und Politik, 1979.

Bühler, Charlotte. "Das Schwärmen als Phase der Reifezeit." *Zeitschrift für Psychologie* 100 (1926).

Demos, John. "Developmental Perspectives on the History of Childhood." *Journal of Interdisciplinary History* 2 (1971).

Demos, John. "Adolescence in Historical Perspective." *Journal of Marriage and the Family* 31 (1969).

Ehalt, Hubert Ch. "Das Wiener Schulwesen in der Liberalen Ära." In *Wien in der Liberalen Ära. Forschungen und Beiträge zur Wiener Stadtgeschichte*, 1 (Vienna, 1978).

Ehmer, Josef. "Frauenarbeit und Arbeiterfamilie in Wien: Vom Vormärz bis 1934." *Geschichte und Gesellschaft* 7, 3/4 (1981), 438–73.

Evans, Richard. "The History of European Women: A Critical Survey of Recent Research." *Journal of Modern History* 52 (December 1980).

Fairchild, Cissie. "Female Sexual Attitudes and the Rise of Illegitimacy: A Case Study." *Journal of Interdisciplinary History* 8, no. 4 (Spring 1978).

Fischer, Walter. "Jugend und Autorität." *Der Kampf*, 23, October 1930.

Fuchs, H. "Die Sprache des Jugendlichen in seinem Tagebuch." *Zeitschrift für Angewandte Psychologie* 29 (1927).

Graff, Harvey J. "Early Adolescence in Antebellum America: The Remaking of Growing Up." *Journal of Early Adolescence* 5, no. 4 (Winter 1985).

Gruber, Helmut. "History of the Austrian Working Class: Unity of Scholarship and Practice." *International Labor and Working Class History*, no. 24 (Fall 1983).

Haberda, A. "Gerichtärzliche Erfahrungen über die Fruchtabtreibung in Wien." *Vierteljährsschrift für gerichliche Medizin u. öffentliches Sanitätswesen* 56, 3 (1918). Berlin.

Hanisch, Ernst. "Arbeiterkindheit in Österreich vor dem Ersten Weltkrieg." *Internationales Archiv für Sozialgeschichte der deutschen Literatur*, vol. 7, 1982.

Hänsel, Ludwig. "Staatsbürgerliche Erziehung in der Ersten und in der Zweiten Republik Österreichs." *Österreich in Geschichte und Literatur* 2, 3 (1958).

Hausen, Karen. "Familie als Gegenstand historischer Sozialwissenschaft." In *Geschichte und Gesellschaft*, 1, 1975.

Hausen, Karen. "Family and Role-Division: the Polarisation of Sexual Stereotypes in the Nineteenth-Century—An Aspect of the Dissociation of Work and Family." In Richard J. Evans, *The German Family*. London: Croom Helm, 1981.

Hetzer, Hildegard. "Sexualleben und Interessenrichtung pubertierender Mädchen." *Zeitschrift für pädagogische Psychologie*, 30, 1929.

Hetzer, Hildegard. "Das vernachlässigte Kleinkind." In *Die Quelle*, 1925.

Hetzer, Hildegard. "Das volkstümliche Kinderspiel." In *Wiener Arbeiten zur pädagogischen Psychologie*, 6, 1927.

Hetzer, Hildegard, and Fritz Frisch. "Die religiöse Entwicklung in der Reifezeit." *Archiv für die gesampte Psychologie*, 62, 1928.

Hetzer, Hildegard, and B. Reinsdorf. "Sprachentwicklung und soziales Milieu." *Zeitschrift für angewandte Psychologie*, 29, 1928.

Jacobi-Dittrich, Juliane. "Growing Up Female in the Nineteenth Century." In John Fout, ed., *German Women in the Nineteenth Century*. New York: Holmes & Meier, 1984.

Jones, G. Stedman. "Class Expression vs Social Control." *History Workshop* 4, (1977).

Kanitz, Felix. "Mieterschutz und Erziehung." *Die Sozialistische Erziehung*, 8 (September 1928).

Kaufmann, Albert. "Soziale Schichtung und Berufsstatistik." In Leopold
    Rosenmayr and Sigurd Höllinger, eds., *Soziologie Forschung in
    Österreich*. Vienna: Böhlaus, 1969.
Kett, Joseph F. "Adolescence and Youth in Nineteenth-Century America."
    In Theodore K. Rabb and Robert I. Rotberg, eds., *The Family in
    History: Interdisciplinary Essays*. New York: Harper & Row, 1971.
Klenner, Fritz. "Die sozialen Probleme der ersten Republik." *Österreich in
    Geschichte und Literatur* 2, 2 (1958).
Kohoutek, Rudolf, and Helene Maimann. "EXOTIK DES ALLTAGS? Zur
    Konjunktur eines Begriffs." In Norbert Kremeyer et al., *Heute schon
    gelebt? Alltag und Utopie*. Offenbach: 2000, 1981.
Langewiesche, Dieter. "Arbeiterkultur in Österreich: Aspekte, Tendenzen
    und Thesen." In Gerhard Ritter, ed., *Arbeiterkultur*. Königstein:
    Athenäum, 1979.
Lapsley, Daniel K., Robert D. Enright, and Ronald C. Serlin. "Toward a
    Theoretical Perspective on the Legislation of Adolescence." *Journal
    of Early Adolescence* 5, no. 4 (Winter 1985).
Lazarsfeld, Paul. "Geistige und Körperliche Entwicklung bei Volksschul-
    kindern." *Die Quelle*, 1929.
Maimann, Helene. "Bemerkungen zu einer Geschichte des Arbeiterall-
    tags." In Gerhard Botz et al., eds., Bewegung and Klasse. *Studien zur
    österreichischen Arbeitergeschichte*. Vienna: Europa, 1978.
Meissl, Gerhard. " 'Für mich wäre es Freiheit, wenn ich in die Fabrik
    Gienge.' Zum Wandel der Arbeitsorganisation und Arbeitserfahrung
    in Wien zwischen 1890 und 1914." In *Archiv 1985: Jahrbuch des
    Vereins für Geschichte der Arbeiterbewegung*, 1, 1985, 18–31.
Meissl, Gerhard. "Industriearbeit in Wien 1870–1913. Die zeitgenössische
    Industriestatistik als Quelle für die Analyse industriebetrieblicher
    Entwicklung und Arbeitsorganisation." *Jahrbuch des Vereins für
    Geschichte der Stadt Wien*, 36, 1980.
Minge-Kalman, Wanda. "The Industrial Revolution and the European
    Family: The Institutionalization of Childhood as a Market for Fam-
    ily Labor." *Comparative Studies in Society and History* 20 (1978).
Niethammer, Lutz. "Wie wohnten Arbeiter im Kaiserreich." *Archiv für
    Sozialgeschichte*, 16, 1976.
Otruba, Gustav, and L. S. Rutschka, "Die Herkunft der Wiener Bevölker-
    ung in den letzten hundert-fünfzig Jahren." *Jahrbuch des Vereins für
    Geschichte der Stadt Wein*, 13, 1957–58.
Pattermann, F. "Die Gedankenwelt der Arbeiterin." *Der Kampf*, 2, 1908–9.
Peller, Sigismund. "Die Ernährungsverhältnisse der Wiener Arbeiterschaft
    im Jahre 1925." *Archiv für Soziale Hygiene*, offprint from vol. 13, no.
    1–2 (1919).
Philippovich, E. V. "Wiener Wohnungsverhältnisse." *Archiv für Soziale
    Gesetzgebung und Statistik*, 7, 1894.
Pirhofer, Gottfried. "Linien einer kulturpolitischen Auseinandersetzung in
    der Geschichte des Wiener Arbeiterwohnbaues." *Wiener Geschichts-
    blätter*, 33, 1, 1978.
Pollak, Marianne. "Aus der Geschichte des Prügelns." *Die Sozialistische
    Erziehung* 6 (April 1926).

Rabinbach, Anson. "Politics and Pedagogy: The Austrian Social Democratic Youth Movement 1931–32." *Journal of Contemporary History* 13 (1978).

Rabinbach, Anson G. "The Politicization of Wilhelm Reich: An Introduction to 'The Sexual Misery of the Working Masses and the Difficulties of Sexual Reform.' " In *New German Critique* 1, no. 1 (Winter 1974).

Rainwater, Lee. "Some Aspects of Lower Class Sexual Behavior." *The Journal of Social Issues* 22 (April 1966).

Ritter, Gerhard. "Workers Culture in Imperial Germany: Problems and Points of Departure for Research." *Journal of Contemporary History* 13 (1978).

Ross, Ellen. " 'Not the Sort that Would Sit on the Doorstep': Respectability in Pre-World War I London Neighborhoods." In *International Labor and Working Class History*, no. 27 (Spring 1985), 39–59.

Rudolf, Richard. "The Pattern of Austrian Industrial Growth from the Eighteenth to the Early Twentieth Century." *American Historical Review* 11, no. 1 (1975).

Schiff, Walter. "Die Kinderarbeit in Österreich." *Archiv für Sozialwissenschaft und Sozialpolitik*, 37, 1913.

Schlesinger, Therese. "Krise der Jugend." *Der Kampf*, 25, April 1932.

Schlesinger, Therese, and Paul Stein. "Leitsätze für die sexuelle Aufklärung der Jugend." *Bildungsarbeit* 19, no. 12 (December 1932).

Sieder, Reinhard. "Gassenkinder." In *Aufrisse: Zeitschrift für politische Bildung*, 5, 4 (1984).

Sieder, Reinhard. "Geschichten erzählen und Wissenschaft trieben." *Mündliche Geschichte und Arbeiterbewegung. Eine Einführung in Arbeitsweisen und Themenbereiche der Geschichte "geschichtsloser" Sozialgruppen*. Vienna and Cologne: Böhlau, 1984.

Sieder, Reinhard. "Vata, derf i aufstehn?" In Hubert Ch. Ehalt and Hannes Stekl, eds., *Glücklich ist, Wer Vergist . . . ?: Das andere Wien um 1900*. Vienna: Böhlau, 1986.

Sieder, Reinhard, and Hans Safrian. "Gassenkinder—Strassenkämpfer." In Lutz Niethammer and Alexander von Plato, eds. *Wir kriegen jetzt andere Zeiten*. Berlin-Bonn: Dietz, 1985.

Stearns, Peter. "The Effort at Continuity in Working-Class Culture." *Journal of Modern History* 52 (December 1980), 626–55.

Stearns, Peter. "Working-Class Women in Britain, 1890–1914." In Martha Vicinus, ed. *Suffer and Be Still: Women in the Victorian Age*. Bloomington: Indiana University, 1972.

Stearns, Peter N., and Carol Z. Stearns. "Emotionology: Clarifying the History of Emotions and Emotional Standards." *The American Historical Review* 90, no. 4 (October 1985).

Tandler, Julius. "Ehe und Bevolkerungspolitik." *Wiener Medizinische Wochenschrift*, 74, 1924.

Tesarek, A. "Strafen in Schule und Haus (Schüleranten)." *Die Sozialistische Erziehung* 2, no. 12 (1922).

Teuteberg, Hans Jugen, and Annegret Bernhard. "Wandel der Kinderernährung in der Zeit der Industrialisierung." In Jürgen Reulecke and Wolfhard Weber, eds., *Fabrik, Familie, Feierabend.* Wuppertal: Peter Hammer, 1978.

Tilly, Louise A. "Linen Was Their Life: Family Survival Strategies and Parent-Child Relations in Nineteenth-Century France." In Hans Medick and David Warren Sabean, *Interest and Emotion: Essays on the Study of Family and Kinship.* Cambridge: Cambridge University, 1984.

Vester, Michael. "Was dem Bürger sein Goethe, ist dem Arbeiter seine Solidarität." *Asthetik und Kommunikation* 24 (June 1976).

Wegs, J. Robert. "Working-Class Respectability: The Viennese Experience." *Journal of Social History* 15 (Summer 1982).

Wiechert, Trude. "Mädchenerziehung von heute—nicht von gestern." *Die Hausliche Erziehung* 10 (November 1930).

Winter, Max. "Wie kommen wir zum sozialistischen Kulturbund?" *Der Kampf,* 19, 1926.

Wislitzky, S. "Beobachtungen über das soziale Verhalten im Kindergarten." *Zeitschrift für Psychologie,* 107, 1928.

DISSERTATIONS AND MANUSCRIPTS

Angerer, Maximilian. "Studien zur Sozialgeschichte der Wiener Bezirke I, VII und X in der Zeit zwischen 1869 und 1910." University of Vienna, 1957.

Astegher, Hubert. "Die Lohnentwicklung in Österreich von 1918 bis 1938." University of Vienna, 1974.

Bauböck, Rainer. "Zur sozialdemokratischen Wohnungspolitik 1919–1934: Mieterschutz, Wohnungsanforderung und kommunaler Wohnbau unter besonderer Berücksichtigung Wiens." University of Vienna, 1976.

Blumberger, Walter. "Konzepte der Arbeiterbildung: Eine historische-kritische Analyse." University of Linz, 1976.

Blunk, Laura Aileen. "The Viennese Working Classes in the 1840's." Kent State University, 1976.

Deters, Frederic. "The Role of the Suburbs in the Modernization of Vienna, 1850–90." University of Chicago, 1974.

Feistritzer, Hildegard M. Ansätze zur Sexualerziehung in der sozialdemokratischen Jugendbewegung in der Zeit ihrer Entstehung." Pädagogisches Institut, Vienna.

Fidesser, Rosa-Maria. "Die soziale Lage der Metallarbeiter Niederösterreichs in der Zeit der Industrialisierung bis 1914." University of Vienna, 1974.

Fink, Manfred. "Arbeiter Jugend in Österreich, 1894–1914." University of Vienna, 1978.

Freiler, Johann. "Die soziale Lage der Wiener Arbeiter in den Jahren, 1907–1918." University of Vienna, 1966.

Hagenhofer, Johann. "Die soziale Lage der Wiener Arbeiter um die Jahrhundertwende." University of Vienna, 1966.

Kaufmann, Albert. "Demographische Struktur und Familienformen der Wiener Bevolkerung." University of Vienna, 1966.

Kosian, Wilhelm. "Das Realeinkommen verschiedener Berufsgruppen des Arbeiterstandes u. das der öffentliche Beamten in Österreich in der Epoche 1910–1949." University of Vienna, 1978.

Krammer, Reinhard. "Geschichte der österreichischen Arbeitersportbewegung von den Anfängen bis 1934." University of Salzburg, 1979.

Kresbach, Robert. "Die Stellung des Arbeiters als Konsument: Eine statistische Untersuchung für die Jahre 1925–1935." University of Graz, 1953.

Melinz, Gerhard. "Hilfe, Schutz und Kontrolle: Versuch zur historischen Genese der öffentlichen 'Jugendfürsorge' in Österreich unter besonderer Berüchsichtigung von Wien (1880–1914)." University of Vienna, 1982.

Neugebauer, Wolfgang. "Die sozialdemokratische Jugendbewegung in Österreich, 1894–1945." University of Vienna, 1969.

Pfoser, Alfred. "Literatur und Sozialdemokratische Offentlich in der Ersten Republik." University of Salzburg, 1978.

Pirhofer, Gottfried. "Wiener Arbeiterquartiere: Geschlichtlichkeit, 'milieu' und soziale Planning." Manuscript in the Institute for Economic and Social History. 1977.

Rabinbach, Anson. "Ernst Fischer and the Left Opposition in Austria Social Democracy: The Crisis of Austrian Socialism 1927–1934." University of Wisconsin, 1973.

Rieger, Philip. "Anderungen in den Lebensverhältnissen und den Verbrauchsgewohnheiten von Wiener Arbeitnehmerhaushalten, 1952/1957." University of Vienna, 1960.

Seiser, Manfred. "Die wirtschaftliche und soziale Lage der Wiener Arbeiterjugend zwischen 1918 und 1934." University of Vienna, 1981.

Sieder, Reinhard J. "The Daily Life of Viennese Working-Class Families during World War I. Manuscript.

Sieder, Reinhard J. "Housing Policy, Social Welfare, and Family Life in 'Red Vienna', 1919–1934." Manuscript.

Viethen, Eva. "Wiener Arbeiterinnen Leben zwischen Familie Lohnarbeit und politischen Engagement." University of Vienna, 1984.

Index